THE ENCYCLOPEDIA OF
CHINESE
MEDICINE

The Encyclopedia of Chinese Medicine reports information and opinions of medical and other professionals which may be of general interest to the reader. It is advisory only and is not intended to serve as a medical textbook or other procedural guidebook for either physicians or patients. The information and opinions contained herein, which should not be used or relied upon without consultation and advice of a physician, are those solely of the authors and not those of the publishers who disclaim any responsibility for the accuracy of such information and opinions and any responsibility for any consequences that may result from any use or reliance thereon by the reader.

THIS IS A SEVENOAKS BOOK

Copyright © Sevenoaks Ltd 1997

10 9 8 7 6 5 4 3 2 1

A CIP catalogue record for this book is available from the British Library

ISBN 1-86200-006-9

Project editors: Heather Thomas, Liz Wheeler
Art editor: Rolando Ugolini
Production controller: Sarah Schuman

Printed and bound in Spain

THE ENCYCLOPEDIA OF
CHINESE MEDICINE

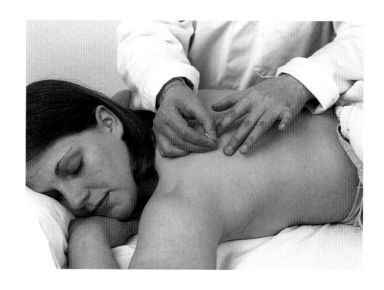

CONSULTANT EDITOR
DR DUO GAO

SEVENOAKS

Acknowledgements

The publishers would like to thank the following individuals and organizations for their help in compiling this book.

Professor Duo Gao, Professor Yilan Shen, and Professor Yi Zhu for reading through and assisting in the editing of the text. Miss Su Ping Xing and Mr Robert White, who assisted with translation and proof-reading. Mr Hui Li, who assisted with the photography. Also, the Society of Chinese Medical Practitioners in the UK.

Picture acknowledgements

All pictures DAVID DALTON with the following exceptions:

AFTCM: pages 128 and 130 (top), 133, 136 and 137

BRITISH ACUPUNCTURE COUNCIL: page 190

DR PAUL LAM: page 143

FRANK LANE PICTURE AGENCY: pages 90 (N J Thomas), 184 (Life Sciences Images), 32 (top)

HUW WILLIAMS: pages 89, 95, 99, 100, 105, 109 and 121

MARY EVANS PICTURE LIBRARY: pages 14, 19 and 26

SALLY & RICHARD GREENHILL: page 138

TONY STONE IMAGES/BRUCE HANDS: page 56

TRU PICTURE: pages 10-11, 22, 25, 28-29, 30, 31, 32 (bottom), 33, 34, 35, 37, 38, 39, 40, 41, 42, 43, 44, 46, 48, 50, 51, 52, 54-55, 58, 60, 68, 75, 76, 86-87, 90, 91, 92, 93, 94, 96, 97, 98, 102, 103, 104, 106, 107, 108, 109, 110, 111, 112, 113, 116, 118, 122-123, 126 and 134

CONTENTS

INTRODUCTION

BY BARBARA BERNIE OF THE AMERICAN FOUNDATION OF TRADITIONAL CHINESE MEDICINE

The philosophy and art of traditional Chinese medicine (TCM) can be compared with that of the ancient Greek philosopher-physician Hippocrates (500 B.C.), the father of Western medicine. Hippocrates believed that man was strongly related to all the natural elements. He believed in treating "the man, not the disease." He examined the individual as a whole, not limiting his observation to merely the organ or body part in which the disorder seemed to be located. When making a diagnosis, Hippocrates observed "the patient's habits, regimen, pursuits, his conversation, manners, thoughts, sleep patterns, sometimes his dreams and tears." According to Hippocrates, it is most important to consider the seasons of the year, the winds, the quality of the water and all other natural phenomena which are part of the individual's environment. Like the Chinese, such considerations are highly relevant to making a medical diagnosis.

Since 3000 B.C., the Chinese practitioners have considered the mental, spiritual, and physical aspects of the person before making a diagnosis, thereby treating the cause of the problem, not the symptom. It is unfortunate that Hippocrates' philosophy of treating the whole person has been lost in this era of medical specialization in the West. On the other hand, the Chinese have consistently treated the whole person during this 5000-year history of medical practice.

From its primitive roots, TCM has developed into a highly effective form of medicine, and is being expanded every day. Its use in surgery as an analgesic with laser and electric stimulation and computerized diagnostic tools are just a few of the new fields which are still being researched and developed in TCM.

In the first chapter, History and Philosophy, you will find a description of the development of TCM and gain an understanding of the philosophy behind it. You will see how these elements point to its future evolution. The following chapter, Causes of Disease, will introduce the reader to a new way of observing the connection between the body, mind, and spirit and the influence that the environment, emotions, and nutrition have upon health. The chapter on Chinese Herbal Therapies provides descriptions of many commonly used herbs and demonstrates the way they are used in combination to achieve the desired results. With Food as Therapy, the reader will note that food as well as illness is described as hot, cold, wet, dry, yin, yang, strong, or weak. The diagnosis of a disease based on these elements determines the treatment. For instance, if a disease is determined to be "hot," cooling foods would be recommended to bring the body into balance. In the chapter on Acupuncture, there is an introduction to the theory of meridians and the way they are used in treatment and diagnosis. The chapter on Acupressure discusses acupressure points on the body that can be used by oneself or with a partner to treat common problems such as headache, back problems, etc. The final chapter on Qi Gong includes breathing and meditative exercises and demonstrates how Qi Gong works to keep the body's system in balance and prevent disease and/or overcome illness.

This book provides a thorough overview of traditional Chinese medicine and points to ways in which it can be used independently or in conjunction with Western medicine. TCM was introduced to Europe about 350 years ago. However, it did not become legal to practice it in the United States until 1975. Since then, many TCM schools have opened. Today medical schools are beginning to include TCM in their curriculum. Furthermore, the office of Alternative Medicine at the National Institutes of Health (NIH) is funding research studies in medical schools and clinics. The interest and knowledge of Chinese medicine is growing at a rapid pace. The integration of TCM with Western medicine will benefit us all by not only allowing alternative treatment for many difficult diseases, but also guiding us toward a better way of preventing illness in the first place.

FOREWORD BY DR DUO GAO

Traditional Chinese Medicine (TCM) originated in the Huanghe Valley in Ancient China. At that time, people had only an elementary knowledge of anatomy, and the specific functions of the different organs of the body were not fully understood. The ancient Chinese based their medical studies on concepts that bore many similarities to modern control theory or to the study of astronomy, climates and plant ecology, rather than specializing in the study of separate organs. They combined the study of the human body with the study of Nature and reduced it to five different systems, exploring the physiological and pathological changes in the human body and its reaction to herbal medicine. This gradually developed into the systematic theory of traditional Chinese medicine.

In clinical practice, traditional Chinese medicine underlines its diagnosis and treatment with an analysis based on the differentiation of symptoms. In effect, this means that TCM does not focus mainly on dealing with symptoms, but seeks out and cures the underlying causes of the disease that are producing these symptoms.

Take, for example, a case of common constipation. In some instances, there are immediate causes, such as acute obstruction, whereas in others the causes are long-term or chronic. Remedies vary from the "direct attack", which is cathartic, to just "mild regulation". At the same time the treatment will contain medicines to ease bowel movement and act on the related nerve system, hormonal system, soft tissues and organs. Traditional Chinese medicine describes this as "different remedies for the same ailment".

As another example, hay fever symptoms include a blocked nose, itchy eyes and a sore throat. This is described in traditional Chinese medicine as "spreading internal heat in the lung system". The prescription will be Powder of Lonicera and Forsythia. However, a virus infection can cause all the same symptoms, and so in each case the same diagnosis will be made and the same remedy given. This works very effectively and in traditional Chinese medicine this is described as "the same remedy for different ailments".

Herbal medicine has been in existence for more than 5,000 years. During its long history, TCM doctors have gained rich theoretical and clinical experience. About 200 years ago, traditional Chinese medicine had already developed very specific specializations in internal medicine, surgery, obstetrics, gynaecology, otolaryngology (ear and throat), pediatrics, ophthalmology, acupuncture and massage. As such, traditional Chinese medicine is a valuable asset that should be available for the benefit of the whole world.

The progress of contemporary medicine and clinical practice is limited by the development of the pharmaceutical industry, where research has still not developed the ideal remedy for many diseases, and no remedy at all for some. The medicines made by the modern pharmaceutical industry are very specific indeed, but unfortunately they are often also the cause of many side-effects, producing a balance of advantage against disadvantage in use, which is now called "double effect" medicine. Different systems in the human body function in coordination with each other to maintain the balance that we call good health. These different organs also interact with each other, and where conflict exists, judgment has to be made as to whether the medicine is good for A but might not be good for B. A proficient doctor should have an overview of the whole system, like a general in a war, to ensure that he or she is in an invincible position.

The ultimate goal of medicine is to eliminate disease and bring benefits to human beings. It was pointed out in classical traditional Chinese medicine books that "what worries the patients most is the fact that there are too many diseases, but what worries the doctors most is the fact that there are not enough remedies." This encourages traditional Chinese medicine practitioners to endeavour to be well learned and well informed, and thus to perfect their skills.

During the last five years, while I have been working in London, I have had the opportunity to come across a wide range of diseases and have been able to help many thousands of patients. I believe that, with cooperation and effort, in ten years' time traditional Chinese medicine will become widely used in the West, and more and more patients who are suffering from illnesses that cannot be cured by contemporary medicine, will benefit from TCM. Also, many other illnesses will be treatable without the current side-effects of many modern drugs.

The aim of all traditional Chinese medicine practitioners, particularly in the West, is to change people's thoughts on healthy living and attempt to achieve a positive outlook whereby we realize that what we eat, how we take mental or physical exercise, and how the world and our environment affect us all have everyday implications on our state of health. That is why this book has chapters on food and diet, and exercises as well as herbal treatments to correct either short-term imbalances or longer-term personal weaknesses – whether these involve Qi, essential essences or replacing losses caused by special events in our lives such as childbirth or other metabolic changes.

My hope is that this book will help those who are interested in traditional Chinese medicine to cross the threshold of understanding. Perhaps, as an old Chinese saying goes, "sometimes one must cast a brick to attract jade". This book will help to initiate an all-important understanding between traditional Chinese medicine and western medicine.

Dr Duo Gao

THE HISTORY AND PHILOSOPHY OF

CHINESE MEDICINE

The Yellow Emperor said:

"Yin/Yang are the way of Heaven and Earth, the great principle and outline of everything, the parents of change, the root and source of life and death, the palace of gods. Treatment of disease should be based upon the roots (of Yin/Yang)."

Nei Jing (first century BC).

OVERVIEW

The birth of medicine in China dates back approximately 5,000 years. Archaeological evidence suggests that as early as the Neolithic period, stone needles were used for medical purposes. In the 1970s, many new discoveries of artifacts deepened our knowledge of medical practice in ancient Imperial China.

The two most significant periods in the early history of medicine in China include the pre-scientific supernatural medicine of the Shang and early Zhou dynasties, and the foundation of rational science and medicine in the late Zhou and Chin dynasties. It is the later Zhou and early Chin periods that established the scientific medical discipline of Traditional Chinese Medicine (TCM) and which are the root of later developments.

To understand the foundation of the ancient pre-scientific Chinese medical system, one must have an appreciation of the various philosophic tendencies and social forces that shaped the *Huang Di Nei Jing* (The Yellow Emperor's Canon of Internal Medicine). Medicine began in China with Ancestral therapy, Wu shamanism and magic practices. These supernatural practices were roughly equivalent to those found in the West in ancient Egyptian, Sumerian and Greek traditions, and they relied heavily on ritual and divination as part of their medical procedures. Also, like the pre-Socratic Greek tradition, philosophical traditions arose to lay the foundation of later scientific inquiry. Those who played their part included followers of Taoist (Dao) alchemy and early empiricism, the astrological soothsayers who plotted in detail the course of the seasons and celestial events, the philosophers of the Five Correspondences and the Yin/Yang School and the Qi vitalists.

It is also important to realize that, like the Western tradition, there was a clear demarcation between early pre-scientific supernatural medical practice and the beginning of the rational and scientific tradition based on the empirical observation of nature. This formulation and reliance on

natural principles formed the foundation for what we know today as modern traditional Chinese medicine. These empirical and rational elements gradually gained ascendancy in the various schools and were eventually all united under the strongly reconciliatory humanism of Confucian social and political theory. It is the Confucians who, around the first century BC, quelled the din of the "hundred contending schools of thought" of the Warring States period and laid the social foundation for both political and scientific theoretical unification. This provided a structure for subsequent scientific inquiry and fostered a true Chinese science – which included medicine.

In this Chinese illustration, the philosopher Confucius (551–479 BC) is shown starting a school.

THE SHANG DYNASTY

*T*his period marked the beginnings of medicine in China. We have discovered the history of the Shang period (1766–1100 BC) mainly through archaeological record. Cheng Tang founded the Shang Dynasty after exiling the previous Emperor Jie, a tyrant. This dynasty lasted until the advent of the Western Zhou in 100 BC. Historical reports from the later Zhou dynasty and current archaeological data comprise what is known about the earlier period. Artifacts found along the lower basin of the Yellow River show depictions of architecture and religious practices, which included divination by fire, human sacrifice and ancestor worship. The most famous artifacts were tortoise shells and "oracle" bones, on which were inscribed various inquiries for divination (including military and political undertakings), as well as matters of hunting and health prospects for the emperor.

Shang culture was a predominantly Bronze Age Neolithic society, based on the domestication of plants and animals. Most members of society lived in small hamlets in which a distinct class structure emerged, consisting of the ruling elite and the peasant craftsman.

Deceased members of the community played a very important role in people's beliefs and so in their everyday lives, interweaving the living and the departed. Through divination, the living consulted their deceased ancestors about all kinds of matters. They were consulted in times of war and peace, questioned about the bounty of the harvest, and their advice sought in matters of sickness and health. The active relationship of the dead with the living consisted of mutual obligations for the well-being of the community. The living had a responsibility to care for the remains of the dead by placing their bones near good wind and water (Feng shui) and honouring them through memory and ritual sacrifice. It was thought to be the responsibility of the dead to assure the living of prosperity and health. In this way the living and the dead lived in mutual harmony.

HEALTH AND HEALING IN THE SHANG DYNASTY

Legend has always attributed the invention of early medicine to two great Celestial Emperors: Shen Nong (the Red Emperor, who invented herbal therapy) and Huang Di (the Yellow Emperor, who invented the art of medicine). The two earliest great classics of medicine bear their names: the *Shen Nong Ben Cao Jing* (Canon of Herbal Medicine) and the *Huang Di Nei Jing*, which laid the foundation for medical theory. Legend has held that they dated back to great antiquity, but the truth is they were compiled in much later periods, by many contributors.

The people of the Shang cultures had concerns for matters of health and had developed a long tradition of healing practices. Health care was relatively simple in structure. A number of illnesses were reported but very few diseases.

Illnesses, as Paul Unschuld points out,

are those disturbances of the individual organism that disrupt normal activity and function, whereas disease is the socially derived explanation of their cause.

THE CURSE OF THE ANCESTORS

In early Shang records, many ailments are listed, including afflictions of the foot, nose, ear, tooth and tongue, diseases of the eye, including blindness, childhood diseases, scabies, and observations about the termination of diseases. However, no drug prescriptions were mentioned. Whether the affliction be a toothache, cough or a headache, only one remedy was mentioned: prayer. What is important to realize is that there was believed to be one cause for all of these afflictions: the curse of the ancestors. So the etiology of a toothache, a broken foot or a crop failure might be the same – an ancestor who is displeased and curses the living. The difference between a toothache and crop failure is, of course,

WIND

a matter of whether it is of individual or community concern. The important thing in healing therefore is to ascertain through divination the origin of the curse and to perform the necessary ritual sacrifices to lift it.

NATURAL EVILS

Natural influences were also mentioned as causes of disease. Wind evil was mentioned as a cause of affliction. These winds may have come anyway, or might have been sent by ancestors to beset the village. If this was the case, then the intervention of the king was required to remove the influence of evil wind by performing the proper rituals for the ancestors. Many of these medical theories would later be abandoned or transformed, serving as the foundation for new theories as Chinese medicine shifted toward empirical investigation and rational medicine under the influence of the various philosophical traditions that emerged in the next phase.

ANCESTOR THERAPY

Ancestor therapy did not necessitate a physical examination, nor did it require any direct attention to the patient. It was a social act, often requiring the king to consult the oracle to determine the will of the ancestors.

The king was the sole practitioner of ancestor therapy and thus had a great responsibility to the welfare of the community. In this way the living were reconciled with the dead and the health of the community was restored. This practice also provided a justification for total political dominance by the Shang ruler, as he took on the role of caretaker for the whole community.

THE ZHOU PERIOD

This period (1100–221 BC) marked the birth of formal systems. Shang culture's central authority dissolved in the twelfth century BC, when it was conquered by the semi-nomadic Zhou. The people of the Zhou period had an advanced agricultural technology. This included a communally managed irrigation system that increased their productive capacity and enabled them to sustain a prolonged armed assault. In this period, which has been compared to the European feudal era, more than 1,000 districts were formed. The capital was moved from Shang to the Shenshi province. The Zhou people were also rooted in ancestor worship, like the vanquished Shang, and they attempted to restore the old traditions. In fact, many of the Shang nobility were absorbed into the new Western Zhou Dynasty.

In 771 BC, the capital was moved further east to Lo-i as the rulers sought eastern support in a bloody battle over succession to the throne. During the following years, all kinds of internal intrigues and bloodshed ensued and the power of the king over outlying lands weakened. The introduction of new technologies, the production of iron and salt, the advent of a money-based economy and an increasingly mobile population, meant that the rulers lost their centralized control and the various states became more powerful in their own right. Many wars took place between the seven provinces and with invaders from the north.

Alliances were formed and then quickly dissolved. The period from 481 to 221 BC was so bloody and rivalries were so strong between provinces that historians have designated it the "Warring States" period. The earlier regard for honour and mutual ancestry was now replaced by a hungry lust for power and success, and the old feudal values of morality, honour and balanced moderation were supplanted by the ruthless values of the rulers of the Chin state. It was the Chin rulers that

succeeded in finally unifying China, in 221 BC.

King Cheng had himself proclaimed Shih Huang Di, the first emperor of a now unified China. He was aware that all vestiges of the early feudal provinces must be eradicated in order to ensure that the unification would remain secure, so the entire empire was reorganized into administrative districts with military governors. Standardization of weights and measures was undertaken and public roads were built between the various districts. The Yellow Emperor Huang Di also ordered the collection, and later burning, of all written materials – except those relating to medical care, drugs, oracles, agriculture and forestry.

MEDICINE BEGINS IN THE ZHOU PERIOD

The period of turmoil and internal strife known as "The Spring to Autumn period" (770–476 BC), including the Warring States period of the Zhou Dynasty, abounded with philosophical, scientific, and spiritual inquiry. This period gave rise to the prac-

tice of what has been termed "Demonic" medicine, which in turn was eventually replaced by the later philosophical schools of Yin/Yang dualism, the Five Correspondences/element theory, and the strong influences of Taoism and Confucianism.

And so ancestral therapy was gradually replaced by Demonic medicine, which put forward the theory of demon attacks. Demons were thought to inhabit the earth and lie in wait in dark corners in the woods or cavern, ready to strike unsuspecting victims. To be "ill" was to be struck by a demon of some kind. The Wu shamans displayed a fascinating repertoire of medical techniques, which included herbal therapy, traditional shamanism and public exorcism for which shamans ran around the outskirts of a village, shouting and waving sticks to drive away the evil spirits.

Public executions were also held as a way of discouraging the demons. The use of talismans for ritual protection was common, and even acupuncture was said to be employed for ridding the body of demonic influence. In the medical treatise, *Prescriptions Against Fifty-two Ailments* (168 BC), Wu Shih Er Pin Fang comments on the sophisticated demon exorcism ritual formulas along with magical procedures, which included the time of day and manner of performance. Herbal formulas were often combined to aid the expulsion of demons, and Pien Chio (407–310 BC), the legendary first acupuncturist, specifically mentions 13 acupuncture points in the treatment against demons.

THE BEGINNINGS OF EMPIRICISM AND EARLY SCIENCE

There were many influences that began to shift philosophy to a more empirical and scientific version of medicine in the late Zhou period. These times saw a true flowering of many diverse philosophies – so much so that it has been termed the period of the "Hundred Schools of Thought". This period also witnessed the birth of Confucius (551–479 BC) and his active, conscious humanism, and it promoted a system of ethics and spiritual development to be employed in public life. He was responding to the moral and political chaos around him as feudal states clashed in war and intrigue. He developed the theory of the "superior man" (junzi) who strove "to love others" as a guiding principle for the basis of order in society. Later philosophers such as Mencius (372–289 BC) and Xun Zi (298–238 BC) embraced Confucianism and were instrumental in its later adoption as the formal political system in the Han Dynasty.

Another figure, called Laozi (sixth century BC), also had political concerns, although his main interests lay in investigating nature, life-prolonging alchemical experiments and biological change. In his *Dao De Jing* (Classic of The Way and of Virtue), he admonished rulers and encouraged them to follow the spiritual practice of the Tao (Dao) in order to improve the lives of all the people.

The Logicians and Mohists worked hard to develop a scientific logic. The Mohists, although interested in a chivalrous community that was not focused exclusively on the family, were also attracted to mechanics and physics. All of these played a part in the establishment of a scientific tradition and development in Chinese medicine as formulated in the *Huang Di Nei Jing*.

MOHIST AND LOGICIAN SCIENTIFIC INFLUENCE

THE MOHISTS

Mo Ti (479–381 BC) preached a social philosophy of universal love not readily applicable to scientific inquiry, as well as a firm belief in spirits and demons. The Mohist philosophers nevertheless promoted ideas that laid the ground for empirical methods, developed much further by later followers. They maintained an empirical attitude towards investigating phenomena and relied on a community of observers to verify the truth or falsity of a claim. For example, the fact that many people reported the witnessing of an event such as a ghost sighting, would gave credence to the possibility of the ghost's existence.

The later commentaries of the original *Canons of Mo Tzu* (Book of Master Mo) illustrate the efforts of his followers to grapple with the logic of investigation. Like the Greeks, the Mohists were aware of the social factors in assigning terminology and they discussed sensation, perception, levels of causality, classification, the difference between first- and second-hand evidence and deductive and

RIGHT
Confucius, also known as K'ung Ch'iu.

inductive logic. Their interest in chivalrous defence of the weak encouraged the study of physics and mechanics in the art of defensive warfare.

THE LOGICIANS

The Logicians, or "School of Names", were developed by Hui Shih and Kungsun Lun in the fourth century BC. The *Kungsun Lun Tzu* was said to represent a pinnacle of Chinese philosophical writing and consisted of dialogues concerning "universals" (such as oneness and twoness, for example). Through his paradoxes and discussion of fundamental principles, Kungsun Lun addressed the idea of change, one of the central problems in empirical investigation.

And so the Logicians, including Hui Shih, began to formulate dialectical rather than formal logic, which would become a central feature of Chinese scientific investigation and medical theory.

TAOIST SCIENTIFIC INFLUENCE

The most important contribution of the Taoists to traditional Chinese medicine was its empirical and scientific theories. Not only did the Taoist alchemists encourage the investigation of life-prolonging substances that formed the basis for herbal science and therapy, but they also encouraged empirical investigation in general, and were responsible for the development of gunpowder and other breakthroughs in chemistry.

Early Taoists were not concerned with the prolonging of life. They maintained that the change from life to death was merely a transition from one state of existence to another. Later Taoists sought intensively to cultivate existence because of the belief that one should make the most of our allotted existence on earth. They thought that immortality might be achieved by using medicinal substances or performing special exercises or meditation techniques. The methods employed to achieve immortality included special breathing exercises, combined with meditation, to develop the strength of Qi within the body. Qi (pronounced "chee") is sometimes translated as "air", "vapour" or "breath" and represents the energy throughout the universe and that which pervades and flows within the human body. This is another significant aspect of Chinese medicine and is very close to the Greek idea of "pneuma", or the Indian "prana".

Manfred Porkert defines Qi as "energy of definite (or definable) quality, energy of a definite direction in space, of a definite arrangement, quality, or structure" and "energetic configuration". It is the vital force that animates a living organism. It is essential for the smooth functioning of the internal organ systems through which it circulates. It gives the power that animates them (whether it be the pumping of blood throughout the body or the power of speech, only two of many such examples). Paul Unschuld refers to Qi as "finest matter" and emphasizes that, even though it is invisible and without form, it is still referred to as a substance in the ancient literature and this is an important consideration when interpreting ancient medical texts.

SYSTEMATIC
CORRESPONDENCES

T he theories of Yin/Yang, and of the Five Elements, developed around the fourth century BC and are often called the theories of systematic correspondences. This is because of their unique contribution to the idea that the universe, as well as the body, consists of dynamic and functional interrelations. It attempts to explain the universe as forces or principles instead of the whims of gods, ancestors or demons. Along with the five-element theory of nature, this helped to create an important link in the development of Chinese science and medical theory. The I Ching (The Book of Changes) is a book about the constant flux and permanence of this process in the universe. The character "Jing" means "great book", and the character "I" is derived from an abstract pictorial representation of the sun and the moon in combination, which signifies Yang and Yin respectively.

YANG AND YIN

Originally, Yang and Yin represented the sunny and shady sides of a mountain. Chinese science later developed this principle to stand for polar opposites of inter-related phenomena. Yang represents the functional energetic qualities of the universe, while Yin represents the structural and substantive qualities of the universe. This has been explained in the following way: "in modern terms, yang corresponds to all that is active, expansive, centrifugal, aggressive, demanding, (polar) negative, and yin implies all that is structural, substantive, contractive, centripetal, responsive, conservative, (polar) positive". These inter-related phenomena are expressed in terms of corre-spondences between qualities of any identifiable object. One cannot exist without the other. For example, the concept of up cannot exist without the idea of down, nor the concept of fast without the corresponding idea of slow.

Change, or "I", in the universe is a dynamic interaction between Yin/Yang, in which the constant interplay of these basic forces creates, and is created by, the universe of which we are all a part. "The universe is in movement or transformation at every moment. Life itself is a process of never-ending change from birth to death...The I Ching is an attempt to find reliable rules for nature, and for human life in relation to changes in the universe."

Actually, the I Ching forms the basis for all Chinese science and is a fundamental part of Chinese cultural expres-sion. In medicine, the theory of Yin/Yang is the organizing principle in the correlation of all medical information (for example, the differen-tiation of syndromes and pulse qualities), and combines with other important theories like the Five Transformative Phase and Channel theories. So, in essence, "The Yin/Yang doctrine is simple but its influ-ence has been very extensive. No aspect of Chinese civilization – metaphysics, med-

icine, government, or art – has escaped its imprint." There were two schools of Yin/Yang theorists. The main difference between them was whether to divide the natural unfolding of change into four or six divisions.

FIVE TRANSFORMATIVE PHASES

Another vitally important philosophical and empirical contribution to Chinese science that was incorporated extensively within medical theory was the principle of Wuxing – the "Five Transformative Phases" or elements. In ancient times in China, it was thought that the universe consisted of five transformative phases, or natures. Tzu-Szu (492–431 BC) was said to have advanced this theory, later redeveloped by Mencius. The world was viewed as a constant interaction and combination of the five transformative phases.

The five basic transformative phases are Wood, Fire, Earth, Metal and Water. This theory was an attempt to classify the basic properties of material things in the process of change. Each transformative phase has a particular nature and a predictable interaction and relationship with each of the others. Originally, the Yin/Yang theorists and Five Element theorists disagreed profoundly about the nature of change, but the concepts were later resolved and are now combined.

So integrated is the Wuxing with Yin/Yang that they may now be considered different elements of a unified concept. "We are aware that Wuxing theory originated from and cannot be separated from Yin/Yang theory, so we can conclude that Wuxing is Yin/Yang, and Yin/Yang is Tao."

In interaction, elements may clash, balance or nurture the others, depending on their own inherent nature as well as their relative strength. The movement of Nature is a constant interplay of the natural assertions, adjustments or adaptations of these basic primal forces

ABOVE

The traditional "Willow Pattern" features the Five Elements: Wood, Fire, Earth, Metal and Water.

through the seasons. In this way Nature achieves an harmonious but vigorous balance. In the theory of Yin/Yang, as well as with the Five Elements, "The outlook is dynamic and not static. And the end is an ordered Nature rather than chaos. In point of process, there is contradiction as well as harmony, and in point of reality, there is unity in multiplicity."

The elements foster balance and harmony with each other. When each transformative phase plays its natural part, all things function smoothly. Each specific transformative phase functions to keep another transformative phase in balance with the whole, and is in turn balanced by yet another. The ancient empirical philosophers observed that the transformative phases also had specific functional relationships in the natural cycle of Nature. Just as seasons change from one to the next, so the various transformative phases of Nature change or "give birth" to the others. All of Nature, including human social and political activity and changes, is explained by these transformative phases and their various corresponding natures.

WOOD

WATER

It was in this light that the human body was seen as a part of Nature. The Wuxing was developed to represent these basic natural principles and forces. Within the body there are "physiological" trans-

formative phases and energies that reflect the basic forces of life. There are tissues and organ functions that resemble each of the transformative phases both physically and energetically, and reflect the same basic interrelationships of Nature. There is a "physiological" equivalent to the actions of Wood, Fire, Earth, Metal and Water functioning within the body. For example, Wood is related to the organs of the Liver/Gall Bladder, Fire is related to the Heart/Small Intestine, Earth is related to the Spleen/Stomach, Metal is related to the Lung/Large Intestine, and Water is related to the Kidney/Bladder.

EARTH

FIRE

Each element nourishes another and they depend upon each other for their growth and support. As the five transformative phases/elements nourish each other, so do the organ systems. As it is in Nature, so it is in the organ system. For example, Water or the Kidney/Bladder system supports growth; Earth or the Stomach/Spleen system can dam Water/Kidney/Bladder, controlling the natural or physiological excess of water. As one transformative phase or physiological system nurtures or controls another, balance is achieved.

METAL

FIRE

Fire is symbolized by the Heart/Small Intestine.

WOOD

Wood is symbolized by the Liver/Gall Bladder.

EARTH

Earth is symbolized by the Spleen/Stomach.

METAL

Metal is symbolized by the Lung/Large Intestine.

WATER

Water is symbolized by the Kidney/Bladder.

CONFUCIAN MEDICINE
IN THE HAN DYNASTY

This was the period when the Huang Di Nei Jing was compiled. In the Han Dynasty, most of the great scientific ideas and precepts were formalized and the foundation was laid for all later developments in traditional Chinese medicine.

The Huang Di Nei Jing is actually the work of many unknown authors in the employ of the first Han Emperor (who took the name Huang Di, the legendary Yellow Emperor) and his successors. They worked to synthesize the best medical thinking of the time and to create a working medical theory and system.

The *Nei Jing* consists of two parts: the *Su Wen* (Essential Questions), which deals with anatomy, physiology and therapy; and the *Ling Shu* (Miraculous Pivot or Canon of Acupuncture), which deals mostly with acupuncture. Certain passages and concepts illustrate the various philosophical roots that now form a complete system.

For example, in the *Su Wen* the Yellow Emperor asks Ch'i Po, the famous physician with whom he has a constant dialogue about medical problems throughout the work: "Why don't men live to one hundred years as they used to?" To which Ch'i Po replies: "The men of antiquity understood the Tao (they therefore strove to adapt their existence to the rules of Yin/Yang [duality] and to live in harmony with numerical calculations. Moderation determined the consumption of food and drink; they arose and slept in accordance with a consistent order. No one depleted his strength through unseemly behaviour. The men of antiquity thus preserved both body and mind in their full power and reached the full extent of life accorded by Nature." This passage clearly reflects the Taoist influence in the *Su Wen*, with its reference to life-preserving techniques and behaviour.

ABOVE

Radish and ginger act on the lung and stomach, and are used to treat the common cold. According to Confucian theory, radish is the "Emperor" and ginger is its "minister", enhancing its action.

CONFUCIANISM

Confucianism, with its complex social networks and elaborate economic framework and interrelations, is reflected in some of the descriptions of physiological functions. For example, the Zang organs (Stomach, Small Intestine, Large Intestine, Triple Burner, Bladder and Gall Bladder) are hollow and are used to store food or waste material for transport through the gastro-intestinal system. The word "zang" means depot or storage facility. There are many such references to canals, waterways, palaces, emperors, ministers and assistants in the names of acupuncture points and in herbal therapy. The chief herb in a herbal formula is called the Emperor; subsequent herbs are ministers and assistants. These descriptions represent a rich Confucian influence in Chinese medicine.

RIGHT
In this illustration, the Chinese philosopher Confucius is supervising the exorcism of evil influences.

An example of conceptual synthesis occurs when we combine the idea of Yin/Yang with the Five Elements theory. In physiology, we find that, not only do we have organ systems represented by elements (for example, the Liver Channel represents the Wood function within the body), but we can also divide this internal function of the Liver into both Liver Yin (blood storage/structural) and Liver Yang (free coursing of Qi/active) aspects. Both help to counterbalance and support the activity of the other. Also, in the theory of Zang-Fu Organs the Gall Bladder (relatively more Qi) functions as an external (Yang) relation to the relatively more internal (Yin) activity of the Liver (relatively more blood), thus making a Yin/Yang coupling of the Wood element.

SCIENCE IN ANCIENT CHINA AND MODERN INTERPRETATION

The early mainstream scientific concepts of the ancient Chinese were different from those adopted by the West, but no less scientific. The logic of the system was built on a different perspective from that of the Western scientific tradition. The logic that created the intricate internal relations of the correspondences of Yin/Yang and the five transformative phases was conceived to represent an active universe of constant change, while the Western logic of the Greeks emphasized the delineation of discrete identities. Actually, some of the pre-Socratic philosophers of ancient Greece, including Empedokles, a physician, postulated a philosophical tradition that was roughly equivalent to the theory of Yin/Yang. For him, Love and Strife symbolized contradictory forces of a dynamic universe that complemented, contradicted and influenced each other. His philosophy was abandoned in favour of the traditional Aristotelian approach of categorization.

Early Chinese medical science as we know it today derives its wisdom from many different sources. Rational empirical medicine began in the fifth century BC, around the time that the ancient Greeks developed their Western version of empirical classification. This signifies the formal development of science and medicine based on natural laws and empiricism instead of medicine based on supernatural principles. Many diverse philosophical tendencies emerged and influenced its development. These included ideas from the Taoist, Mohist, Logician, Yin/Yang and Five Element schools of thought.

Confucian political influence was also a strong organizing force and, by the beginning of the Han Dynasty in the first century BC, a clear synthesis of the empirical traditions had been accomplished and a formal medical scientific tradition had been established, exemplified by the *Huang Di Nei Jing*.

CAUSES OF DISEASE

According to traditional Chinese medicine, we are alive and healthy because our body is in a state of harmony. This state of harmony is a balance between Yin and Yang, between the different organs of our own body, and between our body and the environment in which we live. This harmony is constantly being broken, not only because of our own daily activities, which are accomplished through the functions of the different organs of our body, but also because of the different influences from the outside environment that can affect both our body and the performance of our organs. When a person is healthy, any disharmonies are quickly restored, and thus a dynamic equilibrium is maintained. In this state, the body remains healthy and maintains a normal

EXTERNAL CAUSES
Wind.

physiological balance. When this dynamic equilibrium is broken and is not restored, we will feel ill and then disease will occur. In traditional Chinese medicine, the factors that can damage or break this equilibrium in the human body are the causes of disease.

Since ancient times in Chinese history, practitioners of traditional Chinese medicine have tried to understand and explain the factors *that can cause disease, and to classify them into different categories. Approximately 1,000 years ago, during the Song Dynasty, a medical scientist called Chen Yan classified the causes of disease into three general categories:*

1 External (exogenous) causes
These include the external climatic influences that cause disease.

2 Internal (endogenous) causes
These include emotional distresses that damage the visceral organs, thereby causing disease.

3 Neither external nor internal causes
These include other factors that affect health, such as diet, trauma and sexual activity.

INTERNAL CAUSES
Stress.

This method of categorizing the causes of disease is somewhat simplified and ignores the fact that our own physical constitution plays a very important role in the occurrence of disease. Nevertheless, this method does have significance in clinical practice and provides guidelines for the diagnosis and treatment of disease.

OTHER CAUSES
Diet.

In traditional Chinese medicine, causes of disease are mainly determined by analyzing our symptoms, which is called "differentiating the syndromes to find the cause" or "differential diagnosis to identify the pathogen".

EXTERNAL AND INTERNAL DISEASE

*H*uman beings have always struggled against external and internal threats to health. External factors such as climate and weather changes – called pathogenic or malignant factors in traditional Chinese medicine – do not normally cause disease. However, when the body's ability to adjust to climate changes is diminished or when environmental changes occur too suddenly for the body to adjust, the body's delicate balance is disrupted and ill-health ensues. On the other hand, some diseases are considered to be caused by internal problems. They are the result of a disharmony created by emotional stresses and dysfunctions of our own visceral organs.

THE SIX EXTERNAL CAUSES OF DISEASE

The six external factors that cause disease include the normal climatic elements:

◆ WIND
◆ HEAT/FIRE
◆ SUMMER-HEAT
◆ DAMPNESS
◆ DRYNESS
◆ COLD

Each of these elements is associated with a particular season and, although most of them can cause disease at

any time of the year, it is during their related season that they tend to cause illness. Wind is most common in the spring, heat/fire in the summer, dampness in late summer, dryness in the autumn, and cold in the winter. For example, we tend to contract summer-heat diseases, such as heatstroke, in the summer. Likewise, living in a damp environment makes us more susceptible to diseases related to dampness, such as arthritis.

These six external factors can induce disease individually by themselves, but in

most cases they combine together, two or three at a time, and affect the human body simultaneously. For example, dysentery is caused by both damp and heat in the large intestine, and acute rheumatic arthritis is caused by wind, damp and heat in the joints. During the process of a disease, the six pathogenic factors will not only influence each other, but under certain conditions can also transform into each other. This transformation is seen in a person who suffers from the mild exterior condition of a common cold that goes deeper into the body and develops into pneumonia – or heat in the Lungs as we say in traditional Chinese medicine.

THE FIVE INTERNAL CAUSES OF DISEASE

In order to distinguish these from the six external evils, we call them:

◆ INTERNAL WIND
◆ INTERNAL HEAT/FIRE
◆ INTERNAL DAMPNESS
◆ INTERNAL DRYNESS
◆ INTERNAL COLD

These internal problems also manifest symptoms of wind, heat/fire, dampness, dryness and cold.

OTHER FACTORS RELATED TO THE SIX EXTERNAL EVILS

In modern clinical practice, diseases that are caused by the six external evils also include those that are related to any organic factors (bacteria and viruses), chemical factors (pesticides), and physical factors (nuclear radiation).

WIND

According to the Five Elements, spring is usually the most windy season of the year and therefore wind is considered the major climatic element of this season, although it can also appear at other times of the year. There are two broad categories of wind disease: external wind and internal wind. External wind disorders are influenced by wind from the natural environment outside, and are less serious than internal wind diseases.

Disorders due to external wind can occur in spring as well as any of the other seasons of the year.

SYNDROMES INDUCED BY WIND

EXTERNAL WIND

When pathogenic wind invades the outer layer of our body, it will cause fevers, chills and sweating. Because the skin is related to the lungs, when pathogenic wind invades the body surface, it will also affect the lungs and induce symptoms of coughing, a stuffy and running nose and an itchy or scratchy throat. In traditional Chinese medicine, this condition is called "shang feng" or "invaded by wind".

There are four other external pathogenic factors (heat, dampness, dryness and cold) that usually rely on wind to invade and enter the body. Because of this phenomenon, wind is considered to be the predecessor of all other external pathogens. The other external pathogenic factors often invade the body at the same time as the wind.

◆ When external wind combines with cold, a "wind-cold syndrome" will result, in which the patient's main symptoms will manifest as chills more than fever and an aversion to cold.

◆ When external wind combines with heat, a "wind-heat" syndrome will be produced, in which the patient will feel fever rather than chills and the throat might be red and sore. There may be thirst and dark-coloured urine, and the tongue will be red with a thin yellow coating.

◆ When wind combines with dampness, a "wind-dampness" syndrome will result, in which there will be a fever that is worse in the afternoon, an aversion to wind, sweating and swollen and painful joints in which the location of the pain moves around. There may also be symptoms of oedema on the face or the body.

◆ When wind combines with dryness, a wind-dryness syndrome will occur. Symptoms include a dry mouth, dry nose, dry throat, dry skin and a dry cough.

INTERNAL WIND

The main symptoms of internal wind include spasms, convulsions, a rigid neck, upward-straining of the eyes and opisthonis (muscular spasms). In less serious cases, there will be numbness or tremors of the limbs, blurry eyes and vertigo. In traditional Chinese medicine, these symptoms are all related to the liver and are usually called "liver wind". Because the liver is in

ABOVE

External wind can cause a cold but internal wind can lead to more serious problems – these are usually referred to as "liver wind".

LEFT
External wind shapes our environment; pathogenic wind penetrates our body, influencing our well-being.

RIGHT

Disease caused by pathogenic wind migrates around the body. Arthritis may start in the knees then spread to other joints in the body affecting different areas at various times.

charge of storing the blood and in charge of the ligaments, internal wind conditions are usually caused by deficiencies or dysfunctions of the liver. As the medical theory surrounding liver wind disorders can be very complicated, suffice it to say that such symptoms are due either to a deficiency of the liver Yin, which results in wind disturbing and moving in the upper parts of the body, or to a deficiency of the liver blood, which can cause lack of nourishment to the ligaments.

CHARACTERISTICS OF EXTERNAL AND INTERNAL WIND

1 Wind has the nature of ascending and dispersing. Because of this tendency to move upwards and outwards, wind is classified as a Yang pathogen. Because of this Yang nature, diseases influenced by pathogenic wind tend to affect the Yang areas of the body, including the face and the head (upper areas), and the surface of the body (outer areas). Wind also opens up the pores of the skin and can cause symptoms of sweating and a marked dislike of winds and draughts.

2 Wind has a tendency to move around swiftly and make frequent changes in direction. Because of this, diseases that are influenced by wind are characterized by the special feature of migration. The location of a wind pathogen is never fixed,

but often moves around from one part of the body to another. The most obvious example is a person with arthritis, where the pain moves from the knee to the hip, and then to the elbow. This type of movement indicates that the pain is indeed related to pathogenic wind. Another example of this special moving and changing characteristic of pathogenic wind is urticaria, a skin problem in which the patient suffers from itching and rashes that move constantly from one part of the body to another. Furthermore, diseases associated with wind tend to be acute conditions that occur suddenly and change very rapidly. Examples include strokes or cerebrovascular diseases, which are called "windstroke" in traditional Chinese medicine. The Chinese term "windstroke" reflects the rapid and changing nature of the wind pathogen that causes this type of sudden attack.

3 Wind diseases are also characterized by involuntary movements. The ancient Chinese medical texts say that, when wind prevails, it will produce involuntary movements. Any symptoms that show involuntary movement, such as tremors, spasms, vertigo, dizziness and convulsions, are all symptoms indicating pathogenic wind. These symptoms can occur with both externally caused diseases, such as meningitis or encephalitis, and with internally caused diseases, such as hypertension or epilepsy.

HEAT/FIRE

The difference between fire and heat is one of temperature. Fire is not only higher in temperature, but it always flares upwards, like flames. When fire is inside the human body, it will tend to create symptoms that flare up in the upper part of the body. Pathogenic fire is usually internal and could result from problems with the kidney's Yang energy and function. Internal fire could also be the result of other external pathogenic factors (such as wind, summer heat, dampness, dryness and cold), which could penetrate into the body and transform into fire. Internal fire may also be produced by excessive emotional stimulation or dysfunction of the organs, which can cause stagnation in the body, eventually creating heat or fire.

In traditional Chinese medicine, fire can be associated with several different organs, each pattern displaying specific signs and symptoms. People are frequently diagnosed with the syndromes "stomach fire", "liver fire" and "heart fire".

SYNDROMES INDUCED BY FIRE

EXCESS FIRE

The condition of excess fire is usually acute with a short duration. Patients have a high fever or a strong aversion to heat and are very restless, irritable and thirsty. They have little urine or sweat, a flushed face and red eyes, and may sometimes experience delirium.

DEFICIENT FIRE

Conditions of deficient fire are often chronic. They are caused by the depletion of the body's own healthy energy. The most common syndromes are related to Yin deficiency with deficient fire.

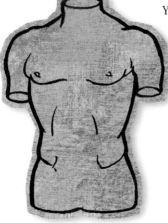

- ◆ Heart fire
- ◆ Liver fire
- ◆ Stomach fire

SYMPTOMS OF YIN DEFICIENCY

Symptoms of Yin deficiency may include:	worse in the afternoon
◆ Flushed cheeks	◆ Irritability
◆ Hot hands and feet	◆ Inability to fall asleep
◆ Low-grade fever that is	◆ Night sweats
	◆ Sore and dry throat

CHARACTERISTICS OF EXCESS AND DEFICIENT FIRE

1 Fire flares upwards and is extremely hot. Pathogenic fire is a sign of heat. In diseases involving fire, the body temperature is higher, and the patient will be restless and irritable, with a flushed face, red eyes and red lips, and a red, sore and swollen throat.

2 The extreme heat from pathogenic fire will exhaust the body fluids. When we put a kettle of water over a high flame, the water in the kettle gradually boils off and diminishes. The same applies to the human body. Because of the exhaustion of body fluids in diseases that are caused by pathogenic fire, patients will feel extremely thirsty. Their mouth and lips will be dry, they will sweat very little, their urine will be scanty and they will also tend to be constipated.

3 Fire and heat can burn and damage the vessels of the body. Symptoms include bleeding from the nose, blood in the urine or stools, bleeding associated with haemorrhoids, or even eruptions or rashes on the skin. In any case, there will always be symptoms of fire and heat, such as fever, irritability or thirst.

ABOVE
Just as boiling water in a kettle evaporates to vapour, the body will lose vital fluids due to the extreme heat of pathogenic fire.

SYMPTOMS OF FIRE FLARING UP

When fire flares upwards, we will usually find symptoms like the following:

Cold sores on the tongue or mouth	Related to heart fire
Swelling of the gums	Related to stomach fire
Red or swollen eyes	Related to liver fire

SIGNS OF PATHOGENIC
FIRE IN THE BODY

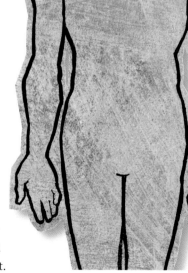

Restless and irritable

Flushed face

Red eyes

Red lips

Red, sore and
swollen throat

High body
temperature

SUMMER HEAT

Like fire, summer heat is a major climatic element of summer. Summer heat is converted from fire and heat. Of the six exogenous pathogenic factors, this is the only pathogen that is seasonal, occurring only in summer, and not in any other season. This is also the only pathogen that is completely external, caused only by the heat from the outside environment. There is no internal summer-heat.

SYNDROMES AND SYMPTOMS OF EXTERNAL SUMMER HEAT

Summer heat disorders happen frequently during the summer months. The main symptoms include fever, excessive sweating, thirst, irritability, fatigue and shortness of breath.

Summer heatstroke is another common syndrome that occurs during the summer. In a mild case, the patient will only experience some dizziness, nausea, tiredness or lack of energy. In more serious cases, when a person is exposed to too much heat for too long, the patient could suddenly faint, lose consciousness, or experience profuse sweating, thirst and shortness of breath. The hands and feet become cold and the patient could go into a state of shock.

CHARACTERISTICS OF EXTERNAL SUMMER HEAT

1 Summer heat is a climatic pathogen that features scorching heat. Both summer and heat are Yang elements of the natural environment, therefore summer heat is also classified as a Yang pathogen. When one is affected by this extreme heat in the summer, the body will develop a very high temperature.

2 Summer heat tends to ascend and disperse. Because of this, it easily exhausts the body's energy and damages the body fluids. We all know that, when we are hot, the pores of our skin open up and we sweat. This is a normal physiological mechanism of the body, designed to regulate body temperature and prevent the body from getting too hot. However, when we sweat too much, we might lose too much body fluid, causing not only dehydration, but also loss of energy. For exam-

ple, people who work outdoors during the summer often crave large amounts of cooling fluids to keep their body temperature down, to replenish the body fluids that are lost from sweating, and to prevent them from getting heatstroke.

3 Summer heat often mixes with dampness. Besides being hot, the summer is also often rainy, and the air humid and damp. Therefore, when we are affect-

ed by summer heat, it is easy to be affected by dampness at the same time, and to contract a case of "summer heat and dampness". In this situation, the patient will have symptoms of summer heat along with symptoms of dampness, including a high fever that is more pronounced in the afternoon, although the body is not hot to the touch. There will also be other symptoms, such as thirst, malaise, heaviness of the extremities, loss of appetite, nausea, fullness and oppression in the chest, loose stools, and dark urine.

Humid conditions caused by summer heat and dampness can give rise to the patient showing symptoms of both simultaneously.

DAMPNESS

Dampness is also divided into external and internal dampness. External dampness is the dampness in the outside environment, including the humidity in the air – the water, rain and fog that we often find around us. According to the Five Elements, the body tends to be especially influenced by external dampness in late summer, because this is often the rainiest season of the year. Besides the weather, working or living in a damp location can also allow pathogenic dampness to affect the body, and consequently induce related health problems. Internal dampness is usually the result of spleen dysfunction, in which this organ becomes unable to transmit and digest the water and fluids in our body, leading to the retention of water and dampness.

Although external dampness differs from internal dampness, they often influence each other in the course of a disease. When a person's spleen is deficient, not only will internal dampness develop, but this condition will also make him or her more susceptible to dampness from the outside environment. Likewise, when outside dampness invades our body, it tends to damage the spleen's functions and create internal dampness.

SYNDROMES INDUCED BY DAMPNESS

EXTERNAL DAMPNESS
When pathogenic dampness damages the surface of our body only, it causes an external or superficial dampness syndrome. The patient shows symptoms of chills, fever that does not recede with sweating, heavy limbs, sluggishness and a suppressed feeling in the chest. Because there is excess dampness already in the body, the patient will not feel thirsty.

If pathogenic dampness affects our joints, then it will cause "shi bi" or "arthritis caused by dampness". The joints will feel heavy and sore, sometimes swollen and difficult to move, and the pain will always be in the same location in the body.

INTERNAL DAMPNESS
Internal dampness is usually related to dysfunction of the spleen. When the spleen's mechanism of transporting and processing water is reduced, a common symptom is difficult urination. If the dampness is mainly in the upper chest (above the diaphragm), the patient may feel tightness in the chest, dizziness or vertigo. If the dampness is in the mid-stomach area, the patient could feel fullness and distended sensations in the stomach and abdomen, nausea, a sticky or sweet taste in the mouth, soft or loose stools and heaviness of the limbs. If the dampness is in the lower abdominal cavity, there will be oedema, difficult urination or vaginal discharge in women.

ABOVE
External dampness is present in our environment: in water and damp air.

CHARACTERISTICS OF EXTERNAL AND INTERNAL DAMPNESS

1 Dampness is a pathogen that is heavy and murky in nature. Any illness that is caused by pathogenic dampness will manifest symptoms that bring a heavy and sluggish feeling to the body and

limbs. For example, if the head is affected by dampness, it will feel heavy and tight, as if it were wrapped in a turban. When an arthritic joint is affected by dampness, the joint will feel heavy and be difficult to move. The problem in the joint will tend to stay in the same place. Any secretions or discharges from syndromes due to dampness are usually murky rather than clear, such as cloudy urine, dysentery with pus in the stools, vaginal discharges that contain pus or

blood or skin problems such as boils and eczema.

2 Viscosity is a feature of dampness. Not only are symptoms of dampness viscous in nature, but also the process of diseases related to dampness tends to be intractable and prolonged. Two examples of this stubborn tendency are seen in the symptom of a strained sensation in the anus after diarrhoea due to dampness in the large intestine, or in the condition of eczema, which is very difficult to remove.

3 Dampness is classified as a Yin pathogen, as it has many Yin characteristics, such as being a form of water, being heavy and turbid and being viscous in nature. Because dampness is considered to be a Yin substance, an excess amount will restrain and damage Yang Qi, as well as impeding vital functioning mechanisms in the body. The organ that is in charge of transporting and processing water is the spleen. When the spleen Qi is deficient, the ability to transport and process water becomes impaired, causing the retention of water and dampness inside the body. Also, when the body is invaded by pathogenic dampness, it will impede the Yang Qi of the spleen and impair the function of the organ, leading to water- and dampness retention, with symptoms of oedema or soft and loose stools. The heavy, turbid and viscous nature of dampness can cause a tight sensation in the chest, bloated feelings and a fullness in the stomach and abdomen.

DRYNESS

According to the Five Elements, dryness is a climatic element of autumn. There is both external and internal dryness.

SYNDROMES INDUCED BY DRYNESS

EXTERNAL DRYNESS

External dryness invades the body through the nose or the mouth, and the symptoms usually affect the functioning of the lungs. If dryness affects us in early autumn, closer to summer than winter, then the dryness tends to exhibit symptoms similar to heat, and is called warm dryness. If we are affected by pathogenic dryness in late autumn, the dryness will tend to exhibit symptoms that are colder, and is called cool dryness.

In the late autumn condition of cool dryness, the patient will not only have the signs of dryness (dry mouth, nose, throat, skin, cough and so on), but will also have some symptoms of cold (fever, chills, headaches, lack of sweating for example). The difference between external cool dryness and that of an external cold is that, in this condition, the patient will show more visible signs of dryness.

When the early autumn syndrome of warm dryness affects a person, the patient will have symptoms of dryness as mentioned above, as well as those of heat (fever, headaches, little sweating, thirst, irritability). This condition can be seen not only in healthy individuals that have been exposed to external dryness, but also in people who were originally deficient in body fluids and were then affected by pathogenic heat or dryness.

INTERNAL DRYNESS

The condition of internal dryness results in lack or loss of blood and body fluids. It can occur after feverish illness, where the high temperature can deplete the body fluids, or after profuse sweating induced by heat or medications. Internal dryness can also occur after chronic diseases, when the body fluids are exhausted, or due to conditions of malnutrition and blood cloudiness in the body, when the body is unable to nourish the tissues. Clinically, the symptoms of internal dryness include thirst, dry skin that can be coarse and flaky, dry hair, constipation, thin and emaciated muscles and a dry tongue.

CHARACTERISTICS OF EXTERNAL AND INTERNAL DRYNESS

The special feature of pathogenic dryness is that it damages the body fluids. When there is a drought in the natural environment, the air will be dry, the water in the streams will turn shallow or dry up and there will be cracks in the soil. Similarly, when dryness invades the body, it will also start to manifest dry symptoms such as dry skin (even cracks or lacerations), dry scalp, dry hair, dry mouth, dry lips, dry nose, dry throat, constipation, scanty urine and a dry cough with little or no phlegm.

ABOVE
A dead tree, withered and twisted, its internal fluids exhausted by external dryness and warmth during severe drought conditions.

COLD

RIGHT
Cold is not just
restricted to winter.
Just as this late frost
and hailstone shower
can damage tender
plants in spring, our
bodies can also be
affected by sudden
climatic changes.

According to the theory of the Five Elements, cold is the main climatic element of winter, although, like pathogenic wind, cold can also exist in the other seasons of the year. There are two distinct ways in which cold can affect the body – externally and internally. External cold diseases are caused by the invasion of the body from the cold elements in the natural environment around us, while internal cold results from a deterioration of the body's functions and indicates that the body's Yang Qi is deficient.

SYNDROMES INDUCED BY COLD

Pathogenic cold can invade our body via two main pathways. External cold invades only the surface of our body and lungs, while internal cold invades at a deeper level – that of the internal organs.

EXTERNAL COLD

When the body is exposed to cold, be it from sudden climate changes or from staying in a cold place for a long period of time, the body will be affected by the cold and become ill. We will have symptoms that include fever, aversion to cold, headaches, body aches, stuffy nose, coughing and lack of sweat. If we overeat cold and raw foods, our abdomen will become

cold. Excessive intake of cold foods can damage the vital mechanisms – or Yang Qi – of the spleen and stomach, causing dysfunction of the digestive system. The symptoms for this condition include pain in the abdomen or stomach, indigestion and vomiting or diarrhoea.

INTERNAL COLD

Internal cold is caused by Yang deficiency, in which the cold is produced from within our own body. Yang deficiency can occur in any of our visceral organs. Depending on the organ that is affected, the patient will manifest symptoms of dysfunctions of the related organ.

CHARACTERISTICS OF EXTERNAL AND INTERNAL COLD

1 Cold is a climatic pathogen that manifests as an excess of Yin, and is therefore classified as a Yin pathogen. When Yin is predominant in the environment or in our body, it will suppress or damage the Yang element or Yang energy. When pathogenic cold invades the body, it will restrict the body surface, suppress the body's defensive energy and induce symptoms of chills and aversion to cold. If pathogenic cold directly attacks the internal organs, the spleen and stomach for example, it will damage the ability of these organs to

INTERNAL COLD

THE HEART

If the Yang energy of the heart is deficient, the patient will have diminished heart function. As we see in patients with heart failure, they feel cold and experience palpitations, shortness of breath and stagnation of Qi and the blood, leading to severe chest pains. The lips and face may turn purple or blue in colour.

THE KIDNEYS

When the kidney Yang is deficient, the patient will feel cold and experience pain in the low back or knees, with cold pain in the lower abdomen. Frequent urination or difficulty with urination are other features. In males, there may also be impotence; in females, there may be thin and clear vaginal discharge.

THE SPLEEN

In Yang deficiency of the spleen, the patient will feel bloated and have soft and loose stools and cold limbs.

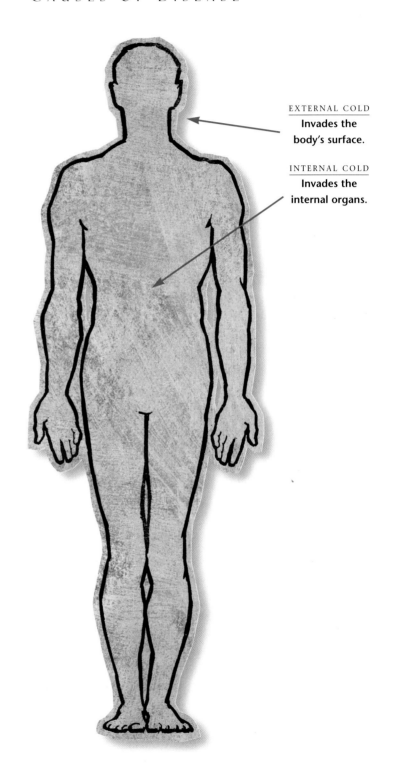

EXTERNAL COLD
Invades the body's surface.

INTERNAL COLD
Invades the internal organs.

digest the food that we eat and cause soft watery stools, clear and heavy or non-stop urination or vomiting of clear water. If pathogenic cold attacks a person's lungs or kidneys, it will affect the person's ability to warm and nurture the body and will cause symptoms such as cold hands and feet, as well as thin and loose phlegm or mucus.

2 The nature of cold is coagulation and stagnation. Pain is the special feature of pathogenic cold. In winter, water turns into ice because the cold temperature causes it to freeze and coagulate. The same phenomenon will appear when cold invades the interior of our body. Because pathogenic cold can damage the body's Yang Qi, it will reduce the body's warmth and slow down the flow of Qi and blood, causing stagnation that can block or obstruct the normal flow of Qi and blood in the meridians. Whenever there is stagnation of Qi or blood, the meridians and the body tissues will not be able to receive adequate nourishment, and pain will result. There is a principle in traditional Chinese medicine that says: "When blockage occurs, pain will occur". Since cold has the property of causing coagulation and stagnation, pain thus becomes the special feature of pathogenic cold. For example, many of us who have aches or pains in our joints and body feel that the discomfort becomes more prominent when the weather temperature drops.

ABOVE
Lower air temperatures cause water molecules to slow down, and eventually water turns to ice. Internal cold has the same effect inside the body, slowing the flow of Qi and blood.

3 Cold causes contractions. When pathogenic cold invades the body and damages the body's Yang Qi, it will also cause the vital mechanisms of the body tissues to close up or contract in order to protect our body from further loss of our warm Yang energy. This contraction of the body can be seen when one shivers in response to the cold. These tremulous contractions of the body surface are actually an attempt to close the pores of the skin, to prevent the body from losing any more of its warmth. In traditional Chinese medicine, one of the main symptoms in judging whether a patient's common cold is the result of external cold, is the absence or presence of sweating. As we have just discussed, external cold will cause contractions and thereby close up the pores of the skin, so that the body will not sweat through these pores.

EFFECTS OF PATHOGENIC COLD ON THE BODY

Contractions can occur in any tissue that is invaded or attacked by pathogenic cold. For example, when it invades the meridians or ligaments, cold can cause contractions of the ligaments and meridians, and induce symptoms of spasm, coldness and numbness in the limbs. If pathogenic cold gets to the blood vessels, as in the case of frost bite or thrombophlebitis (inflammation of the veins), it will cause contractions of the blood vessels and coagulation of the blood, resulting in severe pain and damage to the body tissues.

EMOTIONAL FACTORS

*I*n our daily lives, we react to different situations with a wide range of emotions, each person being affected in their own individual way. For example, what makes one person happy could make another person very sad or angry. These different emotions are the natural responses of the mind to the outside environment. But if we are emotionally upset for a very long time, or go through very sudden or severe emotional trauma, the mind finds it difficult to adjust to these mental disturbances. Significant emotional stress will result in changes in our body, such as Yin and Yang imbalance, Qi and Blood disharmony, or dysfunctions of the organs or meridians, allowing disease to occur.

Traditional Chinese medicine distinguishes seven types of human emotion: joy, anger, anxiety, worry, grief, fear and fright.

These emotions are the main causes of internal disease and, especially when they become excessive and pathogenic, they will directly influence the internal organs and cause disease. In traditional Chinese medicine, a person's mental activities are closely related to the condition of his internal organs. Healthy and productive functioning of the visceral organs will provide the blood and essences necessary to nourish the mind and enable it to think

EPIDEMIC DISEASE

Epidemic diseases are also pathogenic factors from the outside environment, and should be recognized as external pathogens. They are different from the six excessive climatic factors that were discussed previously, in that epidemic diseases are all acute and very infectious by nature. Practitioners of ancient traditional Chinese medicine noted that epidemic diseases would infect the whole family, whatever the age or gender of the individuals, with everyone manifesting the same symptoms. By the Ming Dynasty, two to three centuries ago, it became recognized that the infections were mainly spread through the nose or mouth. Examples of epidemic diseases include measles, mumps, diphtheria, chicken pox, cholera and influenza.

The occurrence of epidemic disease often follows severe natural disasters, such as floods and long droughts, when sudden or prolonged changes in nature create adverse conditions in our living environment and lifestyle. These changes are often so dramatic that it becomes difficult for the body to adjust properly and stay healthy. Furthermore, an unsanitary environment (such as overcrowded living space with poor ventilation or sewage systems) or unsanitary food and eating habits, creates a fertile atmosphere for epidemic disease. These issues, while environmental, are also often socially related. To prevent the spread of epidemic infections, appropriate authorities or governing agencies need to treat each and every episode of infectious disease in a timely and effective manner.

Another very important factor in the occurrence of epidemic disease is our own body's ability to deal with, or to fight against, epidemic factors. When we are strong and healthy, we tend to be less susceptible to pathogens. Even when exposed, a strong body may be immune and will not become sick.

and react to the stimulants from the outside world. Each of the internal organs is associated with one of the seven emotions. The emotion of the liver is anger, that of the heart is joy and that of the spleen is worry. The emotions of the lungs are both anxiety and grief, and the emotions of the kidneys include both fear and fright.

Because of the relationship between our feelings and our organs, excessive emotion can become pathogenic and cause disharmonies in the related organ. For example, excess anger will damage and hurt the liver, worry and

excessive contemplation will hurt and damage the spleen, and fear will hurt and damage the kidneys. These emotions can affect the internal organs because

they can damage the vital mechanism of the organ, disturbing the normal mechanism of Qi and creating an adverse flow of energy in the body. For example, when we get angry, we often experience the sensation of feeling flushed and our eyes and face become red. This is because anger causes the Qi to go upwards to the head and face, and the blood rushes up with it. Another example is the saying "he almost wet his pants" when describing a person who was scared. This is actually true, because fear causes the Qi to drop downwards and brings on urination or diarrhoea. When doing work that is mentally very taxing, our appetite often decreases. This is because excessive deliberation and contemplation causes the spleen Qi to stagnate and our appetite reduces with the stagnation. This shows not only that different emotions affect different organs, but also that the organs will be affected or damaged in different ways. Generally speaking, anger will cause the Qi to accelerate upwards, joy will slow down the flow of Qi, grief will dissipate the Qi, fear will send Qi downwards, fear will disturb the Qi and anxiety will cause Qi to stagnate.

According to traditional Chinese medicine, the heart is the governing organ of all the other organs, and is also in charge of the mind. Although the seven different emotions will specifically affect their related organs, it is the heart that will first register the emotions before influencing the related organs. Because of this, no matter what emotions we experience, they primarily affect the functions of the heart and thereby affect the other organs only because of their relationship with the heart. The special influence that emotions have on the heart is reflected in the many colloquial expressions that mention the heart.

While emotional factors can affect the organs in our body by influencing their vital functions, the reverse is also true. The dysfunctions of our organs could also influence or alter our mentality, causing emotional disturbances. It is not uncommon for someone to experience emotional changes after recovering from a sickness, especially after a long, chronic illness. Typical emotional changes include becoming short-tempered, depressed or listless.

SYNDROMES INDUCED BY EMOTIONAL FACTORS

Diseases induced by prolonged or sudden emotional stimulants usually occur because of damage to the body's internal organs. Each organ has its own physiology, functions and vital mechanisms, and each organ also manifests specific symptoms when it's damaged. In general, emotional factors tend to influence, and more often cause, problems of the heart, liver and spleen. For example, emotional distress affecting the functions of the heart can disturb the heart's ability to govern the mind, causing behavioural changes in a person such as being scared, panicky, forgetful, restless, irritable, hysterical or deranged. There may be an inability to control one's emotions, violence or even insanity. When the liver's functions are affected by emotional factors, symptoms include depression, taking long, deep

sighs and feeling as if something is stuck in the throat, as well as anger and a bad temper. Additionally, in women there can be irregular menstruation, menstrual cramping or lumps in the breasts. Pathogenic emotions can affect the spleen and stomach functions, with symptoms of indigestion, poor appetite, a bloated abdomen and irregular bowel movements.

There could also be either no menstruation or excessive menstruation in the case of spleen and heart deficiency. Nausea and abdominal pains may result if the liver is also affected. In general, diseases that are caused by emotional factors will usually produce symptoms of emotional disturbance, and these emotional disturbances often indicate the progress and outcome of the disease.

MISCELLANEOUS FACTORS

DIET AND EATING HABITS

Food intake is necessary for our body to obtain nutrition and to keep performing the vital activities of daily life. One of the major causes of disease is a poor diet or bad eating habits. In particular, poor diet can cause disorders of the spleen and stomach. In traditional Chinese medicine, the stomach is called "the holder and digestor of water and grains", and is the container for these substances. The spleen is the organ that is in charge of the transportation and processing of water and grains. Food is first received and digested in the stomach, after which it is transformed into essences to be absorbed and transported by the spleen to the other organs and tissues of our body. Because of their digestive functions, the stomach and spleen are most vulnerable to any damage caused by improper food intake. Damage from food could also create complications of cold, heat, dampness or disturbed metabolism, causing other visceral disorders.

SYNDROMES INDUCED BY IMPROPER DIET AND EATING HABITS

IMMODERATE EATING

While the intake of food is necessary for our body to obtain essential nutrients, the amount of food taken should be appropriate. Starving or over-eating can both cause disease. When we do not eat enough, the body will not receive adequate compensation to replenish the Qi and Blood that is consumed through the activities of our daily life. If prolonged, this will lead to Qi and Blood deficiency, which will cause further disease and reduce both our body's healthy energy and its ability to fight against the influence of pathogens. Over-eating is a more common problem in our society. Eating too much, exceeding the body's ability to digest the food, will directly damage the spleen and stomach. Clinically, we see patients with a bloated fullness in the stomach or abdomen, with pain that is aggravated by pressure, belching, nausea, bad breath, acid regurgita-

tion and diarrhoea with a strong odour. This condition is more common in children, because their digestive functions are not as strong as adults, and they have not learned how to control their eating habits. Over-eating can cause undigested food to stay inside the body, which may eventually produce heat, dampness or phlegm. In such cases, we have symptoms of hot hands and feet, a feeling of heat in the abdomen, flushed cheeks, fullness in the chest or stomach, mild fever in the afternoon or excess phlegm. Food stagnation can also create a disharmony between the nutrient Qi and the defensive Qi in our body, reducing the functions of the defensive Qi and making us susceptible to the invasion of external pathogens and the occurrence of disease.

UNSANITARY FOOD

Eating food that is unclean or poisonous will cause food poisoning or other diseases of the digestive tract. Symptoms include vomiting, diarrhoea, abdominal pains or blood and pus in the faeces. In the case of food poisoning, the vomiting, diarrhoea and abdominal pain will be much more intense. In serious cases of toxicity, the patient could lapse into a state of coma.

FOOD ADDICTIONS

Traditional Chinese medicine stresses the importance of a well-adjusted diet that includes different types and different flavours of food, to ensure well-balanced nutrition. Over-indulgence of one particular kind or flavour of food could lead to either lack of certain nutrients or to an imbalance of the body's Yin and Yang, causing disease to occur. For example, over-indulgence in greasy, spicy or sweet foods can cause the body to produce dampness and phlegm, making us feel sluggish and heavy. Over-indulgence of raw and cold foods will impede the Yang energy of the spleen, reducing its functions. Therefore, excess cold and raw food often cause bloated feelings or pain in the abdomen, as well as soft and loose stools. People who like to eat very hot and spicy foods, or drink too much alcohol, are more likely to have heat generated in their body, and will tend to have related symptoms such as haemorrhoids, constipation, boils or acne.

DAMAGE FROM STRESS, FATIGUE, SEXUAL ACTIVITY AND INJURIES

Normal physical labour is a natural part of our lives, and is essential to our well-being. This type of exercise can improve the flow of energy and blood in our body, improve our physical health and prevent the occurrence of disease. But when we exhaust ourselves or deprive ourselves physically, it will influence the physiological functions of our internal organs, disturb the harmony between Yin and Yang and induce disease.

LEFT
Over-indulgence in greasy or spicy or sweet foods can cause the body to produce dampness and phlegm.

ABOVE
Mental stress from excess concentration, often found in the workplace, can cause low Yin and lead to fatigue.

STRESS AND FATIGUE

Over-exertion will exhaust our body's primary energy, or "Yuan Qi" as it is called in traditional Chinese medicine, and deplete the vitality of the internal organs, causing fatigue. This will make us feel tired and listless, with a lassitude in our limbs and a reluctance to talk – even shortness of breath upon exertion. If there is mental stress from excessive contemplation, then the heart will be stressed and the heart and spirit will suffer from a depletion of Yin and blood, resulting in a rapid heart beat, poor memory, restless dreams and disturbed sleep at night. On the other hand, lack of physical activity, and an overly easy and comfortable lifestyle, will also damage the flow of energy and blood in our body, affecting the digestive functions of our spleen and stomach. Such lack of exercise will reduce the body's resistance to pathogens, causing us to feel tired and languid, without vigour or energy, and making us more susceptible to disease.

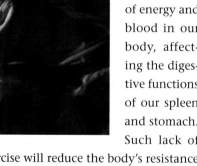

ABOVE

Although sex can be a great stress-reliever, excessive sexual activity can deplete your kidney essence and therefore sap your physical strength, making you vulnerable to disease.

EXCESSIVE SEXUAL ACTIVITY

Excessive sexual activity includes unrestrained sex, marrying too young, or women having too many pregnancies. These activities can deplete our kidney essence, which in turn will deplete our physical strength and diminish our vitality, making us vulnerable to disease. The depletion of kidney essence will cause kidney deficiency syndromes, with symptoms of low back pain, fatigue, listlessness, dizziness, light-headedness or sexual dysfunctions (say, involuntary emission of semen without intercourse or premature ejaculation in men, and irregular menstruation or excessive vaginal discharges in women).

DAMAGE FROM TRAUMA AND INJURIES

This category includes all kinds of injuries, such as sprains and strains of the muscles and ligaments, cuts or wounds to the skin and muscles, fractures of the bones, dislocation of the joints, burns and bruises, lacerations and gunshot wounds. The damage is usually localized, but could be complicated if not taken care of properly, leading to severe bleeding, loss of body fluids, infections or even unconsciousness and death. While most bites from insects or animals mainly cause skin damage, it is possible to contract general toxicity if the bite was from a poisonous snake or an animal with rabies.

DAMAGE FROM PARASITES

Parasites are still a common problem in regions where sanitation is poor, especially food sanitation. When parasites invade the human body, they will cause Qi and Blood deficiency. People infected with parasites often manifest symptoms of pain in the abdomen, poor appetite or emaciation.

DAMAGE FROM PHLEGM

In traditional Chinese medicine, phlegm not only exists in our bronchi and lungs, but can also be contained or retained in any part of our body, such as in the skin or the meridians, in the muscles or the bones, in the internal organs and on the legs or in the head – anywhere and everywhere. Phlegm is produced from pathological changes inside our body. Once phlegm is produced, it could become a pathogenic factor, and either directly or indirectly affect our internal organs or body tissues, causing or influencing the progress of a disease.

Phlegm is formed from the accumulation and coagulation of our body fluids, and mainly affects the functions of the lungs, spleen and kidneys. These are the organs that are in charge of the water metabolism in our body, and when they do not function correctly, the water and fluids inside the body cannot be properly distributed and will accumulate inside the body. Initially, this accumulation of phlegm is considered to be a type of dampness.

However, with the help of other pathogenic factors inside the body (such as heat, cold, fire or stagnated Qi), the dampness will be transformed into phlegm and can cause disease. The spleen is often regarded as the main culprit in this process, because it is the organ that has the most significant role in the transportation and processing of water and body fluids, and is considered to be the organ that produces phlegm in traditional Chinese medicine.

LOCATIONS OF PHLEGM AND ITS EFFECT

Depending on where the phlegm is located, patients will present different symptoms. For example, when the phlegm in congested in our lungs, there will be copious coughing, with large amounts of phlegm. If phlegm is in the stomach, there will be nausea and vomiting. If the phlegm stays in the meridians, there could be phlegm nodules in our tissues. Furthermore, when phlegm stays in the heart orifice, it could disturb the brain and cause the patient to become mentally disoriented.

DAMAGE FROM STAGNANT BLOOD

Stagnant blood is another important pathogenic factor, and includes the following: blood that is not flowing smoothly throughout the body; blood that is stagnated locally in a part of our body; or blood that does not stay inside the blood vessels. When blood cloudiness is formed, it will impede or obstruct the flow of blood in the vessels and meridians of related visceral organs and body tissues.

Symptoms of stagnant blood mainly include pain, but there may also be bruises, rashes and bleeding, with a dull and darkish complexion as well as purplish-blue coloured lips and tongue.

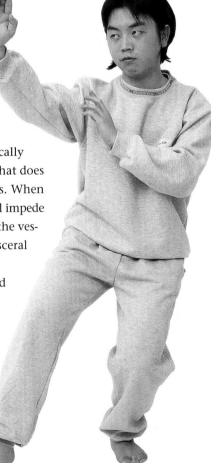

RIGHT
Regular exercise will increase the body's vigour and energy rather than deplete it.

TRADITIONAL CHINESE HERBAL THERAPIES

T*he history of traditional Chinese therapies* *goes back many thousands of years. Herbology, acupuncture, moxibustion (applying heat to an acupuncture point), acupressure, massage therapy, body manipulation, physical and breathing exercises, cutaneous scraping therapy, vacuum cupping, and Qi Gong are some of the popular therapies included in traditional Chinese medicine. However, Chinese herbology is considered to be the main root.*

The wealth of wisdom that springs from Chinese herbology is just as valuable today as it was to the ancient Chinese. It is essential to introduce the inherent philosophy of Chinese medicine to the West, and most importantly to interpret the almost incomprehensible antiquated Chinese classics into modern language and apply their knowledge in a practical and accessible way.

GENERAL CONCEPT OF CHINESE HERBOLOGY

What are Chinese herbs? Some say they are barks and roots. However, the every-day term "Chinese herbs" is not limited just to barks and roots; this simple term has been broadened to encompass many other medicinal agents. In fact, it includes animal products (such as cicada and snake skin, pig's bile or skin, bovine hide, gecko, pearl and oyster shell) and minerals (such as talcum, kaolin, sodium sulphate and magnetic stone). They are all in the realm of Chinese herbology (and its bible, Ben Cao Pharmacopoeia or Materia Medica). The majority of herbal substances are prepared in special ways before ingestion in order to enhance their functions.

Herbs can also be characterized by their origin of growth. In the Chinese language, such herbs are known as "Di Dao" medic-inal herbs. The term "Di Dao" literally means "down to earth", and is understood as the original source of the best growth. Certain areas of China are known for their special growing conditions. Herbs from these areas are considered to be superior in potency and effectiveness because the quality of the soil, the weather and the environment are particularly suitable for the growth of that particular species, just as certain special grapes are used in wine production.

ABOVE
Sandalwood bark.

However, with the increase in the world's population, and following the law of supply and demand, a shortage is devel-oping of the Di Dao medicinal plants. The advancement of science makes large-scale production possible, which is able to ful-fill the market demand.

For many thousands of years, Chinese medical history has registered more than 3,000 species of plants and animal products. Of course, non-Chinese peoples have also contributed to this treasure house, including the Buddhist monks of India, the people of the Middle East and sailors and merchants of the southwest Pacific, the Indian Ocean, Europe, the Mediterranean and North and South America. With the cur-rent development of natural resources and scientific research, many medicinal folk plants from China, and even from other parts of the world, are integrated into the Chinese *Materia Medica*. In conse-quence, the number of medicinal substances is increasing by leaps and bounds and the margin between Chinese herbs and Western medicine is beginning to narrow.

For thousands of years, Chinese medicinal plants have played an important role in disease prevention and in the treatment of the

BELOW
Ginseng root is an example of barks and roots.

Chinese people. Currently, their importance and significance have been recognized by the Western world, and they are now well received by the general public.

THE ORIGIN OF CHINESE MEDICINAL HERBS

The bulk of Chinese herbs are from Nature. So it is possible to say that there are herbs at every corner of the earth that can be incorporated into the Chinese medicinal system.

According to archaeological findings, in the primitive stage of human history, wild fruits and plants were used as food. Peculiar sensations or reactions were noted when ingesting certain plants. In the course of this process, medicinal plants were discovered through keen observation, repeated encounters and accumulation of experience. For example, certain plants may have been found to arrest diarrhoea or relieve headache. Many thousands of years passed before the beneficial ingredients in the plants were determined.

In the Han Dynasty, around AD 200, ancient sages pooled the wisdom and experience of that time and wrote the "bible" of Chinese herbology,

ABOVE
Minerals: talcum (Hua Shi).

ABOVE
Animal products include abalone shell.

known as *Shen Nong Ben Cao Jing* or the *Emperor Shen Nong's Canon of Materia Medica*. This is the earliest comprehensive text of the herbal pharmacopoeia that exists in China.

For more than 30 years the venerable savant Li Shi Zhen (AD 1518–93) reviewed 800 ancient medical works to correct errors of the past. He travelled all over China to gather and identify new medicinal agents. He rewrote his manuscript three times and finally completed the world-renowned *Compendium of Materia Medica*. This manuscript was the most comprehensive classification of that time. At the end of the seventeenth century, this text was introduced to Europe. Since then, it has aided many scientists in the development of *Materia Medica*, botany, zoology and the natural sciences of their countries.

THE PROPERTIES AND FUNCTIONS OF CHINESE HERBS

The properties and functions of Chinese herbs appears to be an esoteric and complex subject. The philosophy and vernacular of Chinese medicine, including the *Materia Medica*, is based on the Yin/Yang theory, which can be traced back to the *Book of I Ching*.

In traditional Chinese medicine, the system of Yin/Yang is backed by meridi-

CAUSES OF DISEASE

The causes of disease in Chinese medicine are categorized into three pathological components:

◆ **EXTERNAL DISEASES**
These are caused by bacteria, viruses and unusual weather changes invading the surface of the body.

◆ **INTERNAL DISEASES**
These are caused by emotional distress, constitutional weakness, toxins, physical stress and exhaustion.

RIGHT
Severe or unusual weather changes are external diseases.

RIGHT
Physical stress and exhaustion can cause internal diseases.

◆ **NON-EXTERNAL AND NON-INTERNAL DISEASES**
These can be due to improper food intake, irregular diet, traumatic injuries and insect or animal bites.

an theory, organ diagnosis, therapeutic strategy, organization of prescriptions and the selection of herbs. Without the latter, Yin and Yang are but an empty spirit, like the American Constitution would be without the state or county codes.

The Yin/Yang system is based on the concept of "imbalance" and "regulation". When talking about imbalance and regulation, the existence of unification and opposition is self-evident, without which, of course, imbalance and regulation cannot exist.

To understand the concrete meaning of Yin and Yang, imbalance and regulation, it is best to start from the etiology of disease, where we can pin down facts rather than deal with abstract terms.

As a whole, the causes of disease are all known as the pathological "Evil Qi" in

LEFT
Insect bites or stings can be classed as non-external/non-internal diseases.

Chinese medicine. From an analytical point of view, they are classified into the three categories listed here (see box, Causes of Disease). However, they may concomitantly affect the body – locally or generally – producing the destruction of tissues and the dysfunction of meridians and organs. This phenomenon is described by TCM as an imbalance of Yin and Yang with manifestations of symptoms.

YIN AND YANG

Yin and Yang concepts can be applied to everything, but when applying the theory of Yin and Yang, they have to be nailed down to a definite subject.

◆ YIN usually represents formed matter, passivity or the static condition. It includes blood, fluids, tissues and organs.

◆ YANG often represents formless action, vitality and potentiality. It represents the systemic function of body, active matter and Qi.

It is essential to understand that all the things in this world are not lined up in two isolated rows of Yin or Yang, without any interaction. In fact, there is a second rule that must be taken into account: within Yin there is Yang, and within Yang there is Yin.

We are using Yin and Yang as a tool to facilitate description and analysis. It is essential to note that Yin and Yang are not separate from each other. In fact, everything is both Yin and Yang, only in varying amounts. For example, we can say that water relates more to Yin than to Yang but it is, in fact, both Yin and Yang. The Yin aspect is its passive state or fluidity, whereas the Yang aspect is its activity or the action of water in the process of transforming into vapour.

There are millions of pairings of Yin and Yang in the body; every element, cell, organ and system has its pair of Yin and Yang. The total of all of these micro-Yin and Yang are manifested as the macro-Yin and Yang of our health. They interact and strike a dynamic balance to achieve normal well-being.

From the above reasoning, "regulation" is used as the basic principle of TCM therapy to counter the imbalance of Yin and Yang and heal the body. This regulation occurs through reconstruction and normalization of the imbalance of Yin and Yang in the meridians and organs, as well as by expelling the body's toxins and repairing whatever damages the body has endured.

BASIC QUALITIES OF HERBS

Chinese herbal therapies possess many specific characteristics, which contribute to their ability to normalize imbalances of Yin and Yang. These basic qualities are as follows:

1 Nature, property or Qi of the herbs.

2 Taste of the herbs.

3 Functional orientation of the herbs (ascending, descending, floating, sinking).

4 Functional site of the herbs' action.

5 Toxicity of the herbs.

Among them, nature (property) and taste are important markers of traditional Chinese medical therapy.

NATURE OF HERBS

Traditional Chinese medicine believes that every herb has a particular nature. The nature is characterized as either cold, hot, warm or cool. Generally speaking, cold and cool are in the realm of Yin while warm and hot relate to Yang. The ancient scholars called this the "Four Qi", as Qi also means action or function. The therapeutic effect and reaction of each herb is understood as cold, hot, warm or cool. Cold herbs are used for hot diseases and vice versa, in order to bring the body back into a neutral or harmonious state of balance.

When a patient is assaulted by an external evil (say, catching a cold) he or she may have symptoms of fever, headache, oral dryness, red tongue with yellow fur and a rapid pulse. In TCM, this set of symptoms is grouped as a pattern, and is seen as a "heat" entity. Two herbs, Honeysuckle Flower (Chinese: Jin Yin Hua; Latin: *Flos Lonicerae*) and Forsythia Fruit (Chinese: Lian Qiao; Latin: *Fructus Forsythiae*) are especially effective for this type of heat pattern. Since these two herbs counteract the heat reaction of the body, we can therefore conclude that they have a cool nature. In other words, they have the power to relieve heat or Yang patterns. As a group, these cold or cooling herbs have the function of clearing heat and relieving toxins.

Another example is of a patient suffering from a protracted course of chronic diarrhoea, with abdominal cold pain, weakness, faeces without foul odour, a pale tongue with scanty fur and a sinking, weak pulse. All of these symptoms indicate that this patient has a slow and low-reacting metabolism. In traditional Chinese medicine, this condition is seen as a cold entity. Dry ginger is indicated to counteract the cold pattern of this patient because it is hot and warm in nature and can alleviate the cold or Yin pattern. As a group, hot and warm herbs have the function of warming the Center (digestive tract) and dispersing cold.

From the above examples, we understand that heat/warm and cold/cool are two totally opposing groups. However, heat and warm or cold and cool differ only in degree. Heat is hotter than warm, and cold is colder than cool. A fifth characteristic of some herbs is that of neutrality. Neutral herbs have a gentle action and can be used in either cold or hot entities or patterns. In clinical practice, we have to differentiate further the status of excess heat or excess cold and mild heat or mild cold, in order to select and measure the right amount of each herb for a given condition. This is the art of differentiation and diagnosis.

ABOVE
Forsythia Fruit (Lian Qiao).

The rule of applying cold or cool herbs to "heat" conditions and warm or hot herbs to "cold" conditions is the basic principle of herbal therapy. However, in practice, absolute heat or cold patterns are the extremes and the majority of cases are mixed heat and cold in various degrees. Thus, it is necessary to determine the correct ratio of heat to cold in the body and administer a certain number and an appropriate dosage of cold and hot herbs in harmonious balance. This is the art of selecting the herbs to include in a herbal prescription.

SUMMARY

Summarizing the empirical experience of the ancients, their actions are discussed as follows:

◆ SOUR constricts or consolidates. Herbs of sour taste are often indicated for use in perspiration due to deficiency, protracted cough, chronic diarrhoea, seminal and urinary incontinence, leakage of spermatic fluid, prolonged menorrhagia (very heavy menstrual bleeding) and leucorrhoea (emission of mucus from the vagina) with a clear discharge. In all the above conditions, the common denominator is hypometabolism (under-performance). In traditional Chinese medicine, they are seen as deficient or cold patterns.

◆ ASTRINGENT herbs are similar in function to sour herbs.

◆ BITTER possesses the function of clearing heat, purging the bowels, lowering the Qi (abnormal rising of Qi is manifested as vomiting, belching and so on), improving appetite and drying dampness or wetness. Bitter herbs are commonly used in fire-heat patterns (such as the acute stage of infectious diseases). They can relieve constipation with foul faecal discharge and can drain excessive fluid retention. Hence, bitter tastes are indicated for use in arthritis

---

TASTES

The tastes ascribed to the herbs in traditional Chinese medicine are:

◆ Sour
◆ Bitter
◆ Sweet
◆ Spicy
◆ Salty
◆ Bland
◆ Astringent

They are more important as markers of each herb's property than of its true taste. Among them, sour, bitter, sweet, spicy and salty are established as the basic tastes commonly known as the "Five Tastes". Bland and sweet tastes are similar to each other. Likewise, astringent and sour tastes have common properties. Sour, astringent, bitter and salty tastes are related to Yin, whereas spicy, sweet and bland are attributed to Yang.

---

or leucorrhoea related to the patterns of damp-heat or damp-cold.

◆ SWEET has the function of toning, improving, moistening and harmonizing many of the important systems of the body, including the digestive, respiratory, immune and endocrine systems. Sweet herbs regulate and moderate the various components of a herbal formula. Sweet tastes also relieve urgency and inhibit pain due to the constrictive action of muscles. They are commonly used for treating deficiency patterns (manifested as dry cough

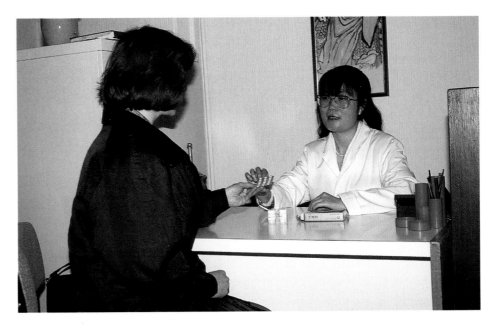

A Chinese herbal practitioner examines the patient and discusses her symptoms before prescribing a herbal preparation.

and constipation related to lack of moisture), dysfunction of the gastro-intestinal tract (often known as spleen and stomach "disharmony"), and in treating pain as the result of muscular spasms.

Licorice (Chinese: Gan Cao; Latin: *Radix Glycyrrhizae*) is a very good example to illustrate the above assertion. It exhibits almost all the aforementioned claims, and is especially remarkable for moderating and harmonizing the herbs in a given formula. It is widely used.

◆ SPICY (pungent) disperses, circulates Qi and vitalizes blood. This group of herbs can stimulate the sweat glands to perspire, circulate Qi, activate the function of meridians and organs and vitalize blood to promote blood circulation. As a whole, spicy herbs have the overall effect of activating and enhancing metabolism.

Clinically, spicy herbs are commonly used in the treatment of external patterns (catching a cold), when the function of the meridians and organs is weakened and circulation of blood has been impeded. In traditional Chinese medical terminology, this is the stage of Qi stagnation and blood cloudiness. Spicy ingredients are also indicated for use in the initial phase of sores and abscesses, when pus has not formed.

◆ SALTY herbs have the function of softening firm masses and fibrous adhesions. The salty taste purges and opens the bowels. Salty agents are often indicated in sores, inflammatory masses, cysts, connective tissue proliferation and faecal impaction.

◆ BLAND herbs can promote the absorption of tissue fluid and drain urine. Hence, they are commonly indicated for use in oedema, urinary tract infection and difficult urination.

FUNCTIONS OF HERBS

Generally speaking, herbs that have a similar nature and taste also have similar functions. When the nature and taste of two herbs differ, their function may be opposite to each other. A certain number of herbs have similar natures but differ in taste; or have similar tastes but differ in nature. The function of these herbs may be similar in particular aspects and different in others.

Huang Lian (*Rhizoma Coptidis*) and Mai Dong (*Radix Ophiopogonis*) are both cold in nature. However, *Rhizoma Coptidis* is bitter, while *Radix Ophipogonis* is sweet. Hence, functionally, *Rhizoma Coptidis* is used to clear heat and dry wet, and is indicated in damp-heat disorders (diarrhoea, abdominal pain, foul faecal discharges and thick yellow tongue fur). On the other hand, *Radix Ophiopogonis* is used to clear heat and nourish Yin (fluids). It is commonly used for heat disorders with thirst and a red tongue with scanty fur, when the body becomes dehydrated and the Yin is damaged.

Raw ginger (Chinese: Sheng Jiang; Latin: *Rhizoma Zingiberis*) and mint (Chinese: Bo He; Latin: *Herba Menthae*) are both spicy in taste. However, the nature of raw ginger is warm, while that of mint is cool. Raw ginger has the ability to disperse wind-cold, and is used in the early stage of this external evil with manifestations of fever, aversion to cold, absence of perspiration and runny nose. Mint can disperse wind-heat, and is used in the initial stage of the invasion of this external evil, manifested by fever, headaches, dry mouth and no aversion to cold.

Thus, to practise Chinese medicine, it is mandatory to master the nature and taste of every herb that is used. Additionally, the herbs must be pre-scribed based on traditional Chinese medical training in "pattern diagnosis", which is not the same as diagnosing disease in Western medicine. Without the appropriate training, incorrect application will result and could even exacerbate the patient's symptoms.

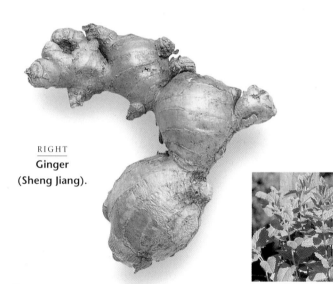

ABOVE
Rhizoma Coptidis (Huang Lian).

RIGHT
Ginger (Sheng Jiang).

ABOVE
Mint (Bo He).

FUNCTIONAL ORIENTATION OF HERBS

The pathology and symptoms of a disease may appear in four main areas of the body.
◆ Symptoms in the upper part of the body include vomiting, coughing and shortness of breath.
◆ Likewise, symptoms may manifest in the lower area, as with diarrhoea, dysen-

tery or rectal prolapse.

◆ Symptoms may also appear mainly on the outer surface of the body, as in the case of perspiration without exertion.

◆ Finally, a patient's symptoms may occur

UPPER BODY
Chest, throat and lungs.

INTERIOR
Internal organs.

OUTER SURFACE
Skin.

LOWER BODY
Bowels and stomach.

mainly in the interior of the body, and include conditions that become worse or spread internally, such as when an external cold (common cold) turns into an internal case of pneumonia.

These four areas indicate the location and orientation of the disease pattern.

Herbs of opposite nature have to be selected to counteract each of the above conditions, and include herbs that ascend, descend, float and sink . Each of these properties has the ability to rectify the imbalance of meridians and organs, and evacuate the evils (virus, bacteria, pathological waste products) along the least resistant route.

◆ ASCENDING is used to describe the raising of the performance of Qi, which elevates the sinking Qi to the normal level of dynamic balance and activates the function of the upper segment of the body.

◆ DESCENDING lowers the Qi or the pathological Qi to the normal level of dynamic balance. In this process, the lower segment of the body is usually activated.

◆ FLOATING (levitating) signifies the action of dispersion towards the exterior, opening the cutaneous pores and promoting perspiration. It excites and activates the surface of the body.

◆ SINKING indicates purging and discharging downwards. The sinking function moves toward the interior and is tranquillizing or sedating.

SOME HERBAL EXAMPLES

Prolapse of the rectum indicates a tendency to sink below. The herb Astragalus (Chinese: Huang Qi; Latin: *Radix Astragali*) has the ability to raise the sinking Qi. Hence, it is the herb of choice to deal with this situation.

◆ DYSPNOEA (DIFFICULT/PAINFUL BREATHING) AND COUGH are related to the lowering of Qi. Radish Seed (Chinese: Lai Fu Zi; Latin: *Semen Raphani*) tends to lower the rising Qi and pacify the cough and dyspnoea.

ABOVE
Radish seed lowers rising Qi.

A common cold that is not relieved by chills and fever is on the verge of invading deeper into the interior of the body and could possibly lead to pneumonia. Before this occurs, herbs for dispersing and relieving the surface should be included in the herbal formula. Depending on the exact symptoms, Forsythia Fruit (Chinese: Lian Qiao; Latin: *Fructus Forsythiae*), Cinnamon (Chinese: Gui Zhi; Latin: *Ramulus Cinnamomi*) or mint (Chinese: Bo He; Latin: *Herba Menthae*) should be administered to expel the external evils (virus, bacteria, toxic metabolic waste products) towards the surface. Since not all common colds are treated in the same way, a practitioner of traditional Chinese medicine should always be consulted before taking any herbal preparations.

◆ HYPERTENSION The cluster of symptoms of a patient suffering from hyperension, such as dizziness, headaches and irritability, is called the pattern of "rising of liver Yang", indicating that an imbalance of Yin and Yang is taking place. In this situation, herbs such as Chuan Niu Xi (Latin: *Radix Cyathulae*) and Magnetite (Chinese: Ci Shi; Latin: *Magnetitum*) have

the effect of sinking and lowering and are used to inhibit the overactive Yang Qi of the liver meridians. These herbs help to achieve a normal cooperative balance of Yin and Yang, with normalization of blood pressure and relief of headache and vertigo.

HERBS WITH TWO FUNCTIONS

There are a number of herbs in which the nature of descending, ascending, sinking or floating is not apparent. With these herbs it is possible to have two functions, such as ascending and descending.

For example, Chuan Xiong (Latin: *Rhizoma Ligustici Wallichii*) can ascend and descend. Ma Huang (Latin: *Herba Ephedrae*) can rise and promote sweating. It can also pacify dyspnoea and drain urine downwards. All the flowers can raise Qi with the exception of Xuan Fu Hua (Latin: *Flos Inulae*), which can lower the Qi of the lung.

ABOVE
Chuan Xiong is a dual-purpose herb, which can ascend or descend.

LEFT
There are now many practitioners of TCM in the West. They should always be consulted before purchasing a herbal preparation.

Heavy doses of Astragalus (Chinese: Huang Qi; Latin: *Radix Astragali*) can lower blood pressure. However, a light dosage can raise the Qi of the spleen and stomach.

It is crucial for us to remember these particular points with respect to herbal preparations. Knowing the precise dosage is the expert practitioner's key to successful prescribing of herbal formulas.

The functions of ascending, descending, floating and sinking are closely related to the nature, taste, texture and weight of each herb. Generally speaking, most herbs that have a raising or floating function are spicy and sweet as well as warm or hot. They are also lighter in weight. The majority of lowering and sinking herbs are sour, bitter, salty and astringent. They are related to cool and cold and are rather heavy.

COMPOSITE FORMULAS

Herbs in a composite formula may restrict or inhibit one another. For example, in a combined herbal formula designed to lower Qi, if all the herbs have a sinking function

PROCESSING AND NATURE

The way in which a herb is processed can affect the herb's nature of ascending, descending, floating or sinking.

◆ Frying herbs with ginger juice aids dispersion.

◆ Frying herbs with vinegar increases the action of astringency.

◆ Frying herbs with salt water encourages the herb's sinking action.

◆ Frying herbs with honey increases the toning effects.

◆ Frying herbs with wine enhances action of ascension.

except one, then the net energy of descending is slightly reduced. This phenomenon illustrates that, under certain conditions, the actions of ascending, descending, floating and sinking can be controlled and modified by the skill of the practitioner. These observations demonstrate the versatility and flexibility of Chinese herbal formulas.

LEFT
Frying herbs in vinegar increases the action of astringency.

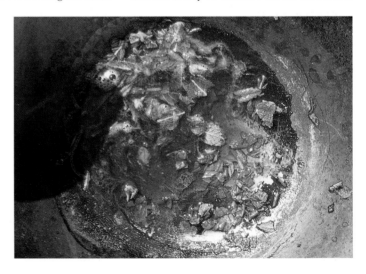

FUNCTIONAL SITES FOR HERBAL REMEDIES

*A*ccording to traditional Chinese medical theory, the physiological coordination of tissues and organs is accomplished by an interconnected web of channels called meridians. During the disease process, a surface lesion or disorder can influence the internal organs via the meridians, and vice versa. Therefore, the symptoms of a certain diseased organ can be comprehensively discerned through the interconnected meridians.

To give an idea of how the meridians work, the stomach meridians originate at the margin of the nose, enter into the oral cavity, pass the gums, descend into the stomach and finally descend down the leg. If a lesion develops along this meridian, then a corresponding group of symptoms will appear on this meridian.

As another example, a red and inflamed swelling is related to the pattern of heat or fire. The gums of the mouth are related to the stomach meridian, so when gums are hot and swollen, the diagnosis is fire (heat) of the stomach meridian. Gypsum (Chinese: Shi Gao) is used to alleviate the pain and relieve the swelling of the gum. Thus it was learned that Gypsum enters the stomach meridian.

The liver meridians traverse bilaterally along the rib region. When there is pain in this area, we can diagnose dysfunction of the liver meridian or stagnation of the Qi of the liver meridian. Bupleurium (Chinese: Chai Hu; Latin: *Radix Bupleuri*) is able to relieve pain in the rib region, and thus it has been inferred that Bupleurium enters the liver meridian.

Recognizing the suitability of certain herbs for a particular region of the body is a fundamental tenet of traditional Chinese herbal medicine. This ability is known as "entering the meridian" of an individual herb. There are 12 meridians in the human body, and each herb does not necessarily enter only one meridian; one herb can often enter many. For example, gypsum (Chinese: Shi Gao) enters into the stomach and lung meridians. Bupleurium (Chinese: Chai Hu; Latin: *Radix Bupleuri*) enters the liver and "triple warmer", gall-bladder and pericardium meridians.

On the other hand, if an ailment along a certain meridian can be healed by a particular herb, it does not necessarily mean that this herb enters the afflicted meridian. Again, painful swollen gums are used as an example. Besides gypsum, Forsythia Fruit (Chinese: Lian Qiao; Latin: *Fructus Forsythiae*) is also effective for treating inflammation of the gums, and can arrest pain and relieve swelling. However, we know that Forsythia Fruit does not enter into the stomach meridian. The nature and taste of

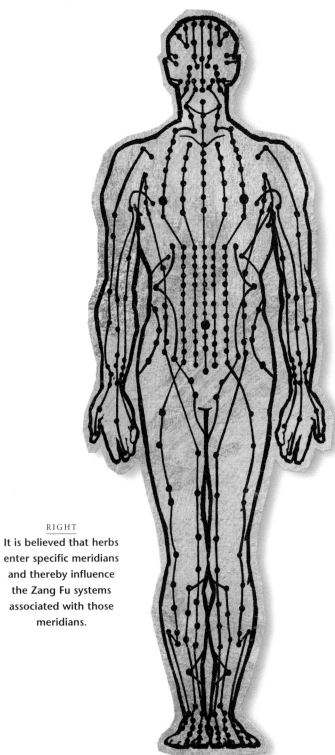

RIGHT
It is believed that herbs enter specific meridians and thereby influence the Zang Fu systems associated with those meridians.

Forsythia Fruit is bitter and slightly cold. Bitter can clear the heat, swelling and fire of inflamed gums. In other words, the nature and taste of herbs fit the specific disease condition. Thus, even though it does not enter the stomach meridian, it can still heal the condition. Comparing gypsum and Forsythia Fruit, the action of the former in clearing heat and purging fire is much stronger than that of the latter. In addition, gypsum enters the stomach meridian. Based on the above rationale and clinical experience, gypsum is the best herb for fire-heat and gum inflammation.

We must also understand that the pathological processes of various organs and meridians can affect one another. Therefore, when formulating a prescription, we do not simply apply the herbs for one meridian – as when a pathological process of the lung meridian is complicated by spleen deficiency. In addition to the herbs for the lung meridian, we must also administer herbs to tone the spleen, which will in turn provide nutrition to the lung meridian and hasten the process of recovery. In this case, the patient may suffer from chronic bronchitis with manifestations of a protracted cough, dyspnoea, asthenia (general bodily weakness) and an erratic pulse, indicating the presence of lung Qi deficiency. The patient will also be affected by spleen Qi deficiency symptoms of poor appetite, a tendency to find all tastes bland and formless stools without foul odour. Combining these two patterns, a diagnosis of lung and spleen deficiency is made. Thus, herbs that affect the lung and stomach meridians should be administered simultaneously. The

NATURE, TASTE AND FUNCTIONAL ORIENTATION

	NATURE	TASTE	FUNCTIONAL ORIENTATION	WEIGHT
Yin	Cool, cold	Sour, bitter, salty	Lowering, sinking	Heavy
Yang	Warm, hot	Pungent, sweet, bland	Ascending, descending	Light

application of spleen-toning herbs is essential to supply much-needed nutrients to the lung and hasten its recovery.

Due to differences of nature and taste, herbs that are related to the same meridian may still be quite different. For example, Huang Qin (Latin: *Radix Scutellariae*), dried ginger (Chinese: Gan Jiang), lily bulb (Chinese: Bai He; Latin: *Bulbus Lilii*) and Ting Li Zi (Latin: *Semen Lepidii*) all enter into the lung meridian. However, *Radix Scutellariae*, which is bitter and cold, can clear lung heat (cough, yellow sputum and dry mouth). Dry ginger, which is hot and spicy, can warm coldness in the lungs (cough, white sputum and bland oral taste). *Bulbus Lilii*, which is sweet, slightly bitter and cool, can tone lung deficiency (chronic cough and shortness of breath). *Semen Lepidii*, which is spicy, bitter and cold, can purge lung excess (cough, excessive sputum, dyspnoea, fast breathing and distended fullness of the chest).

In clinical practice, the disease process is often a multi-factor problem. Therefore, we must understand clearly the thera-peutic selectivity of herbs towards organs, comprehend the physio-pathology of organs and their interrelationship and master the nature, tastes and functions of ascending, descending, floating and sinking.

LUNG MERIDIAN
Huang Qin (above), ginger (left) and lily bulb are examples of quite different herbs used for the same meridian. In this case they are all used to enter the lung meridian.

A comprehensive understanding of the various aspects of herbal function is needed. A TCM herbal practitioner has to take all of this into account before formulating a prescription.

PROCESSING AND ADMINISTERING CHINESE HERBS

From the prehistoric period, when the legendary Emperor Shen Nong began tasting hundreds of plants, until the present, traditional Chinese medicine has placed strong emphasis on methods of processing herbs. The processing of herbs can increase therapeutic results, enhance the quality of herbs for optimum formulation and facilitate administration. Herbs are processed after being picked and before they are sold commercially. What is important to the herbalist is to understand the modified nature of herbs after special treatments. Types of herbal preparation include: stir-baked, stir-fried, and calcined.

Examples include stir-baked Pao Shan Jia (*Squama Manitis*), stir-baked ginger (Pao Jiang), calcined Duan Long Gu (*Os Draconis*), calcined Duan Mu Li (*Concha Ostreae*), stir-fried Zhi Gan Cao (*Radix Glycyrrhizae*), and stir-fried Zhi Huang Qi (*Radix Astragali*).

THE PURPOSES OF PROCESSING

1 TO REDUCE OR ELIMINATE TOXICITY, POTENCY AND OTHER ADVERSE SIDE-EFFECTS.

For example, Ban Xia (*Rhizoma Pinelliae*) is toxic. After processing with ginger, this

Untreated Zhi Mu enters three meridians, but after stir-frying, it enters only the kidney meridian.

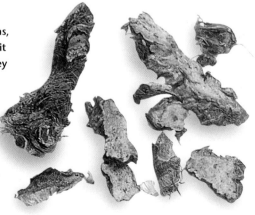

toxicity is eradicated. Zhi Zi (*Fructus Gardeniae*) often causes vomiting in its raw form, but after being char-fried, this adverse effect can be eliminated.

2 TO TRANSFORM THE NATURE OF HERBS TO SUIT THE THERAPEUTIC REQUIREMENT.

For example, Sheng Di Huang (*Radix Rehmanniae*) is cool in its raw form and is indicated for clearing heat and cooling blood. After being steamed in wine and dried under the sun nine times, it is changed into cooked Shu Di Huang (*Radix Rehmanniae*). Its nature becomes warm and it can powerfully tone the blood.

Da Huang (*Rhizoma Rhei*) is very powerful in its raw form for purging the bowels. After processing, its laxative strength is weakened. After char-frying, its purgative effect is almost completely abolished, but it becomes a wonderful agent for arresting bleeding.

3 TO ENHANCE THE THERAPEUTIC EFFECTS OF HERBS.

For example, Ma Huang (*Herba Ephedrae*) is a powerful herb for promoting perspiration. In its honey-prepared form its diaphoretic (perspiration-inducing) effect is considerably reduced while its anti-dyspnoea action is increased.

4 TO IMPROVE THE SENSES OF TASTE AND ODOUR.

Animal products often have an undesirable odour, and an improvement in smell can be achieved after stir-frying in bran or wine. Examples include wine-treated snake skin and bran-fried Chun Pi (*Cortex Ailanthi*).

5 TO FACILITATE THE STORAGE OF HERBS.

Certain herbs tend to become mouldy. In these cases, baking and dry-frying can prevent mildew and putrefaction. For example, boiling Sang Piao Xiao (*Ootheca Mantidis*) can prevent decomposition.

6 TO CHANGE THE ORIENTATION OF HERBS SO THAT THEY ARE DIRECTED TO CERTAIN MERIDIANS.

Untreated Zhi Mu (*Rhizoma Anemarrhenae*) enters three meridians: the lung, the stomach, and the kidney. After this herb is stir-fried in salt, its course is changed and it enters only into the kidney.

7 TO REMOVE IMPURITIES, FOREIGN MATTER AND UNDESIRABLE SUBSTANCES.

For example, the minute hairs of the loquat leaf can cause throat irritation and should be removed to prevent vomiting. The head, legs and wings of certain animal products should also be taken off.

POPULAR METHODS OF PREPARATION

Over thousands of years of empirical practice, Chinese medical practitioners have developed a variety of ways of administering herbal remedies:

◆ DECOCTION

This is the most popular method. Herbs are boiled in water or steamed in wine. The

---

METHODS OF PROCESSING

1 PHYSICAL PROCESSING

◆ Purifying

◆ Pulverizing

◆ Slicing

2 WATER-PROCESSING

Water-processing cleans, softens and reduces toxicity. It also purifies and improves the texture of minerals.

3 FIRE-PROCESSING

Directly or indirectly, the general methods of fire-processing are: stir-

baking, stir-frying, calcine and roasting.

4 SIMULTANEOUS USE OF WATER AND FIRE

◆ Steam

◆ Boil

◆ Stew

◆ Quick-boil

5 OTHER PROCESSING METHODS

This includes sprouting, fermenting and frost-like preparation (such as in the making of Persimmon Frost, see page 99, Food as Therapy).

advantages are: quick absorption, a fast therapeutic effect, and easy modification to suit the ever-changing disease mechanism.

◆ **TEA BAG FORM**

Decoct or steep.

◆ **WINE-PREPARED SOLUTION**

◆ **PILL FORM**

Herbs are pulverized into a fine powder and mixed with honey, water, wine, vinegar or plant juice and rice or flour to form pills.

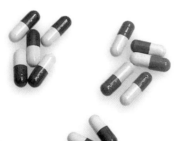

◆ **TABLET FORM**

Pulverized herbs are mixed with binding agents to form granules and are then compressed into tablets.

◆ **POWDER FORM**

A prescription of herbs is made into a fine powder to be taken internally or externally.

◆ **GRANULAR FORM**

Herbs are manufactured into granules, then steeped until dissolved and ingested.

◆ **PASTE FORM**

This includes ointments, salves, creams and adhesives.

◆ **EXTRACTS**

◆ **FROST FORM**

In a series of complex steps, herbs are processed until a frosty crust forms. Examples include apricot frost, deer horn glue frost, dry persimmon covered with white frost and the frost from the bottom of a wok (*Pulvis Fumi Carbonisatus*).

◆ **DEW FRAGRANCE**

Steam the herbs with water and collect the distilled solution.

◆ **EXUDATES**

Collected after applying heat, such as juice excreted from the baked bamboo stem.

◆ **FERMENTED MEDICINAL PRODUCTS**

Various types of yeast.

◆ **SOLUTIONS FOR INJECTION**

In some hospitals in China, certain herbal formulas are administered to ill patients via needle injection into acupuncture points or through an IV catheter. This is just one of the methods where Eastern and Western medicine can work together.

ABOVE

Preparations are also available in paste form, including ointments, salves, adhesives and creams.

ADMINISTERING CHINESE HERBS

It is often said that the treatment of disease is comparable to fighting a war. To gain therapeutic success, the practitioner should attentively observe the following rules.

◆ The practitioner must irrevocably follow the theories and concepts of traditional Chinese medicine, including meridian-organ diagnosis, a rationale that includes the Five Elements and Yin/Yang interaction. These concepts are like the North Star, helping the practitioner to navigate through the rough sea of patient diagnosis.

◆ The practitioner must thoroughly understand the nature and tastes of the herbs, in order to appoint the right herbs to deal with a particular situation.

◆ The practitioner must also take into account correct diagnosis, therapeutic requirement, selection of formulas, matching herbs, contra-indications and optimum dosages to formulate a prescription that fits the particular condition of a given patient.

MATCHING OF HERBS

In the early days of Chinese medicine, single herbs were commonly used to treat diseases. Later, experiences confirmed that single herb therapy was unable to achieve success with many conditions. Rather than giving the patient only one herb, a formula of several herbs was shown to give better results. Hence, the development of herbal formulas began, a great breakthrough and advance in the history of traditional Chinese medicine.

Each herb has its own characteristic action. When herbs are combined, naturally, they interact and synergism (combined effect) is attained.

1 When used together, certain herbs can ameliorate or eliminate adverse effects. Raw ginger (Chinese: Sheng Jiang; Latin: *Rhizoma Zingiberis*) and licorice (Chinese: Gan Cao; Latin: *Radix Glycyrrhizae Uralensis*) are often used to moderate and harmonize a formula.

2 Herbs can also antagonize one another and weaken their net action. For

example, ginseng (Chinese: Ren Shen) tonifies Qi while Lai Fu Zi (*Semen Raphani*) descends Qi. When they are used together, *Semen Raphani* can significantly weaken the tonifying effect of Ginseng. The antagonizing action of herbs should be taken into account when tonifying a deficient patient.

3 Combining herbs of similar action will enhance their original function and achieve better therapeutic results.

COMBINING HERBS

Rhubarb (Chinese: Da Huang; Latin: *Rhizoma Rhei*) is bitter and cold. Mang Xiao (*Mirabilitum Depuratum*) is salty and cold. Both of them are related to the stomach and large intestine meridians, and move towards the inferior. When they are formulated together, a synergistic purging action is achieved. Modern investigation demonstrated that the main ingredient of *Rhizoma Rhei* is rheum emodin, which can increase peristalsis. The main ingredient of *Mirabilitum* is sodium sulphate, which is not easily absorbed. It forms a hypertonic solution and attracts large amounts of water into the intestine to soften the stools, indirectly promoting peristalsis. Rhubarb and *Mirabilitum* complement each other in the process of purging. Thus, clinically, they often appear together in a herbal prescription.

ABOVE
Rhubarb is a bitter and cold food.

4 Some herbs are not toxic by themselves. However, when they are combined with certain ingredients, toxicity or adverse effects may occur and so they should be avoided.

MAIN FOCUSES OF A FORMULA

In the process of formulation, the practitioner should have a clear picture of the best choice of herbs. It is also very important to be aware of changes that occur after combination, changes that can enhance or weaken the total net effect or promote adverse effects.

It is often said that a herbal formula is a mirror that can reflect the knowledge and wisdom of a physician and the degree of mastery of this art.

As early as the period of *The Yellow Emperor's Canon of Internal Medicine*, 722–211 BC, principles governing the formulation of herbal prescriptions have been recorded. This was the era of slavery and feudalism, which is reflected in the terms that are used to describe the position of herbs in a formula (see below). There are four main focuses of a formula, which are described as: Emperor, Minister, Assistant, and Messenger.

◆ EMPEROR is used to designate the main herb(s) of a formula. It focuses on the chief pattern or primary set of symptoms and is the basic ingredient for dealing with the fundamental problem of the patient.

◆ MINISTER indicates herbs that occupy a secondary role, assist the Emperor and enhance the therapeutic effect of the chief herb.

◆ ASSISTANT herbs have three functions:

1 To take care of the associated or secondary symptoms.

2 To restrict and antagonize the potent action of the ruling herbs.

3 To help the body digest the formula. Due to the explosive nature of the disease mechanism, the body may resist the reception of decoction. For example, a patient with extremely high fever and a headache is in the state of "hot" pattern.

Conventionally, a "cold" formula is indicated. However, sudden ingestion of cold herbs could provoke too sudden a reaction and cause vomiting, and the body will resist the cold decoction. Instead, inclusion of a small amount of warm herbs into the cold formula can help the patient to drink the decoction without causing vomiting. These herbs function as a "complying" assistant.

◆ MESSENGER herbs act as guiding herbs and can lead the rest of the herbs in a formula to the diseased site. Messenger herbs can also harmonize the various properties of other herbs.

MODIFICATION OF FORMULAS

It is essential to follow the rules of formula organization; however, in practice, the practitioner also has to consider the constitution, age and lifestyle of the patient, for which further modification of the formula is always needed.

Modification of a formula depends on the number of herbs selected, the dosage and the form of administration. The formula can be modified in the following ways.

MODIFICATION OF THE NUMBER OF HERBS

Generally speaking, the chief herb of the primary pattern is rarely changed. The formula is modified in accordance with the changes of secondary or associated patterns by increasing or decreasing the number of related herbs to suit the requirement of the ever-changing disease process. In traditional Chinese medicine, this is known

REQUIREMENTS FOR SUCCESS

In brief, a formula should fulfill the following requirements to ensure therapeutic success:
1 The formula should accomplish a specific mission, have a definite focus and attain a specific therapeutic result.
2 The formula should be tightly organized.
3 The various functions of the formula should be crystal-clear.
4 The main focus of the formula should be distinctly visible.
5 It should be well balanced.

simply as "plus and minus" according to the evolution of the patterns.

MODIFICATION OF DOSAGE

In this type of modification, the number of herbs is fixed, while only the dosage changes. In doing so, the potency and therapeutic range of a formula are also modified.

MODIFICATION OF THE FORM OF ADMINISTRATION

In this situation, the form of administration is altered to suit different conditions. For example, a decoction is the best for acute conditions. When acute situations become chronic, pill form is recommended for long-term usage. The action of pill-form is gradual and steady.

CONTRA-INDICATIONS OF HERBAL THERAPY

Without a very deep understanding of the concepts of both traditional Chinese medicine and Chinese herbology, it is inappropriate to purchase Chinese patent medications casually, especially those so-called powerful invigorating remedies. It is always beneficial to discuss your problem with an experienced physician who is well versed in the wisdom of Chinese pattern diagnosis.

It is essential to minimize the adverse factors and maximize the potential of recovery. Therefore, the issue of contra-indication should be taken into consideration.

Depending on the patterns, each herb or each category of herbs has certain indications and contra-indications.

For example, Xia Ku Cao (*Spica Prunellae*) is indicated for the treatment of headaches due to "wind-heat evil", while it is contra-indicated for use in headaches and dizziness due to hypertension.

1 MATCHING CONTRA-INDICATIONS

Errors in combining herbs may produce adverse or toxic reactions, aggravate certain conditions and cause therapeutic failure. To avoid improper combinations, the ancient scholars have summarized the contra-indications of commonly used herbs into easily remembered verses, known as "the rhyme of 18 pairs of antagonizing components" and "the rhyme of 19 pairs of opposing inhibition".

2 CONTRA-INDICATIONS IN PREGNANCY

Certain herbs can injure the foetus and cause miscarriage. They should be used with careful deliberation and with extra attention in pregnancy.

Contra-indicated herbs for pregnancy include the following:

- Ba Dou (*Fructus Crotonis*)
- Qian Niu Zi (*Semen Pharbitidis*)
- Hong Da Ji (*Radix Knoxiae*)
- Ban Mao (*Mylabris*)
- She Xiang (*Musk*)
- San Leng (*Rhizoma Sparganii*)
- E Zhu (*Rhizoma Zedoariae*)
- Shui Zhi (*Hirudo*)
- Mang Chang (*Tabanus*)
- Da Huang (*Rhizoma Rhei*)

ABOVE
Cinnamon bark (Rou Gui).

WARNING

The following herbs should be used with care because of their powerful ability to break up and move Qi and stagnate blood, and due to their spicy, hot or sinking natures:

- **Tao Ren** (*Semen Persicae*)
- **Hong Hua** (*Flos Carthamus*)
- **Da Huang** (*Rhizoma Rhei*)
- **Mang Xiao** (*Mirabilitum Depuratum*)
- **Zhi Shi** (*Fructus Aurantii Immaturus*)
- **Fu Zi** (*Radix Aconiti Lateralis Preparata*)
- **Gan Jiang** (Dried ginger)
- **Rou Gui** (Cinnamon bark)

3 ADVERSE INTERACTION OF HERBS WITH FOODS

When taking herbal therapies, some people say that is not necessary to consider the question of negative reactions between herbs and food. Is it good advice to eat whatever one desires? According to Chinese culture and traditional Chinese medical theory, everything in heaven and earth, and in our body, has Yin and Yang. Disease processes have Yin and Yang; herbs are categorized in terms of Yin and Yang. Foods are no exception; they also have Yin, Yang, hot, cold, warm or cool properties.

Many dietitians confirm the therapeutic principles of administering cold/cool agents for hot/warm patterns, and vice versa. The understanding of indications and contra-indications of food is exceedingly important. Proper diet can enhance the therapeutic effects of herbs, whereas an inappropriate regimen will aggravate the condition. Thus, avoidance of certain food is a routine medical practice in traditional Chinese medicine.

◆ Generally speaking, cold, raw food substances are contra-indicated in patients with a previous history of limb coldness, aversion to cold and bland oral taste – all

ABOVE
Hong Hua.

of which indicate the presence of a cold pattern. The patient should keep away from eating ice-cream, iced water, bitter melon, raw fish, cold salads and so on.

◆ Patients with an infectious hot pattern that manifests as fever, sore throat, cough, oral dryness and bitterness, as well as those with "rising liver Yang" patterns that feature vertigo, insomnia and irascibility, should avoid spicy foods (such as pepper, chillies, garlic and alcohol) and greasy foods (butter, beefsteak, pork chops, fried chicken and doughnuts).

◆ Patients with spleen and stomach deficiency, who show symptoms of indigestion, distention and diarrhoea should avoid fried and greasy foods and foods that are difficult to digest, such as fried chicken, beefsteak, pork chops, doughnuts, butter, cheese, ice-cream, prepared sweet rice cookies and beans.

◆ Patients with skin problems should not eat crab, prawns, lobster or duck, because these foods can promote the flaring up of toxins. Peppers, chillies and wine are stimulants and can also aggravate itchiness.

To avoid affecting the nature and action of herbs, it is desirable to eat plain, easily digested food.

LEFT
Bitter melon.

WESTERN MEDICATION

COMBINING HERBAL FORMULAS
WITH WESTERN MEDICATIONS

*low results with herbal therapies may compel the patient to take Western medica-
tions and vice versa. Many patients with chronic, intractable conditions will often
end up taking both Chinese herbal and Western remedies. For hundreds of years,
since the introduction of Western medicine into China, combined administration of herbal
and Western therapies has taken place. Master Zhang Xi Chun (1860–1933), in his book
Yi Xue Zhong Cheng Can Xi Lu, combined gypsum (Shi Gao) with aspirin to treat fevers
of external contraction. He believed that aspirin is pungent and cool and that it can clear
heat. Aspirin and gypsum together are more effective in relieving the surface, clearing heat
and expelling evil to the exterior than using either one alone.*

Today, patients in the majority of Chinese hospitals often receive therapeutic measures from both disciplines, whenever this is appropriate. However, before administration, it is important to understand the advantages and disadvantages, as well as synergistic or antagonistic actions.

Due to the increased reliance upon antibiotics, patients often complain of fatigue, poor appetite, bland tastes, vertigo, tinnitus, chest oppression, vomiting, diarrhoea or constipation. Such symptoms indicate the dysfunction of the autonomic nervous system and digestive system. In traditional Chinese medicine, these symptoms are seen as deficiency and weakness of the spleen and stomach, resulting from the overuse of antibiotics, which can easily injure these organs.

Antibiotics are grouped under cold and cool natures, because, according to traditional Chinese medicine, this group of medications clears heat and relieves toxins.

Therefore, it is wise at the later stage of the disease to incorporate some herbs to circulate Qi and fortify the spleen, or to nurture Yin and benefit Qi. This will regulate and normalize the function of spleen stomach and enhance recovery.

For example, an open wound and soft tissue injury, complicated with infection, advances into a sub-acute inflammatory stage. The usual clinical findings are as follows: diffuse swelling with mild pain and a dull red lesion with a pale yellowish discharge. When antibiotics alone are unable to accelerate the healing, this primarily reflects the weakness of the body's resistance. Practitioners of Chinese medicine believe that this is the pattern of lingering heat-toxins, associated with Qi deficiency and blood stagnation. Antibiotics are still needed to clear the lingering heat and relieve toxins, but herbs should be added to tonify and move Qi, vitalize blood, fortify the spleen and expel damp.

The following herbs are commonly added:

- Huang Qi (*Radix Astragali*)
- Dang Gui (*Radix Angelicae Sinensis*)
- Dan Shen (*Radix Salviae Miltiorrhizae*)
- Chen Pi (*Pericarpium Citri Reticulatae*)
- Fu Ling (*Poria*)

The addition of the above herbs can often accelerate the healing of a wound. A common example is recorded below and is typical of the successful integration of traditional Chinese medicine and Western medications.

However, it is essential to note that, in certain instances, the combination of both systems of medicine is not advisable. For example, digoxin, a cardio-tonic, should not be used with calcium-rich agents such as Mother of Pearl, raw Long Gu (*Os Draconis*) and raw Mu Li (*Concha Ostrea*). They can increase the toxicity of digoxin and cause arrhythmia or conduction blockage. Similarly, herbs that contain large amount of tannic compunds, such as Hu Zhang (*Radix Polygoni Cuspidati*), Jing Jie (*Herba Schizonepetae*), Di Yu (*Radix Sanguisorbae*) and Jin Gou Ji (*Rhizoma Cibotii*), should not be used with ferrous sulphate, vitamin B1, pepsin and pancreatin. The combined use can reduce the potency of the medications and adverse effects are common.

In short, Western medicine and traditional Chinese medicine can be integrated. However, meticulous studying and careful planning should be conducted before administration.

LEFT
Di Yu.

USING CHINESE AND WESTERN MEDICINE TOGETHER

I remember a story my father and elder brother told me when I was a child, about how they saved a critical patient by using Chinese and Western medicine together. The patient was an elderly man, who had contracted lobar pneumonia complicated with heart failure.

Chinese villages at that time were very poor and lacked medical facilities, and the patient was on the verge of dying. His family, not knowing what to do, beseeched a handful of local physicians to save him. My father was appointed to bear the responsibility and take charge of establishing a therapeutic strategy and prescribing a formula. Calmly, he administered a full dose of penicillin, followed by a decoction of aconite, ginseng and raw ginger. Within 12 hours, the patient passed from the critical stage to safety. This case illustrates that penicillin is used as the "emperor" to clear the bacterial heat and toxins and ginseng and aconite as the "ministers", to tonify Qi and invigorate the heart. Raw ginger is used as the "assistant", to enhance the action of aconite.

COOKING HERBS: MAKING A DECOCTION

*T*he last stage of herbal therapy is the cooking and ingestion of the herbs. It is a very important step and one must prepare the herbs with great attention.

1 SELECTION OF COOKING CONTAINER

Earthenware, glass, enamel and electrical porcelain pots may be used. Iron, copper and tin wares can change the chemical consistency of the herbs and therefore should not be used.

2 POINTS TO BE NOTED BEFORE DECOCTION

◆ Place the herbs in a bucket and add an appropriate amount of clean water; stir to wash and pour away the unclean water; repeat the process two to three times.

◆ Place the clean herbs in the cooking container; add enough water to cover the herbs, pressing down with a wooden spoon (not metal) until the water is about 1 cm (¹/₂ in) above the packed surface.

◆ Cover the pot with a lid, and soak the ingredients for about 30 minutes to let the water permeate into the plant tissue. NOTE: the cooking container must be cleaned before and after each use. Assign one pan especially for cooking herbs.

3 GENERAL METHOD OF DECOCTION

◆ Use quick, strong fire to initiate a boil and then reduce to a slow flame; boil for about 30 to 40 minutes.

◆ Herbal formulas for healing external contraction of wind-cold or wind-heat should cook for approximately 15 to 20 minutes. Moistening and tonifying formulas require a longer period of one to three hours, depending on the specific ingredients.

◆ During cooking, do not repeatedly remove the lid. This may cause the excessive loss of volatile elements.

◆ After cooking, immediately strain the solution through some muslin into a bowl or jar made of glass, porcelain or ceramic (not metal). Do not use a metal strainer. If it is necessary to repeat the cooking, add cold water reaching the surface of residue, and boil for 10 to 15 minutes. Strain the liquid again and mix with the first portion.

◆ The entire amount should be divided and taken in separate doses throughout the day.

◆ Once the tea has cooled to room temperature, the remainder should be stored in the refrigerator, and will keep for at least a week before it loses its effectiveness. Note that freshly cooked tea can be left as long as overnight to cool without reducing its effectiveness.

◆ All tea should be warmed before being ingested, so when using tea that has been in the refrigerator, it is necessary to warm it up on the stove first – do not use a microwave. The best way to warm the tea to prevent it from boiling again is to use the double boiler method – placing a non-metal container in a pan of water.

SPECIAL METHODS OF COOKING

The following seven methods are suitable for dense herbs that need extra cooking.

1 Separate the heavy minerals from the rest of the ingredients in the herbal formula. Clean and soak the other herbs, while cooking the heavy minerals, or agents that are difficult to dissolve, in advance. The heavy ingredients are first placed in a container with water, then brought to a boil and cooked for 15 to 20 minutes. Strain to retain the liquid and pulverize or slice the remaining herbs. Add both the strained liquid and the remaining herbs to the rest of the soaking herbs.

EXAMPLES OF AGENTS THAT NEED THESE SPECIAL METHODS OF COOKING
◆ Long Gu (*Os Draconis*)
◆ Mu Li (*Concha Ostreae*)
◆ Shi Jue Ming (*Goncha Haliotidis*)
◆ Gui Ban (*Plastrum Testudinis*)
◆ Bie Jia (*Carapax Amydae*)
◆ Shi Gao (Raw gypsum)

Certain herbs have to be cooked for a longer period to reduce their toxicity:
◆ Fu Zi (*Radix Aconiti Lateralis Preparata*)
◆ Szechuan aconite root (Chinese: Chuan Wu; Latin: *Radix Aconiti*)
◆ Cao Wu (*Radix Aconiti Agrestis*) requires one to two hours of cooking in advance before adding other herbs.

2 Boil to obtain a solution for cooking other herbs. The designated herb is first cooked for 15 to 20 minutes. Then the liquid is strained off (discarding the herb) and the retained solution is used to cook or steam other herbs. For example, Zao Xin Tu (*Terra Flava Usta*) is cooked in advance for 15 to 20 minutes; the solution is retained to cook the rest of the formula.

Alternatively, you can first decoct certain herbs of a formula, and then use the retained solution to steam-cook ginseng. This method will prevent the loss of the effective elements of ginseng while cooking with other herbs.

3 A specific herb is added after the decoction is ready. With some aromatic herbs, we want to preserve the volatile aroma in the decoction. If these herbs are cooked for too long, the aromatic oils will not be retained and the active ingredients may be destroyed.

Therefore it is necessary to add them for the last five minutes, when the decoction is almost ready.

EXAMPLES OF INGREDIENTS
◆ Bo he (*Herba Menthae*)
◆ Sha Ren (*Fructus Amomi*)
◆ Mu Xiang (*Radix Saussureae*)

PURGATIVE HERBS
◆ Da Huang (*Rhizoma Rhei*)
◆ Fan Xie Ye (*Folium Sennae*)
◆ The herb Gou Teng (*Ramulus Uncariae cum Uncis*), which can help to lower blood pressure, should also be added during the last five minutes.

4 Herbs that are in the form of powder, which are relatively sticky, and those that contain minute hairs, should be wrapped with gauze to prevent them sticking to the bottom of pot, irritating the throat or making the tea too cloudy.

EXAMPLES OF HERBS IN A STICKY POWDER FORM
◆ Xuan Fu Hua
   (*Flos Inulae*)
◆ Che Qian Zi
   (*Semen
   Plantaginis*)
◆ Zao Xin Tu
   (*Terra
   Flava
   Usta*)
◆ Pu Huang
   (*Pollen Typhae*)
◆ Xin Yi Hua
   (*Flos Magnoliae*)

ABOVE
Xin Yi Hua.

5 To prevent any loss of effectiveness, certain herbs are often cooked separately. Such herbs include both American ginseng and Asian ginseng. The herb is placed in a special container with a lid and steam-cooked. When ready, it is mixed with the designated decoction and ingested.

6 It is not desirable for certain herbs to undergo prolonged cooking. To ingest, they are pulverized into powder and then steeped in warm water or a hot decoction.

THESE INCLUDE
◆ Hu Po (*Succinum*)
◆ Tian Qi (*Radix Pseudoginseng*)
◆ Chen Xiang (*Lignum Aquilariae*)
◆ Liquid solutions of Zhu Li (*Succus Bambusae*) and raw ginger juice should also be steeped.

7 Sticky herbs should be dissolved with boiling water, or added into the cooked solution (remove residue). Stir over a slow fire until the agent is dissolved.

STICKY HERBS INCLUDE
◆ E Jiao (*Gelatinum Corii Asini*)
◆ Yi Tang (*Maltose*)

TIME OF INGESTING

◆ This is mainly determined by the disease and the nature of the herbs. A herbal decoction is usually taken about one hour after a meal.
◆ Tonifying herbs may be ingested approximately one hour before a meal. A purgative decoction is commonly

METHODS OF INGESTION

◆ The liquid from the herbal decoction for "cold" diseases should be taken warm. But to promote perspiration and expel external evils (cold/flu), it is desirable to ingest while the decoction is hot.

◆ For "hot" diseases, drink it cold, in order to avoid vomiting.

◆ Drinking the decoction while cold is also indicated for use in hot patterns, as it enhances the action of clearing heat.

◆ Drinking the formula while it is still hot is indicated for use in cold patterns, as it enhances their warming effect. However, there are always exceptions, as in certain "deficiency cold" patients that have manifestations of false heat, for example when the patient has body heat and a flushed face but also displays a cold appearance. This condition is known as "genuine cold and false heat". The decoction should be taken while it is cold.

However, a feverish, hot-pattern patient with cold limbs is known as "genuine heat and false cold". The cold nature decoction should be taken while it is hot. These methods of administration can increase the effectiveness of the treatment.

administered on an empty stomach.

◆ Herbs for fortifying the stomach and herbs with a strong irritative nature should be taken about 30 minutes after meals.

◆ One package of tea decoction is generally taken in two divided doses per day. In a chronic but stable condition, once a day is sufficient. In acute cases, two packs of herbs should be divided into four to six doses, with one dose taken every four to six hours, in order to keep the herbs circulating in the body and control the advance of the disease.

CONSULT YOUR PRACTITIONER

The dosages and suggestions discussed on these pages provide only a general guide. It is important to discuss these issues with your herbal practitioner so that he or she can advise appropriate instructions for each individual case.

LEFT
Hou Pi.

FOOD AS THERAPY

Throughout the history of Chinese medicine, doctors have recommended different kinds of food as treatments for their patients' ailments. Many of the doctors recorded the diets, sometimes called prescriptions or formulas, in medical texts. One of the oldest medical books, Shen Nong Ben Cao Jing Herbal Classic, published around 200 BC, lists foods such as sesame seed, Chinese date, Chinese yam, ginger, grape and lily bulb as being therapeutic. The outstanding physician, Zhang Zhong Jing, of the third-century Han Dynasty, recorded the formula to treat Febrile disease – a soup made of Chinese angelica root, fresh ginger and mutton, in the Treatise on Febrile and Miscellaneous Diseases. In the sixteenth-century Ming Dynasty, a great physician, Li Shi Zhen, collected and recorded many recipes for diseases in his masterpiece, Compendium of Materia Medica. In every dynasty, food preparations have been noted as one of the essential therapies of Chinese medicine.

Before suggesting a therapeutic diet, a doctor of Chinese medicine must first

LEFT
A Chinese medical doctor will carefully examine all the aspects of a patient's health and environment that could affect their condition.

take many different factors into consideration. The doctor studies the patient's constitution, the nature of the patient's illness and type of syndrome, and even the season and climate. The doc-tor selects the proper diet for the patient based on all of these factors, not just upon the disease alone.

For example, two people suffering from asthma may not necessarily need the same type of therapeu-tic diet, because in Chinese medicine all diseases are characterized into different types. In the case of asth-ma, the doctor determines whether the asthma is cold-type, hot-type or phlegm-damp type. If the asth-ma is a cold-type, then the doctor might recommend warm or hot types of food, such as fresh ginger and green onion, especially if the weather is cold outside. If the asthma is a hot-type, perhaps occurring during the summer, the patient might need a cold-type of food, such as watermelon, to help eliminate the heat. Additionally, the patient's constitution and the season or climate would be taken into consideration before prescribing a therapeutic diet.

A prescribed diet can be used not only for treating disease, but also for maintaining a person's good health. Garlic, for example, can be used to treat indigestion, diarrhoea, dysentery and whooping cough. But because garlic kills bacteria, detoxifies poisons, strengthens the stomach and promotes digestion, it has also been known to prevent flu and epidemic encephalomyelitis. Fortunately, most of the foods and herbs used in diet therapy have a good taste and are pleasant to take.

THE NATURE OF FOODS

Chinese medicine divides foods into three categories: Yin, Yang and neutral.

YIN FOODS

Foods that are cool or cold in nature are Yin foods, such as cucumber, pear, watermelon, mung bean, chrysanthemum flower or water chestnut. These foods clear away heat, purge fire, remove heat from the blood and remove poison. They treat the heat syndromes associated with excess Yang. Some fruits are not extremely cold, but are considered to be cool or slightly cold, and these include banana and apple.

ABOVE
Cucumber is an example of a cool Yin food.

YANG FOODS

Foods that are hot or warm in nature are Yang foods, such as pepper, onion (red, yellow or white), Chinese green onion, fresh ginger, mutton, Chinese-date and walnut kernel. This type of food has the function of warming the interior, as well as dispelling cold to treat the symptoms linked with excess Yin. Some foods are not extremely hot but are considered to be slightly warm, and these include peaches and cherries.

RIGHT
Red onion is a warm Yang food.

NEUTRAL FOODS

The third kind of food is neutral in nature. Since neutral foods, such as strawberry and lemon, do not influence any hot or cold syndromes in the body, they are useful when it is unclear as to whether one's condition is primarily cold or warm in nature.

THE RELATIONSHIP BETWEEN THE FIVE FLAVOURS AND THE FIVE ORGANS

The flavour of a food influences both the type of action it has in the body and which organ or organs it acts upon.

◆ FOOD THAT IS SOUR, such as black plum, acts upon the liver. It is astringent and can stop abnormal discharge.

◆ BITTER FOODS, such as bitter melon, affect the heart and can remove excessive heat. These foods can correct the direction of the body's Qi, purge pathogenic fire, eliminate dampness and remove toxic substances.

◆ SPICY FOODS, such as red pepper, go to the lungs. Food that is spicy or pungent in nature can disperse and promote Qi circulation.

ABOVE
Seaweed.

◆ FOOD THAT IS SALTY, such as seaweed, acts upon the kidneys and can reduce hard masses or lumps in the body.

◆ SWEET FOODS, such as honey, work on the spleen. They are nourish-

LEFT
Lemon is a neutral food.

ing and invigorating, can regulate Qi and Blood and relieve spasm and pain.

◆ BLAND FOOD, like sweet food, affects the stomach and spleen. Job's-tears seed, a typical bland food, can promote urine, strengthen the spleen and eliminate dampness.

THE RELATIONSHIP BETWEEN THE SEASONS AND FOOD

The season and climate of a region play an important role in choosing what foods to eat for health.

◆ IN AUTUMN, the weather becomes dry. To avoid dryness, a person should eat foods that nourish Yin and moisten the lungs. Chinese doctors often suggest soft, moist foods, such as honey, sesame, dairy products, apples, bananas, grapes, water chestnuts, pears, oranges, tangerines, radishes, kelp and lotus root.

◆ IN WINTER, it becomes cold, so it is better to eat more warm and hot foods, such as mutton, ginger, pepper, onion (red, yellow or white), Chinese green onion, garlic and green leaf vegetables.

◆ IN SPRING, the liver is in hyperfunction, which reduces the digestive function of the spleen. The flavour of the food should be sweet and not sour to nourish the spleen Qi, so choose Chinese dates, honey, malt sugar and carrots.

◆ IN SUMMER, people usually have weaker digestion. It is better to eat lighter food that can be digested easily, such as watermelon and various kinds of vegetable such as tomato and cucumber.

THE RELATIONSHIP BETWEEN FOOD AND COLOURS

Food comes in a variety of colours. Sometimes even the same food can have different colours. For example, onions come in many shades – green, red, yellow and white. Although the colour may be different, the character and function of these four types of onion are almost identical. The differences are mainly seen in the strength and nutritional value of each variety. In general, food that is darker or deeper in colour tastes stronger and has more nutritional value. Another example is black-bone chicken, which has black-coloured bones, meat, skin and feathers. Black-bone chicken has more nutritional value than the regular white chicken, and is used to strengthen someone who is recovering from illness or who is very weak. It is especially helpful after childbirth, when the mother has lost much blood and Qi. A third example of this relationship between food and colour is that of black sesame seeds, which are more effective than white sesame seeds, especially in strengthening the kidneys and treating grey hair.

ABOVE
Red pepper is a warm food for winter.

ABOVE
Tomatoes are a light food for summer.

BEFORE COOKING WITH CHINESE HERBS

When preparing any therapeutic recipes, it is important to use only glass, ceramic or porcelain cookware, as metal pans can alter the chemical constituents of the herbs.

LEFT
Carrots are a sweet food for spring.

INDEX OF FOODS

VEGETABLES

CARROT

This is sweet in flavour and neutral in nature, acting on the channels of the lung and spleen. It contains more than two kinds of carotene, vitamins B1, B2, amino acids, sugar and fatty oil. Its effects include: anti-inflammation, anti-allergy, strengthening the spleen, removing stagnation of food, lowering blood pressure, protecting the stomach and intestines, strengthening the function of macrophages (infection-attacking blood cells) and preventing cancer. It is used to treat indigestion, dysentery, coughs and hypertension.

CELERY

This is sweet and bitter in flavour and cool in nature, acting on the channels of the stomach and liver. It contains organic acid, carotene, vitamin C and sugar. Its effects include: calming the liver and clearing away heat, expelling wind, removing dampness by diuresis and detoxifying. An experiment by Chinese scientists showed that celery has the function of lowering blood pressure. Celery also has the function of contracting the uterus. It is used to treat hypertension, vertigo, headache, flushed face, conjunctival congestion,

ABOVE

Celery is sweet in flavour and cool in nature.

dysentery with bloody stools, carbuncles and furuncles (boils and skin abscesses).

PUMPKIN

This is sweet in flavour and warm in nature, acting on the channels of the spleen and stomach. It contains glucose, sucrose, protein (citrulline and arginine), carotene, vitamins B and C. Its effects include: invigorating the spleen and stomach, replenishing Qi, relieving inflammation and pains, removing toxicity and destroying intestinal parasites. It is used to treat fatigue due to Qi deficiency, dysentery, malaria, intercostal (of the ribs) neuralgia and burns. It is also used to prevent diabetes and colon cancer.

CUCUMBER

Sweet in flavour and cool in nature, cucumber acts on the channels of the spleen and large intestine. It contains amino acid, sugar, carotene, vitamin C, calcium, phosphorus, iron, malonic acid and fibre. Its effects include: clearing away heat, eliminating dampness, inducing urination and bowel movement, relieving pain, lowering cholesterol and preventing cancer. It is used to treat restlessness and thirst, sore throat, conjunctival congestion, dysuria and heat-type dysentery.

Cucumber is especially good in the summer because of its cool nature and ability to clear heat. Those patients with chronic bronchitis and ulcerative colitis should avoid eating cucumber.

GREEN ONION (CHINESE GREEN ONION)

This is pungent in flavour and warm in nature, acting on the channels of the lung and stomach. It contains vitamins C, B1, B2 and nicotinic acid. The effects of green onion are: releasing the exterior, activating Yang and clearing away toxic materials. It is used to treat chills, fever, acute headache, constipation, dysentery, retention of urine, carbuncles and swelling.

ONION (RED, YELLOW OR WHITE)

Onion is pungent, sweet in flavour and moderate in nature. It is rich in vitamins A, B1, B2 and C, calcium, iron and phosphorus. Its effects include: clearing away heat, resolving phlegm, detoxifying and destroying parasites. Onion can also lower cholesterol and triglycerides, so it can be used to treat and prevent arteriosclerosis, enteritis and diphtheria. It can also increase the secretion of the digestive tract to promote digestion, prevent cancer and make the hair strong and shiny.

GARLIC

Pungent in flavour and warm in nature, garlic contains protein, fat, carbohydrate, vitamins and minerals. Throughout the history of Chinese medicine, it has been called the "penicillin in the earth". In ancient Egypt and India, soldiers ate garlic to keep healthy and boost their courage in battle. In the Second World War, the British government shipped several tons of garlic to the infantry to cure the soldiers' wounds. Its effects include: destroying parasites, detoxifying, removing dyspepsia and strengthening the stomach. It is used to treat food stagnancy, cold-pain of the stomach and abdomen, diarrhoea, dysentery, carbuncles, furuncles, swelling, whooping cough, snake-bites and insect-bites. Because it has a warm nature, garlic is especially good to eat in the winter.

LEFT
Garlic is pungent in flavour and warm in nature.

RADISH

This is pungent, sweet in flavour and cool in nature, acting on the channels of the lung and stomach. It contains glucose, sucrose, fructose, various kinds of amino acids and vitamin C. Its effects include: removing food stagnation, clearing away phlegm-heat, reducing nausea and vomiting, regulating the spleen and stomach and clearing away toxic materials. It is

LEFT
Radish is pungent and sweet in flavour, and cool in nature.

used to eliminate the accumulation of phlegm and heat in the lungs, haematemesis (vomiting blood), nose-bleeds, diabetes, dysentery, migraines, headaches and in reducing weight. Radish is also used to prevent both cancer and the formation of gall-bladder stones. It can be helpful in the autumn, as it can also promote the production of body fluid and so help eliminate dryness.

WATER CHESTNUT

This is sweet in flavour and cold in nature. It contains starch, a small amount of protein, fat, calcium, phosphorus, iron and vitamin C. Its effects include: clearing away heat, promoting the production of body fluid, eliminating dampness and phlegm and relieving dyspepsia. It is used to treat restlessness and thirst due to febrile diseases, sore throat, cold sores, conjunctival congestion, dysentery, productive cough, jaundice, indigestion and distention of the abdomen.

RED PEPPER (CHILLI)

Pungent in flavour and hot in nature, red pepper contains protein, carbohydrate, calcium, phosphorus, carotene, iron, vitamins C, B1, B2 and niacin. Its effects include: warming the spleen and stomach, eliminating dampness and cold, promoting appetite and digestion and inducing perspiration. It is used to treat vomiting, dysentery, malaria and pain in the lower abdomen

due to accumulation of cold. It can also prevent cancer. Its warm qualities make it a good vegetable to use in the winter.

MUNG BEAN

This is sweet in flavour and cool in nature, acting on the channels of the heart and stomach. It is rich in proteins (globulin, methionine, tryptophan, tyrosine) and contains phospholipids, small amounts of calcium, phosphorus, iron, carotene, vitamins B1, B2 and niacin. It clears away heat and toxic materials and induces diuresis (increase in urine). It is often helpful in the summertime for treating restlessness and thirst caused by summer-heat oedema, diarrhoea, dysentery, erysipelas (infectious skin disease), carbuncles and for relieving drug toxicity.

CHINESE CHIVE

This is pungent in flavour and warm in nature, acting on the channels of the spleen and stomach. It contains protein, fat, carbohydrates, carotene, calcium, phosphorus, iron and vitamin B. Its effects include: warming the spleen and stomach, promoting and restoring the circulation of Qi, dissipating blood cloudiness, detoxifying, toxifying Yang, and regulating the functions among the viscera. It is used to treat dysphagia (difficulty in swallowing), regurgitation, chest pain and tightness, impotence, premature ejaculation, haemoptysis, haematuria, nose-bleeding, dysentery, insect bites and traumatic injuries. People with heat in the stomach or peptic ulcers should

RIGHT
Water chestnuts are sweet in flavour and cold in nature.

avoid Chinese chive.

Chinese chive is a common vegetable in China and has been used in food therapy for thousands of years. There is a story in the *Compendium of Materia Medica*, written by Li Shi Zhen, about Chinese chives. The story tells of an old man, ill with dysphagia, who vomited instantly after eating. He felt an obstruction behind the sternum during swallowing. Someone gave him some juice made of Chinese chives and salty plums. After drinking the juice, he could take some food and increased his meals gradually every day. One day he suddenly threw up a large amount of thick, ropy phlegm and was relieved of his symptoms thereafter.

CHINESE YAM

This is sweet in flavour and neutral in nature, acting on the channels of the spleen, lung and kidney. Its effects include: replenishing the spleen, lung and kidney, and tonifying Qi and Yin. It is used to treat deficiency of spleen Qi, loose stools or diarrhoea, coughing due to deficiency of the lungs, frequent urination and leucorrhoea (whitish or yellowish vaginal discharge).

LOTUS ROOT

Sweet in flavour and cold in nature, this acts on the channels of the heart, spleen and stomach. It contains starch, protein, asparagine and vitamin C. It is often taken in the autumn to nourish Yin. The effects of raw and cooked lotus root are different:

◆ RAW LOTUS ROOT can clear away heat, cool the blood, dissipate blood cloudiness, quench thirst, dispel the effects of alcohol, arrest bleeding and strengthen the stomach. It is used to treat restlessness and thirst due to febrile diseases, haematemesis, nosebleeding, puerperal metrorrhagia (uterine haemorrhaging at childbirth) and cystitis.

◆ COOKED LOTUS ROOT can strengthen the spleen, promote tissue regeneration, replenish the blood, promote the healthy functioning of the stomach, increase appetite and arrest diarrhoea and coughing.

BELOW
Chinese chives are pungent in flavour and warm in nature.

FRUIT

APRICOT

This is sweet in flavour and neutral in nature, acting on the channels of the lung and large intestine. It contains carbohydrates and sugar, carotene, protein, iron, calcium, phosphorus and vitamins A, B and C. Its effects include: moistening the lungs and relieving asthma and constipation. It is used to treat coughs and asthma due to consumption, and constipation due to dryness of the intestinal tract.

ABOVE
Apricots are sweet in flavour and neutral in nature.

BANANA

This is sweet in flavour and cold in nature and acts on the channels of the lung and large intestine. It contains starch, potassium, protein, fat, sugar, vitamins A, B, C and E, pectin, calcium, phosphorus and iron. It clears away pathogenic heat, cools the blood, promotes the production of body fluid, arrests thirst, moisturizes the intestines, removes poisons and lowers

RIGHT
Banana is sweet in flavour and cold in nature.

blood pressure. It treats restlessness and thirst caused by febrile diseases, constipation and bleeding due to haemorrhoids. It is a good food for autumn because of its moistening quality.

APPLE

Apple is sweet and sour in flavour and cool in nature. It contains large amounts of fructose, malic acid, tannic acid, fibre, pectin, calcium, phosphorus, iron and potassium. It strengthens the spleen and stomach. It invigorates Qi, promoting the production of body fluid and arresting dryness and thirst, which makes it a good autumn food. It treats anorexia, decreased function of the spleen and stomach, mental fatigue, thirst and oppressed feelings in the chest.

RIGHT
Apple is sweet and sour.

PEAR

This is sweet, slightly sour in flavour and cool in nature and acts on the channels of the lung and stomach. It contains fructose, sucrose, glucose, malic acid, vitamins B1, B2 and A, calcium, phosphorus, iron, a trace of protein and fat. Its effects include: promoting the production of body fluid, moistening dryness, clearing away heat, arresting coughs, eliminating phlegm, enriching Yin and blood, lowering blood pressure and removing alcohol toxins. It is used to treat restlessness and thirst due to imbalance of the body fluids during febrile diseases, diabetes, coughs of the heat type, madness due to phlegm-heat, dysphagia and constipation. Pears are a good food to eat in autumn to alleviate dryness.

ABOVE
Pear.

CHERRY

This is sweet in flavour and warm in nature, acting on the channels of the spleen and stomach. It contains a large amount of iron (the highest percentage of iron of all the fruits), protein, sugar, phosphorus, carotene and vitamin C. Its effects include: invigorating the spleen and stomach, expelling wind and removing dampness and inducing the eruption of measles. It is used for the treatment of anaemia, weakness after illness, imbalance of the function of the spleen and stomach and rheumatoid arthritis.

GRAPE

This is sweet and sour in flavour and neutral in nature, acting on the channels of the lung, spleen and kidney. It contains glucose, fructose, a small amount of sucrose, xylose, protein, calcium, phosphorus, carotene, vitamins B1, B2, C and nicotinic acid. Its effects include: invigorating Qi and enriching the blood, strengthening the bones and muscles, nourishing Yin, promoting the production of body fluid and inducing diureses. It is used as a cure for Qi and Blood deficiency, coughs due to deficiency of the lungs, palpitation, night-sweats, arthralgia (neuralgic joint-pain) due to wind-dampness, slow and painful discharge of the urine, weakness of the spleen and stomach, fatigue and oedema. It can be helpful in the autumn to alleviate dryness.

ABOVE
Grapes are sweet and sour in flavour and neutral in nature.

WATERMELON

This contains proteins (citrulline, alanine, glutamic acid, arginine), vitamins A, B and C, glucose, fructose, sucrose, potassium, calcium, phosphorus and fibre. It is sweet in flavour and cold in nature, acting on the channels of the heart, stomach and urinary bladder. It can clear away summer-heat, relieve restlessness and thirst and induce diuresis. It treats restlessness and thirst caused by summer-heat, consumption of body fluid due to excessive heat, difficulty in urinating, mouth ulcers and inflammation of the throat.

RIGHT
Watermelon helps eliminate heat because it is a cold type of food.

STRAWBERRY

This is sweet and sour in flavour and neutral in nature, acting on the channels of the lung and spleen. It contains protein, fructose, sucrose, glucose, citric acid, malic acid, amino acid, carotene, fibre, various vitamins, a large amount of vitamin C, calcium, phosphorus, potassium and trace minerals. Its effects include: moistening the lungs, promoting the production of body fluid, strengthening the spleen, regulating the stomach, enriching the blood, invigorating Qi, cooling heat in the blood and detoxifying. It is used to treat lung-dryness due to consumption of body fluid, weakness of the spleen and stomach, insufficiency of Qi and Blood, dysentery, haematuria (blood in urine), furuncles and menoxenia . It is used in preventing hypertension, arteriosclerosis and colonic cancer.

PINEAPPLE

This is sweet and sour in flavour and neutral in nature, acting on the channels of the spleen and stomach. It contains fructose, glucose, protein, various kinds of vitamins, calcium, iron, phosphorus and potassium. Its effects include: strengthening the spleen and stomach, promoting the production of body fluid, regulating the function of the stomach, tonifying Qi and Blood, reducing swelling and eliminating dampness. It is used to treat dehydration due to excessive summer-heat, thirst and dry throat, rest-lessness, fatigue, anorexia, weakness in the back and knees, hypertension, coughs with profuse phlegm and swelling due to nephritis (kidney disease).

CHINESE DATE (RED DATE)

This is sweet in flavour and warm in nature, acting on the channels of the stomach and spleen. It contains carbohydrate (20–40 per cent in fresh dates and more than 60 per cent in dried dates), protein, fat, a large amount of vitamins B and C, carotene, calcium, phosphorus and iron. Its effects include: strengthening the spleen and stomach, replenishing Qi, promoting the production of body fluid, increasing immunity, promoting the metabolism of white cells in the blood and lowering blood cholesterol. It can be used to treat fatigue due to weakness of the spleen and stomach, diarrhoea, insomnia, thirst, anaemia, leukopenia (decrease of white blood cells) and thrombopenia (decrease in number of blood platelets).

Chinese date is a very popular fruit in China. Long ago, there was a patient who could not eat or drink and had diarrhoea every day. Despite visits to many doctors, he did not improve. A monk at a nearby temple suggested that the patient be fed Chinese date gruel every morning. One month later, the patient was cured.

PERSIMMON

Sweet in flavour and cold and astringent in

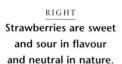

RIGHT
Strawberries are sweet and sour in flavour and neutral in nature.

ABOVE
Pineapple is sweet and sour in flavour and neutral in nature.

nature, persimmon acts upon the channels of the lung and stomach. It contains sugar, protein, fat, high amounts of vitamin C and iron.

The effects of persimmon include nourishing the lungs to arrest coughs, clearing away heat and promoting salivation, resolving phlegm and softening hard masses. It is used to treat coughs due to tuberculosis or any deficiency, as well as diabetes. Because persimmon is cold, those who suffer from spleen Yang deficiency (diarrhoea with undigested food in the stools and cold hands and feet) or phlegm-dampness should avoid eating it.

Persimmon frost is made by first peeling persimmons that are not quite ripe and tying a string around them in order to hang them outside from a tree for one month. After the persimmons have been dried for one month, leave them outside for another month on a plate that is covered in a layer of grass. The white powder that forms on the surface of the persimmon cake is called persimmon frost.

TANGERINE

This is sweet and sour in flavour and neutral in nature and acts on the channels of the lung and stomach. It contains hesperidin, malic acid, citric acid, glucose, fructose, sucrose, vitamins B1 and C, carotene and cryptoxanthin. Its effects include: promoting and regulating the function of the stomach, regulating the flow of Qi, relieving thirst, moisturizing the lungs, eliminating phlegm, inducing diuresis, increasing the level of blood pressure and reducing capillary fragility. It is used to treat the accumulation of Qi in the chest and diaphragm, vomiting and poor appetite, insufficiency of stomach-Yin, dry mouth and thirst, coughs due to retention of pathogenic heat in the lung and dysuria (pain when passing urine).

ORANGE FRUIT (SARCOCARP)

This is sweet in flavour and cool in nature. It contains glucose, fructose, sucrose, very little protein and fat, niacin, carotene, vitamins A, B2, B1 and C, malic acid and citric acid. The effects of the fruit include: clearing away heat and promoting the production of body fluid, the flow of Qi and Blood circulation. The fruit of the orange is used to treat Yin deficiency, fever and sweating, dry mouth, disorders of the Qi of the liver, hypochondriac pain, mental depression and cessation of lactation in women, especially with redness and swelling.

ORANGE PEEL (PERICARP)

This is pungent, bitter in flavour and warm in nature. It contains hesperidin. The effects of the orange peel are to promote

the flow of Qi and eliminate phlegm. The peel is used to treat productive coughs accompanied by chest distress.

DOGWOOD FRUIT (CORNELIAN CHERRY FRUIT)

This is sour in flavour and warm in nature, acting on the channels of the liver and kidney. Its effects include: invigorating the liver and kidney, inducing astringency, and arresting discharge.

LONGAN FRUIT

This is sweet in flavour and warm in nature, acting on the channels of the heart and spleen. It contains glucose, sucrose, vitamins A and B, a little fat, protein and amino acids. Its effects include: invigorating the heart and spleen, promoting body fluid, moistening the five viscera (spleen, lung, kidney, liver and heart), nourishing the blood and Qi and tranquillizing the heart and mind. It is used to treat post-illness weakness, ageing, palpitations, insomnia and amnesia.

HAWTHORN FRUIT

This is sour, sweet in flavour and slightly warm in nature, acting on the channels of the spleen, stomach and liver. It contains sugar, malic acid, citric acid, protein, iron, calcium, carotene, riboflavin, niacin and a large amount of vitamin C. Its effects include: promoting digestion, strengthening the stomach, promoting blood circulation, removing blood cloudiness and destroying parasites. A Chinese experiment showed that hawthorn fruit can dilate the coronary artery and excite the central nervous system, giving it the function of lowering blood-lipids and blood pressure. It is used to treat retention of meat and food in the stomach, mass in the abdomen, phlegm retention, feelings of fullness in the chest and upper abdomen, diarrhoea, dysentery, haemafecia (blood in faeces), lumbago, hernia, post-childbirth abdominal pain, lochi-orrhoea (discharge after childbirth) and infantile dyspepsia (indigestion).

TOMATO

This contains a large amount of vitamins A, B1, B2 and C, carotene, calcium, phosphorus and iron. It is sweet and sour in flavour and slightly cold in nature, acting on the channels of the spleen and stomach. Its effects include clearing away summer-heat, promoting the production of body fluid, arresting thirst, strengthening the stomach, relieving dyspepsia, invigorating the kidney and inducing diuresis. It can be used to treat anorexia, summer-heat and impairment of fluids in the lung and stomach due to high fever.

FISH AND SHELLFISH

BUTTERFISH

This is sweet in flavour and warm in nature. It contains protein, fat, carbohydrate, calcium, magnesium, phosphorus, iron and cholesterol. The sugar content in butterfish is the highest of all fish. Its effects include: invigorating Qi, enriching blood and relieving rigidity in muscles and joints. It is used for treatment of anaemia, indigestion, arthralgia, myalgia (muscle pain), dizziness, palpitations, insomnia, amnesia and numbness of the limbs.

CRAB

Crab is salty in flavour and cold in nature. It contains protein, calcium, fat, cholesterol, phosphorus, iron, vitamins A, B1, B2, and niacin. It acts as an anti-inflammatory and detoxifying agent. It is used to treat the syndrome of damp-heat, dermatitis and puerperal (connected with childbirth) blood-arthralgia.

OYSTER

This is sweet and salty in flavour and neutral in nature. It contains protein, fat, 10 kinds of essential amino acid, vitamins A, B1, B2, D and E, iron, copper, phosphorus, calcium, zinc, magnesium and barium. Most of these components are good for the skin. Its effects include: retaining Yin and suppressing the asthenic Yang, suppressing sweating, arresting seminal emission, resolving phlegm and softening hard mass. It is used to treat fever accompanied by restlessness, insomnia, mental confusion, night-sweating, spontaneous perspiration and seminal emission, as well as slow and painful urination.

ABOVE
Oysters are sweet and salty in flavour and neutral in nature.

SHARK

This is sweet and salty in flavour and neutral in nature. It contains a large amount of protein, unsaturated fatty acids, various inorganic salts and vitamins. The shark's liver contains vitamins A and D; the brain and ovaries contain lipids and cholesterol. Its effects include: enriching Qi and tonifying the five viscera, relieving swelling and dissipating blood cloudiness. It is used to treat weakness of the five viscera (spleen, lung, kidney, liver, heart), consumptive disease and blood stagnation.

LEFT
Crab is salty in flavour and cold in nature.

CLAM

This is salty in flavour and cold in nature. It contains protein, carbohydrate, fat, inorganic salt, vitamins A, B1, B2 and niacin. It invigorates Yin, combats dryness, induces diuresis, relieves swelling and softens hard lumps. It aids diabetes caused by Yin deficiency, dry coughs, insomnia, oedema, hyperthyroidism, soreness of the waist, oliguria (reduced urination), metrorrhagia leukorrhagia (uterine haemorrhaging/discharge), haemorrhoids and lymphadenectasis (dilation of lymphatic vessels).

SHRIMP (PRAWN)

RIGHT
Shrimp is sweet in flavour and warm in nature.

This is sweet in flavour and warm in nature, acting on the kidney channel. It contains protein, fat, carbohydrate, calcium, phosphorus, iron, iodine, vitamins A, B1, B2 and niacin. It invigorates the kidneys, strengthens Yang and promotes lactation and pus discharge. It also aids impotence due to kidney Yang deficiency, weakness in the back and knees, fatigue, hypogalactia (deficiency of milk secretion), measles, chicken-pox and skin problems. People with allergy problems should avoid shrimp.

MEAT AND POULTRY

RABBIT

This is sweet in flavour and cool in nature, acting on the channels of the stomach and spleen. It is rich in protein and carbohydrate, potassium, sulphur, calcium, phosphorus, iron, sodium, vitamins and fine fibre that is easily digested and absorbed. It contains less fat than beef, chicken or pork. Its effects include: invigorating the spleen and stomach, cooling blood and detoxifying the body, clearing away heat in the stomach and intestines, increasing the phospholipids in the blood, inhibiting the adverse effects of LDL and preventing hypertension and arteriosclerosis. Rabbit meat treats deficiency of the spleen, malnutrition, fatigue and diabetes, and can help soften the skin.

MUTTON

This is sweet in flavour and warm in nature, acting on the channels of the spleen and kidney. It contains protein, carbohydrate, fat, calcium, phosphorus, iron, vitamins B1 and B2, nicotinic acid and cholesterol. Mutton invigorates Qi, warms the spleen, kidney and stomach, and relaxes the bowels. It is used to treat:

consumptive disease, weakness in the back and knees, child-birth, periumbilical colic (acute stomach pain around the navel) due to invasion of cold, and regurgitation due to a deficiency of the spleen and stomach. Because of its warm nature, mutton is a good winter food.

BLACK-BONE CHICKEN

This is a kind of chicken whose bones and skin are black. Sweet in flavour and neutral in nature, it acts on the liver and kidney channels. It contains protein, fat, calcium, phosphorus, iron, nicotinic acid and vitamins B1 and B2. It tonifies the liver and kidney, nourishes Yin and reduces fever. It is used to treat hectic fever (usually accompanied by night sweating, as seen in pulmonary tuberculosis due to Yin deficiency), diabetes, lingering diarrhoea due to hypofunction of the spleen, dysentery, metrorrhagia and leukorrhagia (profuse whitish discharge from the vagina and uterus).

DAIRY PRODUCTS

MILK

This is sweet in flavour and neutral in nature, acting on the channels of the heart, lung and stomach. It contains protein, fat, carbohydrate, calcium, phosphorus, iron, magnesium, sodium, potassium, and vitamins A, B1, B2, B6 and C. It treats consumptive disease, reinforcing the lung and stomach, promoting the production of body fluid and moistening the intestinal tract. It is used to treat debility and internal injury caused by overstrain, regurgitation, dysphagia, diabetes and constipation. Milk can combat the dryness that is associated with autumn.

EGG

This is sweet in flavour and neutral in nature, acting on the channel of the spleen. It contains protein and eight essential amino acids. It also contains fat, carbohydrate, vitamins and minerals. Its effects include: nourishing Yin, moistening dryness, enriching the blood, invigorating the spleen and regulating the stomach. It is used to treat hypogalactia due to blood deficiency, dizziness, night blindness, weakness after illness, insomnia, palpitations, sore throat, aphonia (loss of voice), malnutrition and vomiting.

CHAPTER FOUR

OTHER FOODS

PEPPERTREE SEED

This is pungent in flavour and warm in nature, acting on the channels of the stomach and spleen. It contains various kinds of volatile oil. The effects include: dispelling cold and removing dampness, strengthening the stomach to promote digestion, detoxifying, destroying parasites and promoting the circulation of Qi. It is used to treat myalgia, arthralgia, vomiting, indigestion, toothaches, diarrhoea and dysentery, to induce diuresis and relieve asthma and the toxicity of fish. A person with Yin deficiency should avoid peppertree seeds, since they can produce heat.

COIX SEED

This is sweet in flavour and slightly cold in nature, acting on the channels of the spleen, stomach and lung. Its effects include: promoting diuresis to eliminate dampness, strengthening the spleen and clearing away heat. It is used to treat oedema, diarrhoea due to deficiency of the spleen, arthritis, myalgia and appendicitis.

GINKGO (GINKGO SEED)

This is bitter in flavour and neutral in nature, acting on the channel of the lung. It contains carbohydrate, protein, fat, calcium, phosphorus, iron, carotene, various kinds of amino acid and riboflavin. Its effects include: inducing astringency and arresting discharge, spontaneous emission and leukorrhagia. An experiment done by Chinese scientists showed that, to a certain degree, ginkgo could inhibit staphylococcus, streptococcus, bacillus diphtheria, bacillus anthraces, bacillus subtilis, colibacillus, typhoid bacillus and fungus. It is used to treat asthma attacks, spontaneous emission, enuresis (involuntary urination), frequency of urination and gynaecological disease.

CAUTION

Fresh ginkgo seeds have shoots or sprouts that can be toxic and must be removed. Ginkgo must be cooked to avoid toxicity. Poisoning symptoms are vomiting, abdominal pain, diarrhoea, fever and cyanosis (bluish skin due to oxygen-deficient blood). Severe poisoning affects the nervous system and can result in mental trauma, coma and convulsion.

SESAME

This is sweet in flavour and neutral in nature, acting on the channels of the liver and kidney. It contains 60 per cent fatty acids, most of which are unsaturated (oleic acid, linoleic acid and arachidic acid). Sesame invigorates the liver and kidney. Because of its moisturising properties on the five viscera, it is a good food for combating dryness in the autumn. We use sesame to treat deficiencies of both the liver and the kidney, dizziness due to internal wind of a deficiency type, migratory arthralgia, paralysis, dry stools and difficult defecation, weakness during convalescence, early greying of hair and lack of lactation in women.

HONEY

This is sweet in flavour and neutral in nature, acting on the channels of the lung, spleen and large intestine. It contains fructose, glucose, a little sucrose and maltose. Its effects include strengthening the spleen and stomach, moistening dryness, relieving spasm and clearing away toxic materials. It is used to treat cough due to lung dryness, constipation due to intestine dryness, epigastralgia (pain in the middle abdomen), turbid discharge from the nose, aphtha (ulceration), scalds and burns.

Honey is especially good during the dry autumn months because it helps to moisten the five viscera (spleen, lungs, kidneys, liver and heart).

GINGER

This is used in both its fresh and dried forms. Although they both act upon the channels of the spleen, stomach and lung, their temperature and functions are somewhat different.

◆ FRESH GINGER is pungent in flavour and slightly warm in nature. The effects of fresh ginger are: dispersing cold, arresting vomiting and reducing sputum. It is used for treating the wind-cold type of common cold, in which there is no sore throat or thirst.

◆ DRIED GINGER is pungent in flavour and hot in nature. It contains volatile oils. The effects of dried ginger are: warming the spleen and stomach, eliminating cold, recuperating depleted Yang and promoting blood circulation. It is used to treat cold-pain in the chest and stomach, vomiting and diarrhoea, cold extremities and a faint pulse, asthma and coughs due to fluid retention of a cold type, arthralgia due to wind-cold-dampness, haemoptysis (spitting blood), nose-bleeds and haemafecia due to Yang deficiency. The warming nature of both fresh and dried ginger makes this an ideal food in winter.

ABOVE
Ginger, fresh and dried, is pungent in flavour.

LEFT
Honey is sweet in flavour and neutral in nature.

MALTOSE

This is sweet in flavour and warm in nature, acting on the channels of the spleen, stomach and lung. Its effects include strengthening the spleen and stomach, promoting the production of body fluid, moistening dryness, clearing away heat and tonifying the lungs to stop coughing. It is used to warm the spleen Yang, treat abdominal pain due to contraction of the genital organs and nourish deficiency of the lung Yin. Maltose is also good for certain types of thirst, haematemesis, sore throat, constipation, asthma and folliculitis (inflamed follicles).

DARK BROWN SUGAR

This is sweet in flavour and warm in nature, acting on the channels of the spleen and stomach. It contains a large amount of glucose, sucrose, a little protein, various kinds of amino acid, fat, riboflavin, carotene, niacin, iron, phosphorus and calcium. Its effects include: strengthening and regulating the spleen and stomach, dispelling cold and promoting blood circulation to remove blood cloudiness. It is used to treat cold pain in the abdomen, dysmenorrhoea (difficult or painful menstruation), lochiorrhea, and also the wind-cold type of the common cold.

GINSENG

This is a sweet and slightly bitter root that is well known for its ability to tonify the body. Chinese, Korean and American ginseng all have different natures, based on where they grow and are prepared. Wild ginseng, collected from the forests and mountains, is the most expensive and is the most esteemed commercial variety. The individual functions of each are described below. For the cooking of ginseng, it is important to use only glass, ceramic or porcelain cookware, rather than metal. One should avoid taking coffee, tea, radishes and turnips immediately before or after drinking ginseng tea, as these could decrease the tea's effectiveness.

◆ CHINESE GINSENG is slightly warm and acts upon the channels of the lung and spleen. Its warm nature makes it appropriate for cold and deficient syndromes. Chinese ginseng strongly tonifies the lungs and is used for shallow or short respiration, cold extremities, profuse sweating and a minute or weak pulse. It also tonifies the spleen, and is used for fatigue, lack of appetite and chest and abdominal distension. It is able to promote secretion of

RIGHT
Ginseng tonifies the body.

the body fluids and relieve mental stress. It also benefits the heart, and is useful for palpitations due to fright, insomnia, amnesia and irritability – all due to deficiency of the body's Qi and Blood. The best-quality Chinese ginseng comes from Jilin province in China and is very large in size.

CONTRA-INDICATIONS: only use if there are signs of fatigue and Qi deficiency, otherwise this herb may generate heat in the body. Chinese ginseng is not to be used with any signs of heat (excess or deficient) or with Yin deficiency.

◆ KOREAN GINSENG is produced in Korea and has the same properties and functions as Chinese ginseng, although it is considered hot and should be used very cautiously. It has the same contra-indications as Chinese ginseng.

◆ AMERICAN GINSENG is produced in the United States, Canada and France, with the best quality coming from Wisconsin in the US. It is cool in nature, sweet and slightly bitter in flavour. It acts on the channels of the lung, heart and kidney. American ginseng tonifies the spleen, benefits the lungs and promotes the produc-

tion of fluids in the body, useful for Yin deficiency with heat signs and great weakness of the body.

PEPPERMINT

This is pungent in flavour and cool in nature. It contains aromatic oils. Peppermint oil is mostly menthol. The effects of peppermint include dispelling wind and removing heat, eliminating dampness and heat, relieving sore throat and promoting the eruption of measles to help bring the virus out of the body more quickly.

LEFT
Peppermint is pungent in flavour and cool in nature.

PEPPER

This is pungent in flavour and hot in nature, acting on the channels of the stomach and large intestine. It contains vitamins B and C, carotene and carbohydrates. Its functions are: warming the stomach and spleen, controlling nausea and vomiting and clearing away phlegm and toxic materials. It is used to treat cold-pain in the abdomen, cold phlegm and food stagnation, regurgitation, watery vomit, diarrhoea and dysentery of cold type.

TOFU (BEAN CURD)

This is made from soybean seeds. It contains protein (four times more than milk), fat, carbohydrates, calcium (twice that of milk), phosphorus and iron. It is sweet in flavour and cool in nature, acting on the channels of the spleen, stomach and large intestine. Its effects include: invigorating Qi, replenishing the blood and strengthening muscles and bones. Tofu is used to treat acute conjunctivitis and diabetes. It also cools the effects of sulphur and alcohol, by removing their toxic and hot properties through the urine.

BELOW
Tofu is sweet in flavour and cool in nature.

WALNUT KERNEL

This is sweet in flavour and warm in nature, acting on the channels of the kidney and lung. It contains 40–50 per cent fatty acids (mainly trilinolein), protein,

ABOVE
Walnuts.

carbohydrate, calcium, phosphorus, iron, carotene, vitamins B1 and B2 and nicotinic acid. Its effects include: warming the lungs to relieve asthma and moisturizing the intestines to relax the bowels. It is used to treat symptoms due to deficiency of kidney Yang, asthma, coughs, lumbago and beriberi, impotence, frequent urination, slow and painful urination due to the passage of urinary stones, constipation and dry stools.

VINEGAR

This is sour and bitter in flavour and warm in nature, acting on the channels of the liver and stomach. It contains higher alcohol levels (3–5 per cent acetic acid, formaldehyde, acetal, succinic acid, oxalic acid and sorbose), a little amount of calcium, phosphorus, iron and vitamins B and C. Its effects include: dissipating blood cloudiness, arresting bleeding, clearing away toxic materials, destroying intestinal parasites and promoting the digestion and absorption of food. It is used for treating postnatal bleeding, blockage in the abdomen, jaundice, tawny sweat, haematemesis, nose-bleeds, haemafecia, pruritus genitalium (gential itching) and skin and external diseases. It can remove the poisonous quality of fish, meat and vegetables.

KELP

This is salty in flavour and cold in nature. It contains protein, fat, nitrogen, zosterin, pentosan and vitamin B2. It is often called the "vegetable in the sea" or the "vegetable for long life". Its effects include: softening hard masses and removing phlegm, inducing diuresis, expelling pathogenic heat, preventing hyperthyroidism (over-active thyroid gland) and preventing cancer. Because it helps to moisten the body, it is a good autumn food. In Japan, where kelp is a mainstay of the diet, the incident of breast cancer in women is lower than anywhere else in the world.

ROUND-GRAIN RICE

This is sweet in flavour and warm in nature, acting on the channels of the spleen and stomach. It is made up of 75 per cent starch, 8 per cent protein, a little fat and vitamin B. Its effects include: invigorating and regulating the spleen and stomach, nourishing Yin and promoting the production of body fluids. It is used to arrest dysentery and diarrhoea.

HYACINTH BEAN

Sweet in flavour and warm in nature, hyacinth bean contains large amounts of protein, fat, carbohydrates and minerals. It acts upon the channels of the spleen and stomach. The effects of hyacinth bean include invigorating the spleen to eliminate dampness. It is used to treat spleen deficiency with dampness, fatigue, anorexia, diarrhoea, leukorrhagia due to hypofunction of the spleen and diseases caused by summer-heat and dampness.

CHRYSANTHEMUM FLOWER

This is pungent, sweet and bitter in flavour and slightly cold in nature, acting on the channels of the liver and lung. Its effects include: dispelling wind, clearing away the heat, detoxifying and improving eyesight. It is used, along with other herbs, to treat wind-heat types of common cold , conjunctival congestion due to wind-heat in the liver or flaming up of liver-fire and headaches and dizziness due to hyperactivity of the liver Yang.

LEFT
Chrysanthemum flower is pungent, sweet and bitter in flavour and cold in nature.

RECIPES FOR COMMON DISEASES AND SYNDROMES

THE COMMON COLD

Chinese traditional medicine holds that the common cold is caused by external pathogens attacking the body. When your immune system is low or under stress you are more apt to catch colds. A cold can be treated with food therapy, to shorten the course of the disease and relieve its symptoms.

THE THREE TYPES OF COMMON COLD

1 WIND-COLD COMMON COLD
Wind-cold is marked by a strong aversion to cold, slight fever without sweating, headache, stuffy nose, watery nasal discharge, coughs, expectoration of thin and white sputum, thirst and a desire for hot drinks, pain in the limbs, thin and white fur on the tongue and a floating or floating and tense pulse.

2 WIND-HEAT COMMON COLD
Wind-heat is marked by a high fever, slight aversion to wind, distending pain in the head, light sweating, a sore throat, stuffy nose, yellow and thick nasal discharge, a cough with yellow and sticky phlegm, thirst and a strong desire for drinks. There may also be thin and white fur or light yellowish fur on the tongue and a floating and rapid pulse.

3 SUMMER-HEAT AND DAMPNESS COMMON COLD
Summer-heat and dampness is marked by fever, a light aversion to wind, heaviness and distending pain in the head, aching pain in the limbs, thirst but little or no desire to drink, chest distress, loss of appetite, nausea, yellow urine, thin, yellow fur or yellow, greasy fur on the tongue and a soft, floating and rapid pulse.

TYPES OF SYNDROME

The common cold occurs in any season of the year, but most often in winter and spring. The incubation period is about one day. The symptoms begin around the nose and throat areas, with a stuffy or running nose, sneezing, sore throat or tingling in the throat. Sometimes there may be a slight fever.

FOOD THERAPY FOR THE COMMON COLD

RECIPES FOR WIND-COLD COMMON COLDS

Fresh ginger and sugar tea

1 Take 5 pieces of fresh ginger and 2 tablespoons dark brown sugar.
2 Infuse the above ingredients in 2 cups of boiling water.
3 Strain and drink the remaining tea, while it is still warm or hot.

Ginger rice soup

1 Take 10 g (5 slices) fresh ginger, 100 g (3^1/$_2$ oz) polished round-grain rice or glutinous rice and 30 g (2 pieces) green onion.
2 Cook the fresh ginger and rice in 4 cups of water for 30 minutes.
3 Then add the green onion and simmer for 30 minutes.
4 Drink the entire amount while it is still hot.
5 After drinking, lie in bed and under a thick blanket to sweat out the cold that has entered the body.

Chinese green onion

For plugged ears or a stuffy nose, wrap a piece of green onion in a thin tissue and insert it gently into the ear or nose.

Green onion rice soup

1 Take 50 g (1^3/$_4$ oz) fresh green onion and 75 g (3 oz) polished, round-grain rice.
2 Cut the green onion into 2.5-cm (1-in) long pieces.
3 Cook the rice with 3 cups of water for 40 minutes.
4 Add the green onion and simmer for another 10 minutes.
5 Drink the entire amount, while it is still hot.
CONTRA-INDICATIONS: do not take if you are already perspiring. Also avoid if you are allergic to green onion or in the case of severe skin disease.

BELOW
Fresh ginger and polished round-grain rice are used in ginger rice soup.

RECIPES FOR WIND-HEAT COMMON COLDS

Peppermint gruel

STEP 1

1 Take 30 g (1 oz) fresh peppermint or 15 g (¹/₂ oz) dried peppermint.
2 Add 2 cups of boiling water to the fresh or dried peppermint.
3 Cover and allow to steep for 5 minutes.
4 Strain and then save the liquid to add to step 2.

STEP 2

1 Take 90 g (3 oz) round-grain rice, 3 cups of water, and 1 teaspoon honey.
2 Bring the rice and water to the boil, then allow to simmer for 30 minutes.
3 When the rice is cooked, add the peppermint tea and 1 teaspoon of honey.
4 Stir and allow to boil for 5 minutes.
5 Divide the gruel into 2 servings, and take one in the morning and one in the evening.

Chrysanthemum flower tea

1 Take 8 g (¹/₃ oz) chrysanthemum flowers.
2 Add 2 cups of boiling water to the chrysanthemum flowers.
3 Cover and allow to steep for 10 minutes.
4 Strain and drink the remaining liquid once or twice a day until the symptoms of wind-heat common cold subside.

RECIPES FOR SUMMER-HEAT AND DAMPNESS COMMON COLDS

Gruel of Job's-tears seed and hyacinth bean

1 Take 30 g (1 oz) Job's-tears seed, 30 g (1 oz) white hyacinth bean, 100 g (3¹/₂ oz) round-grain rice.
2 Bring the above ingredients to the boil in 4 cups of water.
3 After bringing to the boil, reduce to a simmer and allow to cook for 40 minutes.
4 Separate the gruel into 2 servings, and take one in the morning and one in the evening.

ASTHMA

According to Western medicine, asthma results from bronchospasm, mucous oedema and increased secretion due to an allergic reaction. It is characterized clinically by breathlessness, wheezing, coughing and expectoration.

In Chinese medicine, the causes of asthma are differentiated according to the specific symptoms of the individual. The first distinction made is whether or not the asthma is due to excess or deficiency of the body. Excess cases of asthma are usually less severe and are short-term reactions. There are three common types of excess asthma syndrome: cold-type asthma, hot-type asthma and phlegm-type asthma. It is also possible to have a mixture of symptoms, in which the individual has symptoms from two categories, such as cold-phlegm or hot-phlegm asthma. An attack can last a few minutes or a few hours and produce much phlegm.

Asthma that is due to deficiency of the body is chronic in nature and takes longer to treat. Common types of deficiency asthma syndromes include deficiency of the lung Qi, spleen or kidney. Mixed symptoms are not uncommon, such as asthma due to spleen and kidney deficiency. A therapeutic diet that is tonifying and nourishing to the organs will certainly help these conditions. However, acupuncture and herbal teas are recommended for complete treatment of these chronic syndromes.

ASTHMA DUE TO EXCESS

1 COLD-TYPE ASTHMA

Cold-type asthma often occurs in cold weather. The symptoms may include any of the following: rapid breathing, headache, stuffy nose, wheezing sound in the throat, chest distress, difficulty in breathing, cold extremities, thirst and desire for hot drinks, a cough with clear and thin phlegm, white thin fur on the tongue and a tense pulse.

2 HOT-TYPE ASTHMA

Manifested as breathlessness, hot-type asthma may cause any of the following symptoms: an aversion to heat, thirst and desire for cold drinks, wheezing sounds in the throat, a cough with yellow, ropy and thick phlegm, difficult expectoration, a flushed face, restlessness, sweating, dry and red mouth, thin and yellowish fur on the tongue and a rapid, slippery pulse.

3 PHLEGM-TYPE ASTHMA

This type of asthma occurs mostly in old people and children. Its common symptoms include: white, sticky and frothy sputum, a poor appetite, nausea, white greasy fur on the tongue and a taut and slippery pulse.

FOOD TREATMENTS

◆ Asthma of the cold-type demands taking food that is warm or hot in nature, such as ginger and green onion.

◆ For hot-type asthma, a person should take food that is cool or cold in nature, such as watermelon.

◆ A person with phlegm-type asthma should adhere to a diet that can eliminate dampness.

FOOD THERAPY FOR ASTHMA

RECIPES FOR COLD-TYPE ASTHMA

Peppertree powder

1 Grind peppertree seeds into powder and use to fill capsules. Three grams of powder can be used to fill 7 to 8 capsules.
2 Take 8 capsules 3 times a day for 3–7 days.
CONTRA-INDICATION: this is not for the patient with Yin deficiency or with hot-type asthma, since peppertree seeds can produce heat.

Walnut kernel with ginger

1 Take 10 g (1/3 oz) walnut kernel and one slice of fresh ginger (skin removed).
2 Chew and swallow both before sleeping.
CONTRA-INDICATION: hot-type asthma.

Vinegar soup

1 Take 7 tablespoons vinegar, and 30 g (1 oz) dark brown sugar.
2 Boil the vinegar and dark brown sugar with 150 ml water for a few minutes.
3 Take 4 teaspoons of the soup 3–4 times a day.

Chinese chive and egg

1 Take 100 g (3 1/2 oz) Chinese chives, 2 eggs and 2 tablespoons peanut oil.
2 Cut the chives into 2.5-cm (1-in) long pieces; beat the eggs for 30 seconds.

3 Heat the peanut oil in a pan. Add the chives and eggs and stir-fry for 2 minutes.
4 Eat at meal-time.
CONTRA-INDICATION: hot-type asthma.

RECIPES FOR ACUTE ATTACK OF HOT-TYPE ASTHMA

Sweet tofu with radish

1 Take 200 g (7 oz) tofu, 60 g (2 oz) malt extract and 30 g (1 oz) raw radish.
2 Make some radish juice with a juicer.
3 Add the tofu and malt extract, and boil the mixture for 15 minutes.
4 Take the entire amount warm at meal-times.
CONTRA-INDICATION: cold-type asthma.

RECIPES FOR PHLEGM-TYPE ASTHMA

Ginkgo nut

1 Take 3-9 g (5-10 pieces) ginkgo nuts (shelled).
2 Cook the shelled ginkgo nuts with 1 cup of water for 15 minutes.
3 Add 1 tablespoon of honey.
4 Drink the soup and eat the ginkgo nuts.

CAUTION: ginkgo nut is slightly toxic. Pay attention to the dosage, and do not use raw. It should be cooked or stir-fried.

ASTHMA DUE TO DEFICIENCY

1 **DEFICIENCY OF THE LUNG** This is marked by catching common colds easily, a low voice, shortness of breath, an aversion to wind, spontaneous perspiration, a pale tongue and a weak and erratic pulse. A change of weather can easily induce asthma due to lung deficiency.

2 **DEFICIENCY OF THE SPLEEN** This is marked by fatigue, fullness in the stomach, poor appetite, loose stools or diarrhoea, a pale tongue and a weak pulse that is moderate in rate. Asthma due to spleen deficiency is aggravated by improper diet.

3 **DEFICIENCY OF THE KIDNEY** This is marked by shortness of breath, especially with difficulty inhaling, dizziness, weakness in the loins and legs and tinnitus. This type of asthma is aggravated by exertion or overwork.
◆ When the kidney is deficient in Yang energy, the symptoms include aversion to cold, cold limbs and a thick and tender tongue.
◆ In Yin deficiency of the kidney, the symptoms include feverish sensation in the palms of the hands and soles of the feet, flushing of the cheeks, a red tongue with little or no fur and a rapid and erratic pulse.

FOOD TREATMENTS

RECIPES FOR ASTHMA DUE TO SPLEEN AND KIDNEY YANG DEFICIENCY

Chinese date and pumpkin gruel

1 Take 500 g (1 lb) fresh pumpkin, 15 pieces Chinese dates and 1 tablespoon dark brown sugar.
2 Cook the pumpkin and Chinese dates with 600 ml/1 pint water for 50 minutes.
3 Add the brown sugar to this mixture.
4 Divide into 2 portions and take one portion in the morning and the other in the evening.
CONTRA-INDICATION: constipation, abdominal distension and interior heat.

RECIPES FOR ASTHMA DUE TO DEFICIENCY OF KIDNEY YIN

Sweet nuts

1 Take 15 g (1/2 oz) sweet apricot kernel, 6 g (1/5 oz) walnut kernels and 5 g (1/6 oz) spinach seeds.
2 Boil these three ingredients with 500 ml (18 fl oz) water; simmer for 50 minutes.
3 Take the mixture once a day for 15–20 days.
CAUTION: do not use more than 15 g, as an overdose can cause dizziness, nausea, vomiting and headaches.

Radish and honey soup

1 Take 100 g (3¹/2 oz) radish, and 1 table-spoon honey.
2 Boil the radish with 2 cups of water for 30 minutes.
3 Add the honey to this mixture.
4 Take the whole amount once a day, then repeat every day for 15–20 days.

Walnut kernel gruel

1 Take 30 g (1 oz) walnut kernel, and 100 grams (3¹/2 oz) round-grain rice.
2 Cook the above ingredients with 600 ml (1 pint) water for 50 minutes.
3 Take it at breakfast and dinner time, and repeat the same procedure every day until the symptoms subside.

Sweet sesame syrup

1 Take 250 g (8³/4 oz) sesame, 200 g (7 oz) fresh ginger and 200 g (7 oz) honey or 200 g (7 oz) crystal sugar.
2 Stir-fry the sesame in a heated pan until it crackles.
3 Make some ginger juice in a blender or by smashing the fresh ginger.
4 Melt the crystal sugar in a little water, then stir-fry the sesame in ginger juice until the juice dries up.
5 After cooling, mix with honey and crystal sugar syrup.
6 Stir and store in a bottle.
7 Take one tablespoon every morning and evening with water.

RIGHT
Radish and honey soup.

ESSENTIAL HYPERTENSION

Therapeutic diets can be used not only as a supplementary treatment for essential hypertension but also to prevent it in the first place.

TYPES OF SYNDROME

Chinese medicine divides hypertension into three types, according to its various symptoms: flaming-up of the liver-fire, deficiency of both the liver Yin and kidney Yin and hyperactivity of Yang due to Yin deficiency.

1 FLARING-UP OF THE LIVER-FIRE
The main symptoms of this type include distending pain in the head, dizziness, flushed face, conjunctival congestion, irritability, bitter taste in the mouth, dry throat accompanied by tinnitus, deafness, vexation, insomnia, red tongue with yellow fur and taut and rapid pulse.

2 HYPERACTIVITY OF YANG DUE TO YIN DEFICIENCY
This is marked by more serious distending pain in the head, an occasionally flushed face, irritability, vexation, red tongue with thin and yellow fur and a taut, erratic and rapid pulse.

3 DEFICIENCY OF BOTH LIVER YIN AND KIDNEY YIN
This type mainly manifests as dizziness, headache, dim eyesight, dry mouth, tinnitus, a dryness and uncomfortable feeling in the eyes, insomnia, dreaminess, feverish sensation in the palms of the hands and soles of the feet, lassitude in the waist and knees, fatigue, amnesia, red tongue with little fur and a erratic and taut, or erratic, taut and rapid, pulse.

FOOD TREATMENT

CELERY TREATMENTS

Celery soup

1 Take 30–60 g (1-2 oz) fresh celery and 2 cups of water.

2 Cut the fresh celery into small pieces.

3 Boil the celery in the water for 10 minutes.

4 Drink the soup and eat the celery.

5 Make this celery soup each day, and take until the blood pressure returns to normal.

Celery juice

1 Take 250 g (¹/₂ lb) celery.
2 Cut up the fresh celery and make celery juice.
3 Separate into 2 equal quantities and drink one in the morning and one in the evening.

Celery gruel

1 Take 120 g (4 oz) fresh celery and 120 g (4 oz) round-grain rice.
2 Cut the fresh celery into small pieces.
3 Cook the rice with 1.2 litres (2 pints) water for 30 minutes to make a gruel.
4 Add the celery to the gruel and boil for another 10 minutes.
5 Separate into 2 equal quantities and eat one in the morning and one in the evening.
6 Continue this treatment for 7 to 10 days.

RECIPES FOR HYPERTENSION DUE TO FLARING UP OF LIVER-FIRE OR LIVER YIN DEFICIENCY

Chrysanthemum flower

1 Add 200 ml (7 fl oz) boiling water to 9 g (¹/₃ oz) chrysanthemum flowers.
2 Cover and allow to steep for about 10 minutes.
3 Drink one cup every day until the symptoms subside.

PREVENTION AND TREATMENT OF HYPERTENSION

HAWTHORN FRUIT

Take 9–15 g (¹/₃–¹/₅ oz) hawthorn fruit every day.

ONION – RED, GREEN, YELLOW OR WHITE

1 Make onion juice from one medium-sized onion.
2 Drink every day, or stir-fry with any vegetables.

GARLIC AND VINEGAR

1 In a bottle, cover 10 cloves of garlic with 2 cups of vinegar. The vinegar should cover the garlic by about 2.5 cm (1 in).
2 Add 100 g (3¹/₂ oz) of sugar to the vinegar and garlic mixture.
3 Cover and seal the bottle for one week.
4 Take 1–2 pieces of garlic in the morning on an empty stomach, and 2 tablespoons of the vinegar for 15 days.

GARLIC

The Alliin in garlic can lower blood pressure. Eat garlic raw, stewed or cooked in gruel.

CARROT

1 Carrot can be taken raw, cooked or stir-fried.
2 Take 100 ml fresh carrot juice each day.

ABOVE
Garlic and vinegar can be used to prevent and treat hypertension.

RECIPES FOR NOURISHMENT AND LONGEVITY

*Recipes for nourishment and longevity are mainly used to treat various syndromes
of debility as well as building up health for a prolonged life. Throughout the history of
traditional Chinese medicine, doctors have accumulated thousands of prescriptions
for diet tonics to strengthen the body. The prescriptions most often apply to people
with deficiency syndromes.*

*For people who show Qi deficiency, the upper part of the body should be reinvigorated,
and for this purpose, ginseng and astragalus root can be used. For those who show deficiency of essence, the lower part of the body should be reinvigorated, and for this purpose
rehmannia root (shudihuang) and wolfberry fruit (gaoqi) can be used. Those who show
Yang deficiency should take foods that are replenishing and warming, and for this purpose, cinnamon bark and dried ginger can be used. For those who show Yin deficiency,
the vital essence should be replenished, and for this purpose, dried rehmannia root and
peony can be used.*

1 INVIGORATING QI RECIPE

The following recipe has the
functions of invigorating Qi, enhancing
the function of the immune system,
building up health, increasing the
adaptability to the environment and
strengthening the function of the
tissues and organs in the body. Please
refer to the main index for information
on the type of ginseng that should be
used in the following recipes.

Ginseng gruel

Indications: dyspepsia due to dysfunction
of the stomach and spleen, marked by
poor appetite, distention in the stomach,
loose or soft stools or diarrhoea.
1 Take 100 g (3¹/₂ oz) polished round-
grain rice, and 10 g (¹/₃ oz) ginseng.
2 Cut the ginseng into small pieces, or
buy ginseng that has been pre-cut.
3 Soak the ginseng along with 3 cups of
water for 60 minutes, in a Chinese ceramic pot (or glass pot).
4 Bring to the boil, then reduce the flame
and simmer for about 1 hour.
5 Add the rice to the ginseng soup.
6 Boil and simmer again for 40 minutes.
7 Separate into 2 servings and take one in
the morning and one in the evening.

2 NOURISHING THE BLOOD RECIPE

The following foods have the functions
of nourishing both the blood and liver
and also replenishing the heart and
spleen.

Candied ginger, Chinese dates and longan fruit

INDICATIONS: anorexia, pale complexion and palpitations due to deficiency of the spleen and blood.

1 Take 250 g (1/2 lb) longan fruit, 250 g (1/2 lb) Chinese dates, 250 g (1/2 lb) honey and 1/2 cup ginger juice.

2 Boil the longan fruit and Chinese dates in a clay pot with 3 cups of water or enough water to cover these foods by about 1 cm (1/2 in).

3 After boiling, keep simmering for about 40–50 minutes.

4 Add ginger juice and honey to the mixture.

5 Mix and cook for another 20 minutes.

6 Let it cool, seal and store in a bottle in the refrigerator.

7 Take 6–8 pieces each of the longan fruit and Chinese dates, 3 times a day.

3 NOURISHING YIN RECIPE

The food chosen has the functions of nourishing Yin and tonifying the kidney, replenishing the vital essence to promote the generation of bone marrow.

Gruel with dogwood fruit (cornelian cherry fruit)

INDICATIONS: soreness in the lower back, tinnitus, dizziness, seminal emission, enuresis, sweating due to debility, frequent urination and leukorrhagia due to deficiency of the kidney Yin.

1 Take 15–20 g (1/2–2/3 oz) dogwood fruit, 60 g (2 oz) round-grain rice, 2 tablespoons white sugar and 600 ml (1 pint) water.

2 Cook the dogwood fruit and rice with the water in a clay pot for 40 minutes to make a gruel.

3 Add the white sugar when the gruel is done, stir, and simmer for 5 minutes.

4 Divide into 2 equal portions and take one in the morning and one in the evening.

4 RESTORING YANG RECIPE

Choose foods that have the effect of warming the kidney, invigorating Yang, strengthening the constitution, exciting sexuality and enhancing sexual function. These foods apply to a deficiency of Yang, mainly that of the spleen and the kidney.

Gruel with Chinese chives

INDICATIONS: cold pain in the abdomen, loose stools or constipation, dysentery of a deficiency-cold type, dysphagia and regurgitation, impotence, premature ejaculation, frequent urination, leukorrhagia in women, weakness in the back and the knees, dysmenorrhea, metrorrhagia, metrostaxis (slight but persistent escape of blood from the uterus) and other symptoms due to Yang deficiency of the spleen and kidney.

1 Take 30–60 g (1–2 oz) fresh Chinese chives, 60 g (2 oz) round-grain rice and 0.5 g (1/10 teaspoon) refined salt.

2 Cut the Chinese chives into small pieces.

3 Cook the rice with 600 ml (1 pint) water for 40 minutes to make a gruel.

4 Add the Chinese chives to the gruel and cook for another 10 minutes.

5 Add salt and stir.

6 Divide the gruel into 2 equal portions and take one in the morning and one in the evening.

CONTRA-INDICATIONS: those who have a fever due to deficiency of Yin or any kind of sores and eye and skin diseases are prohibited from taking this gruel. It is also not advisable to take it in the summer, as it is warming to the body.

5 REPLENISHING THE QI, BLOOD, YIN AND YANG RECIPE

The foods chosen have the effects of recuperating both Qi and Blood, replenishing essence and nourishing marrow, tonifying Yin, warming Yang and treating deficiency of Qi, blood, Yin and Yang.

Gruel of "pearl and jade"

INDICATIONS: anorexia, low fever in the afternoon, night sweating, night cough and a hollow, rapid and taut pulse caused by deficiency of Qi and Yin of the spleen and lungs.

1 Take 60 g (2 oz) Chinese yam, 60 g (2 oz) coix seed and 24 g ($^5/_6$ oz) dried persimmon with persimmon frost.

2 Break up the Chinese yam and pound into coarse pieces along with the coix seeds.

3 Cook the above ingredients with 4 cups of water for 40 minutes.

4 Cut the dried persimmon into small pieces.

5 Mix them into the gruel and cook for another 10–15 minutes.

6 Divide the amount made into 2 equal portions and take one in the morning and one in the evening.

BELOW
Fresh Chinese chives can be used in a gruel to restore Yang.

QI GONG

Today people all over the world *are searching for a way to keep fit and healthy and to prolong life. Throughout the ages, people have tried to find ways to reach this goal. "Deep Breath" or "Qi Gong" (pronounced Chi Kung) is among the most popular methods used to promote fitness.*

In this chapter we explain the theory and practice of Qi Gong, especially the style developed by Master Professor Peng-si Yu, who began his martial arts training in Shanghai, became a master of the Shaolin martial art and later studied another form Xingyi, under the Xingyi master Xiang-Zhai Wong. In the Xingyi school records one quickly finds Professor Yu, Master Wong's favourite student. Peng-si Yu also earned an M.D. in Western medicine in China and a Ph.D in Germany prior to the Second World War, thus giving him the ability to combine Buddhist Qi Gong, martial arts and medical treatment to develop his own system, known as Yu's Xingyi Qi Gong. Professor Peng-si Yu and his wife, Simu Min Ouyang, were brought to the San Francisco Bay area in 1980 by a Stanford professor who had been studying Qi Gong with them in Shanghai each summer. From that point on, Professor Yu became an extremely popular Qi Gong teacher.

What is Qi Gong?

Qi Gong is a method of managing health that has been practised since ancient times in China. It has been known in Chinese martial arts for many years and millions of people all over the world practise it. In order to define the word Qi Gong it is necessary to understand the concepts of "Qi" and "Gong".

◆ *"Qi" is a Chinese word that means "air", "breath" or "steam", describing the outer, external part of the body. When Qi is used to describe the internal part of the body, it refers to breath. The word "Qi" in martial arts means vitality, life-force or energy. In TCM it is understood that health results from the harmonious flow of Qi throughout the body. In performing Qi Gong exercises, the goal is to build up internal Qi. In TCM, all disease is considered to be a lack of Qi, an imbalance of Qi, or an interruption of Qi flowing smoothly throughout the body along the 12 major meridians.*

◆ *In martial arts, the term "Gong Fu" (Kung Fu) means the diligent practice of exercises. The word "Gong" means effort.*

Putting them together, Qi Gong means the conscious and systematic development of vital energy. The well-known Chinese martial arts, such as Taiji (Tai chi), Xingyi (Hsingyi) and Ba Gua (Pakua) all come from the practice of Qi Gong. Yoga and Indian meditators also refer to Qi as Chiti, Kundalini and Prana. In Japanese, Qi equals "Ki" as in Aikido, a Japanese form of martial arts.

Thus Qi Gong is composed of these two words, indicating that it is not only how long a person practises that matters, but also the quality of the practice. The student's commitment and persistence in learning how to practise the various forms correctly will determine how effective the practice becomes.

Origins of Qi Gong

Several thousand years ago, the famous Chinese philosophers Laozi (the father of Taoism; sixth century BC), Confucius (Spring and Autumn and Warring States Periods, 551–479 BC), and Zhuangzi (sixth century BC) were all practising "Neigong", which is now being interpreted as "Qi Gong". An historical relic, "Jade Pendant inscription on Qi flowing" (of the early Spring and Autumn and Warring States Period, 770–221 BC) records the training method, the theory and the health-preserving principles of Qi Gong. *The Yellow Emperor's Canon of Internal Medicine*, the earliest extant general medicine collection in the Han Dynasty (206 BC–AD 200) in China, systematically describes the principles, the training methods and the effects of practising Qi Gong.

The Theoretical Basis of Qi Gong

Qi Gong is closely related to TCM, which includes the theories of Yin/Yang, channels and collaterals (the meridian system) and organ systems (Viscera/Zang-Fu). It is also closely tied to the practice of martial arts.

QI GONG AND YIN/YANG THEORY

Yin/Yang theory is a philosophy as well as the basis of TCM. In this philosophy, everything has Yin and Yang properties (for further discussion see the sections on History and Philosophy, Acupuncture and Causes of Disease). Breath (respiration) includes exhalation (expiration) and inhalation (inspiration). Exhalation is Yang, while inhalation is Yin. Exhalation is sedation, while inhalation is tonification.

When practising Qi Gong, it is important to understand the Yin and Yang properties of the four seasons and to plan your training accordingly. Spring and summer are warm and hot respectively and so they nourish Yang. Autumn is considered cool and winter cold, and so they nourish Yin.

ABOVE
Autumn is cool and nourishes Yin.

QI GONG AND THE CHANNELS AND COLLATERALS

Qi Gong was developed on the basis of the channels and collaterals theory of TCM. The goal of the person who practises is to enable the Qi to ascend, descend, open, close and circulate freely through the 12 main channels, the Ren and Du channels, the eight extra channels and the collaterals. One particular practice, Tongqi, asks the student to learn to move the "tip" of the inhalation lower and lower until it reaches a point that is the width of three fingers below the navel. This point, known as the Dantian, is the main source of energy throughout the body. The practice of Qi Gong enables the student to experience the existence of these channels and collaterals.

ABOVE
Spring is warm and therefore nourishes Yang.

ABOVE
Summer is hot and therefore nourishes Yang.

ABOVE
Winter is cold and therefore nourishes Yin.

QI GONG AND THE ORGAN SYSTEM

One of the Qi Gong exercises involves concentrating in such a way that you bring the brain into a tranquil state that will regulate and rejuvenate the mental activities.

THE HEART

In TCM theory, mental activities are regulated by the heart, which also governs blood circulation. The outward manifestation of these is in the face, so practising Qi Gong can affect the exuberance of the heart and result in a ruddy and lustrous complexion and a forceful, even pulse.

THE SPLEEN

This is the foundation of life in that it produces the Qi and the blood and is responsible for the activities of the extremities. The spleen transports and transforms the nutrients necessary for the blood and also creates saliva. By strengthening the up-down movement of the diaphragm, Qi Gong exercises can directly increase saliva and the appetite and promote the peristaltic and digestive functions of the stomach.

THE KIDNEYS

The reception of air is governed by the kidneys. When the student of Qi Gong sinks the inspired air to Dantian through deep abdominal respirations, he can further strengthen the lungs and receptive functions of the kidneys.

THE LUNGS

The lungs dominate Qi, control respiration, send down the inspired (inhaled) air and are related to the skin and hair. The practice of Qi Gong can enrich the genuine Qi, which is the Qi that circulates through the channels and organs of the body.

THE LIVER

The liver serves to activate the vital energy of other organs, regulate the activity of vital energy, store and regulate the blood and control thinking. Stagnation of liver Qi through such experiences as frustration or anger may interfere with the normal smoothing and regulating function of the liver. Qi Gong exercises can stabilize moods and help the liver to regain its normal smoothing and regulating function. These exercises can also calm a hyperactive liver-Yang and liver-fire through relaxation and tranquillity.

THE DANTIAN

This is the main source of energy throughout the body. This point is located three fingers' width below the navel.

TECHNIQUES OF QI GONG

T here are many systems involving Qi Gong techniques taught in China. They can be roughly divided into five categories: ◆ TAOIST ◆ BUDDHIST ◆ CONFUCIAN ◆ MEDICAL ◆ MARTIAL ARTS-RELATED. *In actual practice, many of these categories overlap.*

TAOIST METHOD

The principal aim of the Taoist method is to strengthen both the body and mind. It is called the "dual cultivation of nature and life" because it stresses the relationship between the individual and the environment.

BUDDHIST METHOD

The Buddhist system gives precedence to the cultivation of the mind to improve moral discipline. Dr Yu studied the meditations of Mizong Buddhism (Tibetan) extensively and he learned from his Buddhist master the secret of lowering the Qi until it reached Dantian. From there it could be pushed through to completely open the body's natural Qi-carrying channels. The Buddhist Qi Gong exercises greatly increase a person's health and physical abilities.

CONFUCIAN METHOD

The Confucian exercises emphasize regulation of the mind to achieve a state of tranquility that will promote moral character.

MEDICAL METHOD

The medical techniques of Qi Gong are designed to prevent disease, promote health and prolong life.

MARTIAL ARTS METHOD

The aim of martial arts Qi Gong is to build up the student's inner strength to the point that he or she is totally protected against both moral and physical attack.

THE THEORY OF QI CIRCULATION

*B*eginner students have a tendency to emphasize quiet meditation for longevity, but this *very quietness is not sufficient to make the Qi circulate. Others concentrate too much on deep, thin, long or balanced Qi circulation, which causes holding of the breath and will also fail to make the Qi circulate.*

According to modern medical research, human life could be extended for as long as 150–200 years. There are more than 100 billion nerve cells in our brain, but in daily activities only one-tenth of them are used. Similarly, there are 20,000 capillaries throughout the body carrying blood. However, during a normal resting state, only about five capillaries are carrying blood. When the body is exercising, the blood is flowing through approximately 200 capillaries. The human body has about 7.5 billion lung cells. But without stimulation through exercise these cells may atrophy and become useless. With the practice of Qi Gong and the regulation of the breath, genuine Qi is circulated, enhancing brain cells, capillaries and lung cells.

WHAT IS GENUINE QI?

Genuine Qi is the energy of body movement, the substantial foundation of active life and the main motive force which protects the body against disease, strengthens the immune system and improves health and longevity. If you have abundant genuine Qi, you will be healthy and have a long life, while if the genuine Qi is insufficient, the body becomes weak and ill. Should genuine Qi diminish completely, then life ends.

We can say that genuine Qi is the motivating force of life. The five viscera (Zang) and six hollow viscera (Fu), the extremities and the body can work normally because of the energy from genuine Qi. If there is no genuine Qi, there is no regeneration of essence or vitality, and life ceases.

THE SOURCE OF GENUINE QI

There are two kinds of genuine Qi: prenatal Qi and postnatal Qi. The pre-natal genuine Qi comes from our parents. It is called Yuan-Qi or original Qi. Yuan-Qi is consumed gradually throughout our lifetime. The oxygen and nutrition we absorb join the circulating bloodstream to produce postnatal genuine Qi.

DANTIAN AND ITS FUNCTION

Dantian is a very important concept that people take seriously in the world of TCM and the martial arts. Those who practise the art and techniques of health preservation place their hopes on the Dantian. Singers believe that, if they can sing with Qi from the Dantian, their voice will be sonorous. People who practise martial arts also believe that if their Qi reaches

Dantian, they are unmatched anywhere in the world.

It is said that there are three areas of Dantian: upper, middle and lower. Different schools of thought believe these to be located in different areas. Some believe the upper Dantian to be located on the top of the head at the acupuncture point "Baihui" (Du 20). Others believe the upper Dantian to be located inside the acupuncture point "Yintang" (Extra 1), between the eyebrows. This is called "ZuQiao". The middle Dantian is thought to be in one of two places. The first being inside the acupuncture point "Shanzhong" (Ren 17) on the chest, between the nipples, and the second being in the navel. The area of lower Dantian is considered to be in the lower abdomen, three finger widths below the navel or at the acupuncture point "Huiyin" (Ren 1) or "Yongquan" (Kidney 1).

According to Professor Yu, in Qi Gong practice the most important Dantian area is about three fingers' width below the navel. This is where the genuine Qi is stored. TCM theory states that Dantian is the starting point of the circulation of the Qi in the Ren Channel, the Du Channel and the Chong Channel. It is also "the root of the twelve channels", "the progenitor of life" and "the confluence of Yin and Yang", as well as the location where the male stores the reproductive essence and the female nourishes the foetus. So an excess of sexual activity can consume the genuine Qi and cause weakness and lower back pain.

In Qi Gong, the practice of focusing the mind on the Dantian usually refers to concentrating on lowering genuine Qi to the Dantian to accumulate Qi. When we were born, everyone enjoyed prenatal Qi located below the navel. As we mature, however, the position of the Qi rises and there is a continuous loss of this genuine Qi – unless we practise Qi Gong, which will lower the Qi down again to the Dantian position. When inhaling, we obtain the oxygen to push the Qi down. When exhaling during meditation and standing, keep the focus on Dantian. When the genuine Qi is sufficient and strong, it moves up along the Du meridian and all over the body to supply energy.

FOCUSING ON THE DANTIAN POINT

Remember that the best place to focus your concentration is the Dantian point below the navel. Mind concentration on middle Dantian can cause chest distress and focusing on the upper Dantian can cause hypertension.

BASIC TECHNIQUES OF QI GONG

*P*rofessor Yu's system for improving the flow of Qi combines the techniques of martial arts and meditation to form a unified series of exercises. The aim of these exercises is to lower the Qi to the Dantian point below the navel.

EXERCISE 1: STANDING (ZHAN-ZHUANG)

Standing relaxes the muscles and quietens the mind. The effect on circulation and general body tone can be seen after only a few weeks of practice. Other changes, including relaxation, that begin to permeate an individual's daily life, come gradually over a period of months. The beginner should start by remaining in the posture as long as he or she can manage comfortably, usually 10 to 15 minutes for a healthy adult. After two or three months, the student works up to a minimum of 20 to 30 minutes.

PREPARATION FOR STANDING

◆ Wear flat shoes.
◆ Do not stand with your stomach empty, but neither should you overeat before standing.
◆ Evacuate the bowels and bladder before standing.

THE FORM OF STANDING

1 Stand with your feet absolutely parallel, at shoulder width, with hands held by the side.

2 Slowly bend your knees while raising your hands, palms down, to chest height in front of you in one smooth, coordinated movement until they are parallel to the ground.

3 Look straight ahead while adjusting your posture so that your nose is directly in line with your navel, your neck is relaxed, your arms are spread with hands relaxed (but not limp), your back is erect and your legs stand firmly anchored.

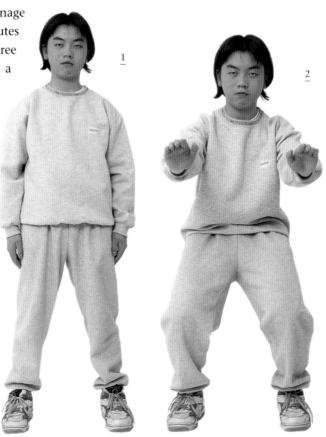

1

2

BREATHING

When comfortable in this position and looking straight ahead, close your eyes gently and concentrate on your breathing. If concentration is difficult, try counting breaths up to ten and then start over again (to avoid being distracted, count with large numbers). No attempt should be made to change the rhythm of the breath, which will come naturally. Be relaxed enough so that your abdomen expands and contracts with each breath (not your chest!). While inhaling and exhaling, you should feel as though the breath is surging through your body.

WHAT DO YOU FEEL?

Eventually, you will begin to feel a warming of your hands. This is the first sign of the deep relaxation that comes with the practice of Standing. If the sensation does not occur the first few times, do not worry – more practice will help you to feel it.

Later, this sensation of warmth permeates the body until distinct sweating occurs; this is also normal. Because of the sweating, it is important that draughts be avoided during and after the exercise.

Most beginners experience a trem-

THE SIGNS FOR THE CORRECT FORM

There are two main indications that you are standing correctly.
1 Your hands should become warm on both sides (right and left, medial and lateral). If they are not warm, or only one side is warm, it indicates that your muscles are not relaxed and the Qi is not flowing smoothly, allowing for good blood circulation. Try consciously to relax your shoulders, letting them drop, and relax your arms, letting them sag slightly while maintaining the basic standing posture.
2 The second indication that things are going well with your standing is the experience of moderate to heavy sweating. This means that Qi is flowing smoothly and the circulation is good.

bling of their legs and body and a temporary soreness of joints and tendons around the knees. This too is normal as the body releases tension, and it should be ignored as much as possible. As Professor Yu would say: "Never mind, never mind." For

WHERE AND WHEN TO PRACTISE

The Standing exercise is best practised twice a day: first thing in the morning and last thing before going to bed. Look for a quiet place where you will not be disturbed, especially where you will not be startled. Avoid draughts so that you will not be chilled after sweating. Within a few weeks you should be able to stand for 20 minutes at a time if you practise every day.

advanced practitioners, this movement progresses into a purely internal vibration that is also a beneficial way to relieve tension and to ease the remaining effects of old injuries.

REMEMBER to hold your hands flat but not tensed. As your legs become tired, they may begin to shake, another normal reaction.

CONCLUDING THE STANDING EXERCISE

1 If you are a beginner, stand erect for 10 minutes then rub your hands together and stroke your forehead and down each side of your face with your warm palms. This massage will improve circulation and help soften wrinkles.

2 Continue rubbing with a downward stroke on each arm and the hands. Using your thumb and fingers, continue down to the knees, the muscles of the shoulders and the arms.

3 Next, rub the chest and abdomen.

4 With your knuckles, massage the back.

5 Finally, sit down and rub the thighs and calves. With the thumb and fingers, massage the muscles on the tops of the thighs and the tendons around the kneecaps. Rub the area again until the soreness caused by standing is erased.

Whatever stress and strains your body carries can be rubbed away by this massage. The combination of rubbing and massage reduces fatigue, closes pores and promotes Qi and Blood circulation. They can also be used after work to relieve strain and tension.

BENEFITS OF STANDING

Many years ago, the standing exercise was one of the secrets passed down from a master to only one or two advanced students. Master Xiang-zhai Wong began to teach it at the beginning of training because he believed it provided a good foundation for later work. Professor Yu also believed it should be taught widely and in no way held secret. He made some modifications to the exercise to allow the student to feel the flow of

TIPS

◆ Be sure to dry off the sweat with a towel after standing, to avoid becoming chilled.

◆ Avoid drinking anything cold after standing and sweating.

◆ Occasionally, the site of an old injury will begin to hurt after standing. If this happens and the pain is severe, stop immediately. If it is very mild, continue standing and rub the area with your palms. It will go away gradually.

Qi more easily. Standing is the most efficient method for mobilizing Qi as a defensive force. Standing also trains one's endurance. Beginner students are usually able to do the exercise for only a few minutes at first. By enduring the fatigue and the strain caused by holding the bent knee position (squatting), they learn to do it for longer periods. The best part of the training is that you learn to endure strain and pain while at the same time trying to relax. Therein lies the secret of success. As you know, many sports champions seem to go into a kind of trance to win effortlessly. They arrive at a natural "high" and make contact with their great inner power and strength – which is Qi.

EXERCISE 2: QUIET SITTING MEDITATION

After the standing exercise, you may find it beneficial to do a sitting meditation.

1 Sit erect on the front edge of a chair with your feet flat on the floor. Your legs should be shoulder-width apart and perpendicular to the floor.

2 Place the palms of your hands over your knees.

3 With your head erect and back straight, relax, close your eyes and concentrate on breathing.

4 Breathe deeply, expanding the abdomen and not the chest.

NOTE: This meditation can also be done

with your eyes open if you are in a place where you do not wish other people to see that you are meditating, such as on a plane or in a boring meeting. It is also a way for you to refresh your body and mind during a break at work or in your lunch hour. You can use this seated exercise frequently throughout the day to relieve tension and practise self-healing.

QUIET MEDITATION – SITTING WITH LEGS CROSSED

This is another form of sitting meditation that you may find beneficial after completing the standing exercise.

1 BOTH LEGS CROSSED
Place the left foot on the right and then move the right foot onto the left leg. Relax both hands on knees or place them in front of the lower abdomen with palms up and overlapped.

2 SINGLE LEG CROSSED (RIGHT)
Place the left foot on the right leg or place the right foot on the left leg. Overlap both hands in front of the lower abdomen with palms up.

3 FREE LEG CROSSED
Place the left foot under the right leg and the right foot under the left leg. Overlap both hands in front of the lower abdomen with palms up.

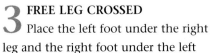
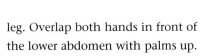

EXERCISES TO IMPROVE YOUR GENERAL QI

QI GONG — EXERCISE 1

1 Start this exercise by assuming the standing position with your arms hanging relaxed by your sides.

2 Slowly raise your hands (palms up) over your chest, breathing in as your hands move up.

3 Once your hands are level with your shoulders. turn the palms down and lower them, breathing out at the same time.

4 Hold this position briefly at the starting position and then repeat the movement. This should be done a total of eight times.

NOTE: As your hands move up and down your should imagine they are gathering up your Qi and moving it to your abdomen.

QI GONG—EXERCISE 2

1 Start this exercise by assuming the standing position with your arms bent from the elbows, your hands level with your shoulders and palms facing forwards.

2 Slowly push them out sideways, level with your shoulders, and then back again to the starting position and repeat the exercise. This should be done eight times in total.

QI GONG – EXERCISE 3

1

1 Start this exercise by putting your left leg forwards, with your arms relaxed by your sides.

2 Slowly raise your hands over your chest.

3 Once your hands are level with your shoulders, slowly push them straight out in front of you and then back again. Then bring your hands down your body to the starting position and repeat the exercise. This should be done eight times in total.

NOTE: Take slow, controlled breaths throughout the exercise, imagining you are moving your Qi to your abdomen.

2

3

RELAXATION

*R**elaxing is an art, as the following story of Professor Yu will illustrate. While he was a hospital intern, a woman had been in labour for several hours but did not seem to be able to deliver. Dr Yu tried to induce delivery but failed. Finally, he had an idea. He brought in the woman's three-year-old daughter and whispered something to her. The little girl then announced in a loud voice: "Little sister, little sister! Better come out!" At this moment the woman gave a hearty laugh and, as she laughed, her body relaxed and the baby was delivered.*

One of the side-effects of relaxing is that things long forgotten begin to come to mind. For example, one of Professor Yu's mature students remarked that he was suddenly able to remember the forgotten names of people who owed him money! That is possible, but try to put these kinds of thoughts aside. The real point is to empty the mind as completely as possible, a practice that can increase one's powers of concentration in every area of life.

When your mind is calm and your body relaxed, you will feel your Qi travelling down from your hands to your knees and then to the bottom of your feet. This sensation is a surge of warmth that seems to travel with your breathing. It goes to your feet during exhalation or inhalation. Initially it may not reach the bottom of your feet, but after practice, it will. After you finish your meditation, your body and mind will feel refreshed and you will look younger, with pink cheeks. This fresh and bright feeling can be achieved by this technique after only a few weeks of practice.

ADVANCED TECHNIQUES AND BENEFITS

Qi Gong exercises differ from normal exercises because they do not require any visible body movements. A person doing the stand-ing exercise can work up a sweat from head to toe, even around the eyes, between the fingers, around the fingertips and places where one does not normally sweat. Many people sweat so much during standing that sweat drops off their body and forms a small puddle at their feet. Of course, the amount of sweat varies from person to person. What is especially impressive is that your sweat pours out by just doing something totally relaxing, without any visible motion.

Beginners, of course, may shake a little during standing. The more tense you are at the start, the more you will shake. After a time, you will relax more and your

THESE BENEFITS WILL LAST THROUGHOUT YOUR LIFE

All of these benefits can either be observed directly, or felt and experienced. The flow of Qi is responsible for some basic functions of your body cells – such as when to regenerate, grow or repair. The flow of Qi may also determine how the body's defence system is maintained. Thus the study of Qi Gong can enhance the immune system to keep you well. You can age, but remain younger internally.

People with stiff joints or arthritis should avoid the leg-crossed forms of meditation. Those forms are more difficult to do before certain training, especially before developing Tongqi.

legs and back will become stronger and shaking will stop. Then you will feel only the vibration in your body that generates heat and produces sweat. Still later during your practice, you will become aware of the heat your body can generate without sweating. The significance of sweating is to clear up obstructions so that Qi can flow smoothly throughout the body. With con-

FEELINGS DURING STANDING MEDITATION

In an advanced state of standing meditation, the genuine Qi is active and the meridians are open. The following are some feelings you can expect to experience.

1 "Big": because the genuine Qi is circulating smoothly throughout the body and more of the capillaries are expanded, you will feel as though the body has become very "big" and full.

2 "Light": sometimes there is a light feeling, as if you are going to fly. This is a phenomenon of inhalation. The genuine Qi is rising when you are inhaling.

3 "Heavy": sometimes your body will feel as heavy as a huge rock. This happens with the exhalation of genuine Qi.

4 "Tickling or itching": occasionally you will feel tickling or itching of the skin and scalp. This is normal. Before you began the practice of Qi Gong, the meridians were closed. Once the genuine Qi is flowing, you may feel the tickling. However, it will usually subside after a couple of weeks.

When you want to solve a problem, try practising Qi Gong. The answer may come to you in a flash, totally unexpectedly.

tinuing practice, you can bring up this warm feeling with your breathing and eventually acquire the sensation that your whole body is breathing.

The first step in attempting to gain this control is to lower your Qi down to your Dantian, located three fingers beneath the navel, by letting your breath go deeper and deeper. You should think of it as being a long, thin and continuous breath. Once your Qi is down to the Dantian, the next step is to let it flow to your limbs and finally throughout every part of the body. Breathing with your whole body is what Qi-Gong exercises teach you. This "total body breathing" may only be a metaphorical way of describing the flow of Qi to every part of the body, but with practice, you can experience this flow of Qi and direct it with your thoughts.

It is very important to learn how to quiet your thoughts by "emptying" your mind. With your eyes closed, it is easier to achieve a meditative state. You can look inward instead of outward. Professor Yu used this technique to control thoughts that come into the mind. He cautioned his students not to dwell upon thoughts, but simply to let them slip away. For beginners, counting each breath may be useful. As your mind becomes calm and "empty" of thoughts, your awareness of what is taking place within your body sharpens and you begin to learn how to control the flow of Qi. However, too much attention should not be focused on the Qi flowing. Just let it happen.

Since your legs are bent while standing, they must carry the full weight of your body. By learning to relax your legs under this pressure, you can strengthen the muscles, tendons and ligaments of the legs. After a long period of training, the strain you feel in your legs will lessen, as they grow stronger. Your back does not support as much of your body weight as your legs but your back will become stronger too.

Qi Gong and healing

Qi Gong and acupuncture work in much the same way. You can use acupuncture and Qi Gong to prevent illness and facilitate healing. Healing is the result of removing obstructions to allow Qi to flow freely. Once a person is ill or injured, even though he recovers completely, a scar is left behind. The injury or illness might reappear over time when a person becomes weakened. Qi Gong can be used to remove some of these negative bodily memories that might work on the mind and body in this weakened state. There is no similar method in meditation or exercise that is as effective. That is because two very powerful techniques, meditation and martial arts, are combined into one in Yu's Qi Gong.

Many of Professor Yu's students who were injured in accidents years earlier said they felt no sensations for years until they began practising Qi Gong. Then some of the pain from the old injuries appeared again during practice. This could have been caused by one of two factors: first, they may have become more aware of their body during Qi Gong practice; secondly, the memory of the illness lingered on, almost as in a dream of something once experienced in the past. However, by massaging the once-injured area immediately after each practice session, such symptoms disappear.

The best time to do massage is after each of the Qi Gong exercises. You should always massage in a downwards direction. The more you practise Qi Gong, the healthier and stronger you will be. If you do become ill, you will find that you are able to recover more rapidly by directing your Qi to the part of your body that has been affected. Professor Yu's wife, Simu Ouyang Min, who was 90 years old in 1997 and still teaching Qi Gong, said that, since practising Qi Gong, she has never had flu.

Focusing Qi Gong

Professor Yu fell and broke his left hip on a snowy day in 1979. All the doctors said that he would lose the leg if he refused to have an operation. That operation would have left his broken leg two inches shorter than his right leg. Professor Yu decided to refuse the operation and concentrated instead on practising Qi Gong every day. Three months later he stood up with the help of canes. Six months later, he could walk as a normal person without canes and his two legs were the same length. In the X-rays the doctors could find only a thin line at the place where the leg had been fractured.

QI GONG AND ACUPUNCTURE

A cupuncture has been practised in China for thousands of years. It is based on the idea of balancing the flow of Qi along the meridians. Many diseases can be treated by inserting needles into points along the meridians to stimulate and direct the flow of Qi. One of the important procedures in this process is called "Deqi" (getting hold of Qi). This is done by twirling the needle a few times until the patient feels numbness, tightness, dull pain, the muscles squeezing the area around the needle and the flow of Qi away from the needle to another part of the body – as indicated by a tingling sensation emanating from the needle.

Focusing Qi from the practitioner's palm onto the needle from a distance of several inches while it is being twirled can increase the effectiveness of acupuncture treatment. The patient feels these sensations more easily and sooner and is therefore able to provide the acupuncturist with stronger, positive feedback. Because the patient is receiving energy from the Qi Gong-practising acupuncturist over a large area surrounding the needle, any blockage of Qi may be overcome more easily and the proper balance required for health can be restored more quickly. Since the acupuncturist is using and giving Qi to his patients, it is very important for him to do standing meditation after his work to regenerate his own Qi.

There was once a young man who tried to join the army in Shanghai but was rejected because of colour blindness. He was then treated by Professor Yu's sister, who had practised Xinyi with Xiang-Zhai Wong and Qi Gong with Professor Yu. After several treatments with acupuncture and the application of Qi, the young man passed the colour perception test and was accepted into the army.

This example demonstrates that there is a close relationship between acupuncture and Qi Gong. In order to use this technique the practitioner must first study Qi Gong until he can release Qi from the acupuncture point in his palm. Then, he learns to release Qi from an area one inch in diameter from the middle of his palm while focusing it onto the body surface of the patient.

After practising Qi Gong, you will find that you are becoming more intuitive and more sensitive. You may sense the changes in temperature and feel draughts. Your concentration will improve and your perceptions will become sharper.

The only way to really profit from doing Qi Gong is to consider it a long-term project. These are the highly worthwhile major goals you can expect to achieve: to feel better, to live longer, to be stronger, to experience a natural "high", to be calm, to improve yourself, to correct bad habits and to recover from illness.

Qi Gong is a discipline and when it is practised every day, the results are amazing! You will look and feel younger, with more energy, better health and a calmer, more peaceful state of mind.

TAI CHI

*T*ai Chi is a martial art that is widely practised in China. Like other Chinese
martial arts, it has developed out of the practice of Qi Gong. It helps promote
inner relaxation and strength, if practised regularly. Tai Chi blends the internal
meditation associated with Qi Gong with an external exercise system. Many Chinese
practise it on their way to work in the morning in city parks.

Here is a simple Tai Chi exercise that you can practise at home.

1 Stand relaxed and upright, feet shoulder-width apart and hands held loosely. Gently stretch the body and concentrate on breathing, feeling the breath going in and out.

2 Raise your bent arms to upper chest height, then hold this position for a couple of minutes, still focusing on the inner breath.

3 Still focusing on the flow of Qi, raise one arm to direct the Qi down through your head and body into the Dantian. Many experienced people who practise Tai Chi regularly attribute their good health and well-being to their ability to sink the Qi down into the Dantian. However, it can take many years to become proficient.

LEFT
Tai Chi can be practised anywhere. It involves slow, graceful movements and promotes inner relaxation and harmony.

ACUPRESSURE

指壓

We know **that acupuncture** developed over a period of at least 5,000 years from its first beginnings. Acupressure, which preceded acupuncture by at least another millennium, can claim to be the more ancient healing art. How this wonderful therapy came into being is unknown. Perhaps it started because a sage with a severe headache banged himself against a tree by mistake and found relief. Or it might have begun with a mother pressing points that somehow soothed her crying child. In any case, knowledge was accumulated, shared and passed on so that future generations could enjoy its benefits.

At some point, acupressure lost favour in China; it came to be considered inferior to acupuncture in the same way that acupuncture was considered inferior to herbology. This was not because of lack of efficacy but because of the class structure of ancient China. In order for a physician to show appropriate respect for his more aristocratic patients, he would touch them as little as possible and, as a scholar himself, he would probably handle his patients sparingly – the upper classes, who could afford to spend their time in more scholarly pursuits, looked down upon anything resembling manual labor.

The highest, most refined form of medicine then became observation and prescription (herbology), much like today. The next highest was the elegant method of treating with needles (acupuncture), especially acupuncture on the extremities, which could be modestly exposed. The least refined of these techniques was

CONVENIENT AND FLEXIBLE

Because acupressure can be practised by anyone, anywhere, at any time, and without tools, it offers superior availability, flexibility and portability. It is a perfect family – and community – medicine. Patients needn't depend entirely on outside institutions for maintaining their health if they are able to use acupressure techniques.

acupressure – manipulation of the actual flesh with the hands. Those without means or advanced education – the farmers and country people who worked with their hands – were those who used acupressure in their daily lives. Acupressure thus became considered a lower pursuit, something for the peasant class, even though it was effective.

An additional factor obscuring the true value of acupressure as a worthy and effective medicine again lies in the social history of China. The primary way for ordinary people to gain rank in imperial China was for them to become government agents and civil servants. They did this by taking and passing a rigorous civil service exam. Intense academic study of appropriate texts, to the exclusion of other labour, was greatly encouraged by parents hoping their sons would so rise to power. Because the emperor could take away anything he wished from his subjects, the saying was coined: "Nothing is yours except your knowledge."

This emphasis on academic excellence remains a Chinese family tradition today. A great distinction was made between this kind of bookish learning and practical, earthy knowledge, which reinforced the relatively low status of acupressure as medicine.

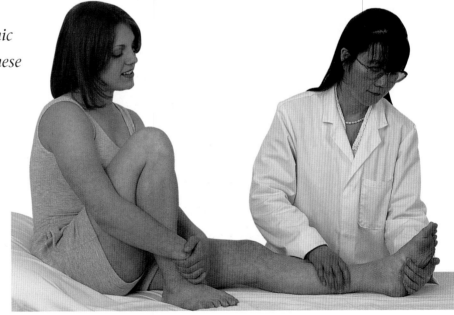

MODERN DEVELOPMENTS

*I*n modern times, two factors have contributed to the rise in status and use of acupressure, which, with acupuncture, had receded in China in favour of Western-style medicine. The first was the Communist revolution, at which time China became a more uniformly poor country. Suddenly China found itself with few Western-trained doctors, with the educated and the elite out of power, and with no money for either drugs or herbs. To cope with this situation, the country's administrators encouraged the resurrection and dissemination of traditional hands-on medical knowledge to serve the basic health needs of the mostly agrarian populace. Because acupuncture requires the additional tool (and expense) of needles, is inherently more invasive, and involves more specialized skill, acupressure became a natural choice for many people.

The second reason for acupressure's rise is that the people of China have been amazed to see how much those in the West are interested in and awed by this traditional medicine, and so began once again to value it more highly. Like a family heirloom that had once fallen out of fashion and into obscurity, only to become a prized collector's item later, acupressure has been rediscovered, refurbished and treasured anew. And, indeed, the study and use of acupressure has now spread throughout the world, along with that of other Eastern healing techniques.

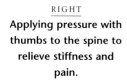

RIGHT
Applying pressure with thumbs to the spine to relieve stiffness and pain.

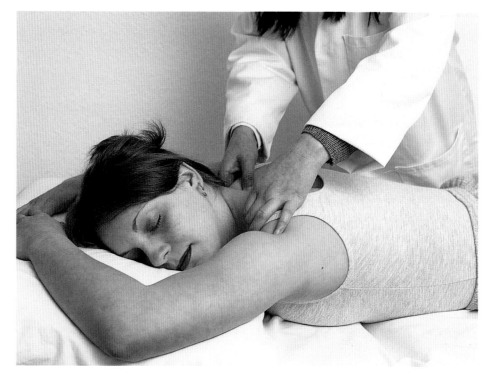

GENERAL THEORY

The acupressure system of therapy uses the same points on the body as does acupuncture to treat or prevent disease. "Acu" means care or precision. The therapist takes care to use the exact point. However, instead of using needles to puncture the skin, the therapist uses hands and fingers (and occasionally another tool) to place pressure on the points. Henceforth, when reference is made to acupressure points, remember that these are the same as acupuncture points.

Treatment with acupressure is based on a theory that includes acupressure points, meridians or channels, and the Zang-Fu organ system.

Acupressure treatment uses different methods to stimulate the points in order to enhance circulation in the meridians and promote the function of the internal organs and the limbs that the meridians traverse.

ACUPRESSURE POINTS

The acupressure points are located in patterns on the surface of the body. They are connected by pathways or channels called meridians. These meridians can be thought of as streets, while the points are various bus stops along the way. The Zang Fu organs are the internal destinations on the meridians. These organs, although similar in some respects to the Western version of the anatomical organs, are actually more like clusters of functions that enable the human organism to undertake its various physiological activities.

Energetic and material substances flow continuously through the meridians, in a single direction. The network of meridians thus eventually connects the entire body together, in much the same way that blood circulation extends throughout the body. The internal organs store and dispense these energies and substances as needed by the rest of the body. These fundamental substances, called Qi (energy), Jing essence (inherited source of reproduction and development), Xue (blood), and Jin Ye (nourishing fluids) are thought to nourish the body in various ways.

In addition to the Qi running through the meridians, Qi takes many forms and performs different functions throughout the body. Qi circulating near the surface of the body, Wei Qi, serves as the body's first line of defence against the invasion of external pathogens. Each organ is infused with its own Qi, which performs the physiological tasks of that organ. The Zong Qi circulates and is stored in the chest. It is a product of air inhaled by the lungs and the food essence acquired by the spleen and stomach. Its function is to control respiration and circulate the blood. The Ying Qi, or nutritive Qi, derived from food essence, circulates with the blood and nourishes the production of blood.

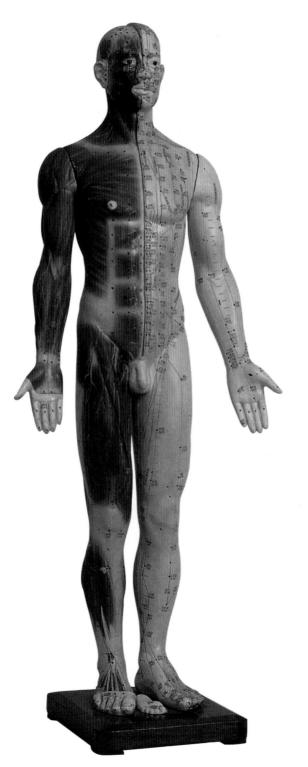

Although strange in concept to the Western view, acupressure theory possesses an internally consistent, unified logic that makes it an excellent, eminently practical therapy. This means that it is possible to extrapolate a healing strategy from a diagnosis or treatment of one part of the body and apply it to another, thus treating causal syndromes as an internal imbalance in need of adjustment. In contrast, Western conventional medicine tends to isolate the parts from the whole of the body system and to neglect the larger context in favour of the current set of symptoms. The interrelations are overlooked, and remote treatment is rarely considered an option. So, while TCM practitioners may view an imbalance of the stomach, liver or gall-bladder as the source of a headache that will disappear when balance is restored to the system, Western medicine is more likely to treat the headache as an isolated, localized problem and treat it symptomatically.

Acupressure tries to adjust two kinds of abnormality – conceptualized in this system of medicine as congestion and weakness. Acupressure serves to normalize body function by clearing away congestion ("sedation") and supplementing weakness ("tonification"). This, in turn, strengthens the body, heals the problem and promotes the recovery of health.

Over its thousands of years of development, acupressure benefited from a constant cycle of learning, from practice to theory to further practice. We now know that acupressure can restore and increase the function of the internal organs and enhance immunity to disease. For example, clinically, we can see acupressure both heal and prevent headaches and colds. Many patients find that acupressure treatment not only helps to heal acute and chronic conditions, but also greatly improves their overall health. It is also a very good self-help method for disease prevention.

POINT AND MERIDIAN RELATIONSHIP

Acupressure points are grouped along the meridians in such a way that pressing points on a meridian affects the flow of substances in the entire channel. To know how to use the points to best advantage, we should know basic meridian theory. We must know where the meridians go, which direction the substances flow in the meridians and what organ systems are attached to the meridian and affected by its flow. We can use this system to isolate the location of a problem, diagnose the problem, and then treat it. Problems anywhere along a meridian can be treated by therapy on that meridian, even when they seem unrelated to each other except by being on the same route. For example, the large intestine meridian passes along the upper surface of the arm and across the shoulder to the face. Pressing the well-known point Large Intestine 4 (Hegu), on the hand in the web between the thumb and forefinger (usually a tender spot), is used to treat shoulder conditions as well as sinus congestion and headaches. The same point will also help with abdominal pain, constipationand dysentery.

MERIDIAN AND ZANG FU ORGAN RELATIONSHIP

According to meridian theory, the channels pass through the limbs of the body and link up with the internal Zang Fu organs. The Zang Fu (solid and hollow) organs have various patterns of internal relationships that govern our functioning, whether in health or disease. These relationships must be maintained in harmony and balance in order to have good health. Zang Fu organs are classified as follows:

◆ The Zang (solid, Yin) organs consist of the heart, liver, spleen, lung, kidney and pericardium.

◆ The corresponding Fu (hollow, Yang) organs consist of the small intestine, gall-bladder, stomach, large intestine, urinary bladder and triple warmer (also called the San Jiao, this is not an organ *per se* but a cluster of functions of roughly the upper, middle and lower body – the three Jiaos).

When an organ becomes congested or weakened in function, other organs are affected. When we pressure the points, we can affect the flow of substances in the meridians to clear congestion (sedate) some organs and supplement weakness (tonify) others, bringing the whole system back into balance and therefore health.

Because acupressure restores balance to the system, it can treat both subtle discomfort and more serious disease – the theory applies equally well to either case. Varying techniques and amounts of time make the difference in treatment for dif-

fering degrees of disturbance to the body's natural state of balance.

THE CITY AND THE COUNTRYSIDE

The acupressure meridians are called the Jing Luo in TCM. The Jing are the 12 regular meridians named after the 12 Zang Fu organs and they traverse the extremities to connect with the internal Zang Fu organs. The Luo are tiny channels that cross between the meridians, allowing this network to reach every place in the body. The Jing may be thought of as the main highways passing from the countryside, our extremities, into the city, our internal organs. The Luo are the connector streets.

Acupressure points are the bus stops along the streets and highways. Buses carry the various passengers, the substances, to their destinations in a continuous one-way circuit throughout the entire country of the body. The Zang Fu organs are the destinations in the internal city. These Zang Fu are important places of commerce and communication that must interact continuously and smoothly in order for the city to function in a healthy fashion. If a building is on fire, we have to send resources to clear up this problem and then rebuild any damaged structures. If there is an accident on a main or a side street that causes congestion, it must be cleared away before traffic can, once again, move smoothly towards its destination. If

ZANG ORGANS

The Zang (solid, Yin) organs consist of the heart, liver, spleen, lung, kidney and pericardium.

FU ORGANS

Fu (hollow, Yang) organs consist of the small intestine, gall-bladder, stomach, large intestine and urinary bladder.

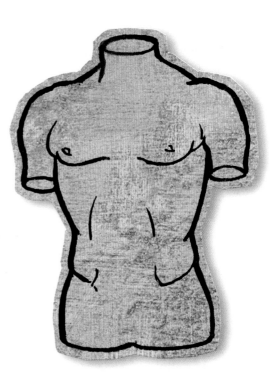

a structure is in danger of collapse, it must be shored up and strengthened before it causes extensive damage.

THE YIN AND YANG MERIDIANS

The meridians are also categorized as Yin and Yang. Using knowledge of the direction of the flow of Qi and other substances in the meridians, the acupressure therapist can adjust the Yin and Yang of the body and its internal Zang Fu organs. The basic idea, once again, is to tonify where there is weakness and sedate where there is congestion. The acupressure specialist uses different techniques and methods to tonify and sedate, adjusting the flow of substances in the meridians to bring the body back into balance.

The theory of Yin and Yang – often misunderstood in the West as simple gender classification – is the highest philosophical source of traditional Chinese medical theory. In brief, just to re-cap a little of the explanation given earlier, everything has both Yin and Yang constituents. An object or being may be more Yin in comparison to one thing yet more Yang in comparison to another; there are no absolutes. An object or being can also be Yin in outer appearance yet Yang in substance or function. Yin and Yang are contradictory yet indispensable to each other, and seek to strike a balance with each other, creating homeostasis. They are wholly complementary, totally interdependent and completely relative aspects of all reality.

Yin, in general, is described as having qualities like elemental water: cold, moist, sinking, slow, dark, material, and so on, whereas Yang is described as having the qualities of elemental fire: hot, dry, rising, fast, bright, non-material and so on.

By studying Yin and Yang, one can come to diagnose and treat diverse, complex conditions. Thorough knowledge of Yin and Yang theory can be of great use in analysing various disease states. For example, surface presentation of excess Yang may very well have an underlying cause of deficient Yin.

Although much can be said about diagnostics, there are some relatively easy ways to distinguish general Yin and Yang syndromes and conditions – one method of determining a possible treatment.

YIN SYMPTOMS

These are apparent in the following signs: the face is dim, dull, pale or grey; not shiny or bright. The extremities are cold and the patient is sensitive to cold. The

patient is often tired, weak, lacklustre, quiet or depressed. The abdomen may be uncomfortable and feels better with pressure or warmth. The urine is commonly light-coloured and frequent or copious. The tongue is often light-coloured and the pulse may be "small" or weak. A common Yin condition is loose bowels and undigested food in the stools.

YANG SYMPTOMS

These are apparent in the following signs: the face may be red and flushed, with red or bloodshot eyes. The body is often warm and the patient prefers cooler tempera-tures and cold drinks. The patient may be restless, active and very loud or irritable. The abdomen may be bloated and uncomfortable, but unrelieved by touch, which is regarded as irritating. The urine is highly coloured and scanty. The patient's mouth is dry and the tongue is red with a yellow coat. The pulse is usually strong. A common Yang condition is dry constipation.

OTHER TENETS OF TCM

From the theory of Yin and Yang spring other philosophical and practical tenets of traditional Chinese medicine – the Eight Principles, the Five Elements and so forth. If you come to understand Yin and Yang, the rest will follow, but if you do not understand this first principle, it is unlikely that the rest will make much sense to you either. However, it is not necessary to have extensive theoretical knowledge to be an effective acupressure practitioner or to help yourself.

The condition of a patient's tongue is an important part of the diagnosis.

THE MACROCOSM
AND THE MICROCOSM

An interesting and vital aspect of acupressure is the concept of the microcosmic maps of the macrocosmic body. The body can be considered a hologram; each part contains the whole, and so treatment of the parts can treat the whole. The body is mirrored in miniature in each part.

In this metasystem of the holographic body, because one part can be used to affect another, if one part is damaged or not appropriate to touch for some reason, then another part can be utilized to help the damaged area remotely as well as to affect the body as a whole.

In contrast, Western conventional medicine tends to treat body parts as separate from each other and from the whole, and as generally untreatable indirectly except by drug action, which often has undesirable and systemic side-effects. When you take a drug, it affects not only the intended part but also the unintended ones, including the nervous system. However, when you treat with acupressure, the benefits go to the needed area and the only "side-effects" are likely to be the rebalancing and harmonizing of the whole body.

THE HOLOGRAPHIC CONCEPT IN ACTION

There are many different versions of this holographic concept in action. The hand, the foot, the ear, the eye, the face, the nose, the scalp and other more or less discreet portions of the body can all be used in this fashion. For instance, the length of the second metacarpal bone, from the knuckle to approximately the web between the forefinger and the thumb, mirrors the length of the body. Therapy can be applied to various points along this bone to affect the head, trunk and extremities. If the hand cannot be used, then there is the ear; if the ear cannot be used, then there is the foot; if the foot cannot be used, then there is the eye and so on.

These holographic body systems are still being explored and mapped today; and they are not the sole province of Chinese scholarship, ancient or modern. New knowledge is being shared, tested, incorporated, put to use and formalized in the same cycle that must have happened in earlier times.

EAR POINTS

The ear points were empirically and extensively mapped by a French doctor, Paul Nogier, of Lyons, between 1955 and 1969. He determined through his own study that the external ear (the auricle) could be viewed as an inverted foetus, with the lobe as the head and the rim, or helix, as the spine. His comprehensive studies in this area added much detail to the current understanding of auricular therapy in China.

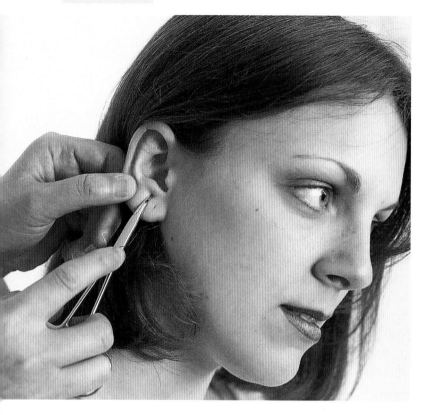

ABOVE
Examining a patient's ear.

traditional Chinese medicine and knew to apply moxa (heat from a burning herb) to the part of the ear that corresponds to this condition. She greatly helped the patient, who then reported his experience to Dr Nogier. From the burn scar, Dr Nogier began to extrapolate from the ear the rest of the body-map. We can easily work on our own ears, which makes this form of acupressure ideal for everyday self-help – something you might try while at work, for example.

EYE SOCKET ACUPRESSURE

In the 1970s, Dr Pang of China developed a form of eye socket acupressure that can be extremely effective. Because the eye is so sensitive (the eyes are said to be the window to the soul, and visual stimuli are strongly felt by the entire organism), this eye socket technique is very powerful, and can be especially helpful for children. By pinching or pressing the flesh around the eye, many different body areas and conditions can be treated. Of greatest immediate use is acupressure of the areas corresponding to the upper, middle and lower body (the three Jiaos). This technique can instantly ease pain and increase function in the selected body zone. Other eye socket sections correspond to the lung, large intestine, kidney, urinary bladder, liver, gall-bladder, heart, spleen and stomach.

Apparently, a patient of Dr Nogier suffered from a painful case of sciatica, and he could do nothing to help this man. Somewhere around Lyons lived a now-unknown woman who had studied

A significant advantage to using this eye socket acupressure is that each meridian is abbreviated yet wholly encompassed in these small eye socket areas, making it possible to treat many conditions and areas simply and effectively.

REFLEXOLOGY

The foot also constitutes a readily available representation of the entire body, which can be treated with acupressure to bring relief for a variety of complaints. This system of acupressure is known in the West as reflexology, and also applies to the hand.

The simplest method of utilizing eye acupressure is to pinch and roll the skin of the areas corresponding to the Upper, Middle or Lower Jiao (upper, middle or lower body). Usually, pinching and rolling is better than pressing because there is more sensation with this method. Other points around the eye socket can be thought of as the applicable meridian in brief, and acupressure will treat problems associated with that organ system and points along the meridian line. For instance, the stomach area of the eye socket will in general treat stomach and digestive problems as well as leg and face problems. Working in a clockwise direction tonifies, while working anti-clockwise sedates.

EYE DIAGNOSIS

Diagnosis can also be done on the eye itself, which can be easier than diagnosis by visual inspection of, for example, the ear. An inspection of the condition of the sclera (the white of the eye), and sometimes the inside of the lid, can give substantial clues to disease states and disharmonies. Some

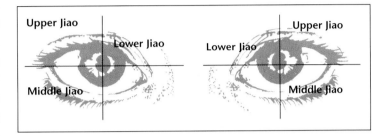

features of eye diagnosis are as follows:

◆ If the vascularization is bright red, it is a sign of new disease, of excess (heat), of a disease that is still developing, or of an acute condition.

◆ If the colour is purple-red, it is a further sign of excess heat.

◆ If the colour is dark red, the condition is getting worse. It is a sign of stagnation and of a heat condition.

◆ If the colour is light red, the Qi and blood are deficient or cold.

POINTS AROUND THE EYE

The Lower Jiao	Treats menstrual cramps, sacrum pain, sciatica and leg pain. Manipulation of all three Jiao areas will help the motility of all limbs and will improve their function.
The Middle Jiao	Treats stomach pain, rib pain, gallstone pain, nausea, vomiting, diarrhoea, constipation and lumbar spine pain.
The Upper Jiao area	Treats headaches, stiff neck, asthma, angina, palpitations, shoulder pain and inflammation, cervical injury and hand and arm pain.
Applicable meridian	Other points around the eye socket can be thought of as the applicable meridian.

- If the colour is dark grey, there is an old disease state in that area.
- If the colour is light grey to red, the person is recovering from an old disease.
- If the shape of the vessel is curved, the disease is more serious and harder to cure.
- If the shape is larger at the tear duct, "has a big root", it indicates a tough, chronic disease.
- If the vessel wanders here and there, it indicates a complex or unstable condition.
- If the vascularization is only on the surface, the disease state is affecting the Fu organs.
- If the vascularization is deeper, the disease state is affecting the Zang organs.
- The origin and destination of a prominent vessel can indicate the organ of disease

origin and where it will manifest.
- If the sclera is blue or dark, it indicates congestion.
- If the sclera is red with black dots, the heat (excess) is going further inside.
- If the sclera is red with yellowish blood vessels, the person will recover. The lighter the yellow colour (associated with Earth and stomach-spleen functions) the stronger the stomach and spleen Qi and consequently the appetite, and the better the person's condition.

ACUPRESSURE'S USEFULNESS

As you can see from the above examples, acupressure can be utilized in many different ways and requires no tools other than the practitioner's knowledge and hands. As an illustration of this usefulness, one day Frank Chung was invited to address a local civic organization on the subject of acupuncture but forgot to bring his needles with which to demonstrate. Nonetheless, he was able to treat everyone who came up with a problem simply by applying some form of acupressure. For the person with spondylosis (inflamed vertebrae), with scarred cervical spine tissue and a constant stiff neck, he treated the area of the eye socket that would affect a twisted Upper Jiao and then requested him to move his neck. He was amazed that he was suddenly able to do so with ease. For a lower back case, he used the corresponding ear points. For a twisted ankle, he used the "extra" sprain point on the forearm. They were all helped. They thought it was magic, but he told them he performs such "magic" every day – it is not a trick.

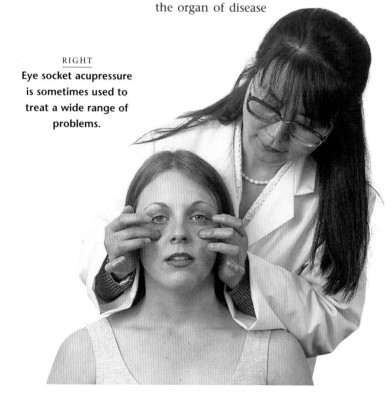

RIGHT
Eye socket acupressure is sometimes used to treat a wide range of problems.

THE IMPORTANCE OF DIRECTING THE QI

When using any technique, it is important to realize that we are directing the Qi to the needed area. Therefore, it can be helpful for the patient/experiencer to visualize what is taking place in order to better direct the Qi by placing attention on the area of concern. The healing thought is very powerful – when we think about something, the energy goes there.

In the practice of another related traditional Chinese healing art, Qi Gong, the power of thought is essential. It is sometimes combined with various forms of acupressure. For instance, a basic exercise involves rubbing the abdomen in a clockwise direction in the vicinity of the Dantian (about three finger-widths below the navel) while breathing slowly and completely and focusing on the area rubbed. (At the same time the tip of the tongue should rest on the top of the palate in order to complete the circuit of Qi in the body.) This exercise helps with menstrual cramps and other abdominal congestions, which are soothed away. Energy blockages are removed with such techniques, making the flow of Qi and blood smoother and therefore creating relief. As it is said in traditional Chinese medicine, the Qi goes where the mind goes, and the blood follows the Qi. In the West, we might say that the circulation improved.

The importance of a strong, directed flow of Qi can be seen in the fate of our leaders. When a president is in power, his Qi is strong – his opinion is sought, crises are coming at him and he has to respond, and he is bolstered in his power by a hive of supporters. So, no matter how bad things get, he carries on because his Qi is aroused and directed – he is strong and vital. However, when he later suddenly finds himself out of power, he often becomes a shadow of his former self – his Qi no longer supports him, and his apparently superhuman vitality collapses. The same thing can happen when we retire. When we are no longer engaged and needed, we can fall apart because our Qi fails and ceases to support us further. To maintain our health, and even our life itself, we should work less but never retire altogether.

Ageing and weakening are associated with chronic long-term problems. As we age, our store of Qi lessens and propensities for problems related to constitutional weaknesses or previous injuries grow. Our weaknesses are no longer covered by the naturally abundant Qi from which we benefitted in our youth. To continue to live well and in good health, we have to address this condition and strengthen our Qi, our vitality, and keep our Yin and Yang in balance.

SPECIFIC ACUPRESSURE TECHNIQUES

There are several major therapeutic techniques using manipulation of acupressure points to achieve results. Other techniques, as well as subcategories of these major techniques, abound. Clinically, the method used is selected according to the patient's condition. For instance, lower back pain is often treated using the "press and release" technique, which is especially good for relieving congestion and spasms in the muscles. Four of the most generally useful techniques are: 1 SUPERFICIAL RUBBING PRESSURE METHOD 2 PRESS AND RELEASE METHOD 3 TAPPING METHOD 4 MERIDIAN METHOD.

SUPERFICIAL RUBBING PRESSURE METHOD

In this technique a slight circular rubbing pressure is applied to a small area, ideally, about 0.5 mm (¹⁄₁₀ in) in diameter, in the centre of the point. The surface of the skin is only slightly depressed. The pressure is applied using the middle or index finger

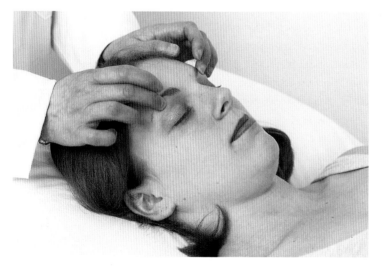

supported by the thumb, index or ring finger. Each depression and circular rub of the skin is counted as one time. Each point is usually massaged in this manner 50–100 times, according to the condition treated (more times for older or deeper condi-

tions; fewer times for newer or superficial conditions).

The patient should feel a sore, slightly numb sensation at the site of the pressure. This assures that the treatment will elicit a change in the internal organ with a corresponding increase in body function and improved resistance to forces that might cause an imbalance.

This technique is especially effective in promoting blood circulation, not just at the site of pressure but throughout the body. The pressure exerted is heavy or light, according to the situation. For a stronger or bigger person, or for an acute or new illness, the therapist uses stronger pressure, which is sedating. Conversely, for a weaker or smaller person, or for a chronic or long-term illness, the therapist uses lighter pressure, which is tonifying.

In general, the press and rub method is used to adjust the Yin and Yang imbalances in the channels. It is an excellent method by which to either tonify weaknesses or sedate excesses (resolve congestion) in order to balance the overall metabolism. Rubbing against the direction of the flow of the meridian is a sedating technique; rubbing with the direction of the flow of the meridian is a tonifying technique.

PRESS AND RELEASE METHOD

In this method, the therapist depresses the skin surface with the finger, pressing deeply into the underlying tissue. Then the deep pressure is released, while contact with the skin and a slight pressure is maintained. Each press-and-release sequence is counted as one time, with each point pressed 50–100 times depending on the condition treated (more times for older, deeper conditions; fewer times for newer, shallower conditions). The therapist presses perpendicularly into the middle of the point for strongest results, using the tip of the middle finger but not the fingernail.

In order to adjust the Yin and Yang with this method, the therapist can slightly angle the pressure on the point either with or against the flow of the meridian. Pressing with the flow tonifies by moving more substances more quickly through the channel. Pressing against the flow sedates by slowing the flow of Qi and other substances through the meridian.

Pressing deeply into the tissue makes the area contract and relax, while releasing the point causes expansion and excitement. Deeper pressure adjusts the Ying substances and shallower pressure affects the Wei.

This method of acupressure is most effective in controlling obvious symptoms of illness. It is commonly used to stop vomiting, relieve pain, reduce sweating and stop bleeding. It is also effective in resolving muscle "knots".

TAPPING METHOD

Using the middle finger and starting 2.5–5 cm (1–2 in) above the point, the therapist quickly taps the surface of the skin at the acupressure point. The pressure from this method is superficial and not deep. Usually each point is tapped 100 times.

This method creates friction and heat, and accelerates metabolism. It is most frequently used to tonify and strengthen the body. It aids the metabolism in dispersing cold and dissolving energy blockages. This method is especially helpful for pain caused by deficiency.

LEFT
Press-and-release method being used on the meridian points down the patient's back.

Warmth is the main property of moxibustion, a treatment method of Chinese medicine that uses a burning herb, moxa (mugwort leaves: *Artemesia vulgaris*), to apply heat to therapeutic points. The acupressure method is always safe for this purpose, while moxibustion has some contra-indications and must be used carefully by a skilled practitioner to avoid burns and their consequences.

The tapping method promotes specific tissue functions, especially the absorption of water. For instance, it is used to stop diarrhoea in children, when dangerous amounts of water can be lost through the stools.

Additionally, the tapping method is used to stop itching and disperse the effects of a common cold, particularly when the person has chills associated with the illness.

MERIDIAN METHOD

Usually the above three methods are adequate to provide therapeutic results. However, when the outcome is not satisfactory, one of the methods should be combined with the meridian method to balance the basic Yin and Yang of the body. Balancing Yin and Yang means that interior and exterior, cold and hot, deficiency and excess are brought into balance. A simpler way of understanding this is that the therapist tries to remove congestion (shi, excess) from an area or to restore its function from a weakened state (xu, deficiency).

The meridian method uses any of the first three methods to achieve results. The therapist uses the middle finger or thumb to move along the meridian, using the rubbing pressure, press and release, or tapping technique. This meridian method strongly affects the flow of substances in the meridians to adjust the Yin and Yang of the body.

In order to sedate or remove congestion, the therapist would move along the channel against the flow of substances in that channel, thereby reducing or slowing the flow. The therapist would tonify, or strengthen, by pressing along the meridian in the direction of the flow of the substances, thereby increasing the flow.

For example, the large intestine channel passes from the hand through the shoulder to the head. To strengthen the shoulder, the therapist would start by pressuring points in the hand, then move along the meridian in this fashion to the shoulder.

In actuality, the therapist will probably press both up and down the channels to get results. If a person has shoulder pain, it is probably caused by a combination of congestion and weakness. The acupressurist must use both sedation techniques (to reduce the congestion) and tonification techniques (to strengthen the weakness). The body will decide what it can use and will disregard irrelevant treatment. The body has a tendency to adjust itself, to achieve balance and homeostasis, whenever it can.

Using meridian theory, there are several ways to tonify and sedate. There are three Yang meridians in which the substances flow from the hands to the shoulder on both the left and right sides of the body. The therapist can follow this flow by pressing along the three channels from the hand to the shoulder, thereby enhancing the flow in these meridians. When there is weakness in the shoulder, this will strengthen the area.

If there is a general problem in an area, such as a headache involving the entire head, the acupressurist can use both hands simultaneously to press down, against the flow, along the three Yang hand meridians to relieve the congestion that is causing the pain.

THE MERIDIAN FLOWS

It is important to know the direction of the flow of substances in the meridians. Remember that pressing points with the direction of the channel flow tonifies the flow, whereas pressing points against the direction of the channel flow sedates the flow. The direction of the flows are as follows:

◆ In the three hand Yang meridians substances flow from the hands to the head.
◆ In the three hand Yin meridians substances flow from the internal organs of the chest to the hands.
◆ In the three foot Yang meridians the flow is from the head to the feet.
◆ In the three foot Yin meridians the flow is from the feet to the chest.
◆ In the Yin conception (Ren) meridian, which runs along the frontal midline, the flow is from the perineum (between the anus and scrotum or vulva) to the chin.
◆ In the Yang governing (Du) meridian, which runs along the posterior midline, the flow is from the tailbone to the upper lip.
NOTE: In both the conception and governing meridians, the direction of the flow is up the body.

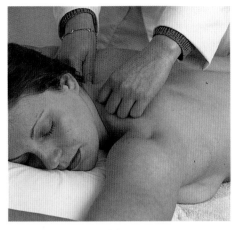

The therapist uses the middle finger or thumb to move along the meridian, using the rubbing pressure, press and release or tapping technique.

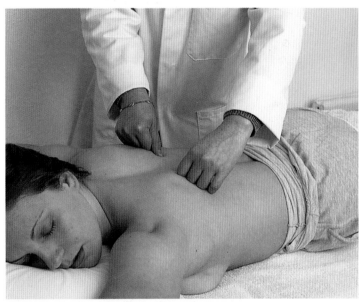

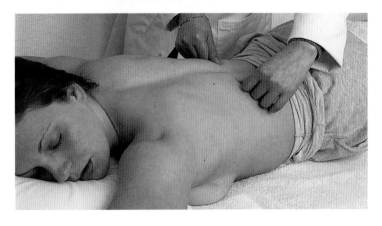

GUIDELINES

In order to treat different conditions in accordance with the principles of Yin and Yang, tonification and sedation and so on, various guidelines, rules and tips have evolved. Many conditions are a combination of congestion and weakness, requiring the therapist to use a combination of techniques to achieve balance.

ABOVE
Yang channel in
the hand.

◆ When more tonification than sedation is required, the acupressurist may tonify by pressing with the channel more times and pressing against the channel fewer times. If more sedation than tonification is needed, the therapist may sedate by pressing more times against the flow of the channel and fewer times with the flow of the channel. For instance, for shoulder pain that is due more to congestion than weakness, one might work down the hand Yang channels three times and up once to sedate the channel.

◆ As another rule, the therapist can press with the flow nine times to tonify or press against the flow six times to sedate.

◆ Another guideline suggests that, for men, better results occur when the meridians on the left side of the body are used first and then those on the right; for women, the right side would be treated first, then the left. This is because men are considered more Yang in general, and the left side is also considered more Yang, whereas women are considered more Yin in general, and the right side is also considered more Yin.

◆ A related idea is that work on the left side treats the Qi more and work on the right side treats the blood more.

◆ Other variations can be used to adjust Yin and Yang imbalance along with meridian therapy. For example, slow and heavy pressure on points sedates while quick and light pressure tonifies.

◆ The meridian method is frequently applied for persistent, hard-to-treat or serious imbalances. For example, it is commonly used to treat numbness and arthritic pain.

◆ In general, one doesn't have to use these particular techniques to get results. However, in serious cases one must follow this system to get satisfactory therapeutic effects.

OTHER TREATMENT METHODS AND TECHNIQUES

*A*nother general treatment method besides the four described above is the Five-Element method. In traditional Chinese medical theory, the internal organs reflect complex interactions between the elements of Wood, Fire, Earth, Metal and Water. There are four major patterns of interaction and a complex acupressure system that uses three methods of manipulation to restore balance to these patterns. It is beyond the scope of this chapter to describe this method in detail, but other methods are outlined.

There are many other acupressure treatment methods and techniques that apply to specific conditions:

◆ A pushing and spreading treatment on the face and head, pushing towards the back of the head, is used for headaches, dizziness, nausea and vomiting.

◆ Pressing the thumbs down along the thoracic spine is a sedation technique used to stop hiccups and vomiting. First the right side of the thoracic spine, along the urinary bladder meridian, is pressed from top to bottom, using lighter pressure at the top and heavier at the bottom; the procedure is then repeated on the left side.

◆ In a localized technique, one palm is pressed by the other into an area with a gentle shaking pressure. This method relieves pain and increases circulation. It is very good for the shoulder and for knee joint problems.

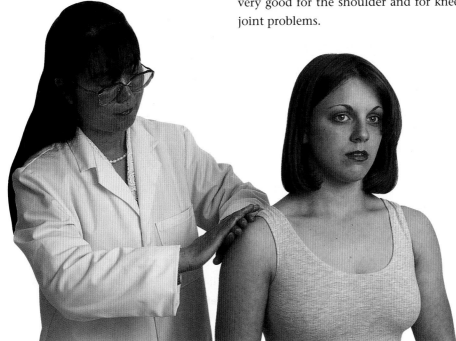

LEFT
In a localized technique, one palm is pressed by the other into an area with a gentle shaking pressure.

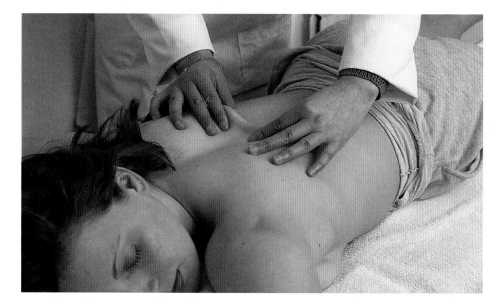

The pinching and pulling method is often employed to help increase blood circulation in the vicinity of a chronic ailment.

◆ A further technique uses pressure on points with a rapid side-to-side movement. In this technique, one presses deeply, stops, and then vibrates the area. This method is used for arthritis or general pain.

◆ Another technique uses a sharp jab with the thumb or another finger directly on a point to relieve congestion in the musculoskeletal system (soft tissue pain). The congestion is treated at a site away from the area affected. This method is usually done through the clothes as it is too painful when applied directly to the skin surface. Often the best points to use for this technique are Stomach 34 Liangqiu or Heart 8 Shaofu, depending on the general area affected, or the overall "extra" sprain point, Niushangxue (a tender point about 1 cm [½ in] lateral to Large Intestine 10 Shousanli) on the same side of the body as the pain.

◆ Other points on the hand (Heart 8), below the nose (Du 20 and on the foot (Kidney 1) are used as first-aid points in the case of fainting or loss of consciousness from injury.

◆ A method of pinching and pulling the local skin area, usually 100 times, is often employed to help increase blood circulation in the vicinity of a chronic ailment.

◆ In another method, the therapist applies pressure with both thumbs down along the cervical spine and then outward along the top of the shoulders to relieve neck stiffness and pain.

◆ A useful technique is to find and pressure tender points local to the site of an injury or problem. Such points are specific therapeutic points for relief whether or not they are known acupressure points or on meridians. They are called Ahshi ("Ahh! Good!" or "That's it!") points.

◆ As a final example of specific treatments for specific problems, the therapist can press with both thumbs downward along either side of the entire spine, excluding the neck region. This treatment can help reduce blood pressure.

Useful clinical and home acupressure treatments

T here are many patients who are apprehensive about needles and do not want acupuncture. For these people, acupressure is the perfect solution. The patient or a friend can learn how to use many of the points for home therapy. What follows are lists of useful treatments. Only the general location of the point is indicated. In order to find the point accurately, please seek professional guidance from a qualified practitioner.

Meridian treatment

First, it is helpful to know what meridians are effective for which general conditions. Sometimes one meridian will be more helpful than another when both theoretically affect the same area or problem; to find out which is best, one can simply test for the desired result. Sometimes a combination of points from different meridians is most effective. And sometimes the use of several techniques are called for. The best way of judging success is empirically and these techniques have repeatedly brought lessened pain, faster recovery and so on. This is an empirical system.

All the meridians can be used therapeutically, not only to treat the associated Zang Fu organ systems but also to help the areas that the meridian traverses. For instance, the lung meridian can also treat the arm, the stomach meridian the face, the urinary bladder meridian the back and so on.

Over the page is a list of the major meridians and the conditions they are commonly used to treat.

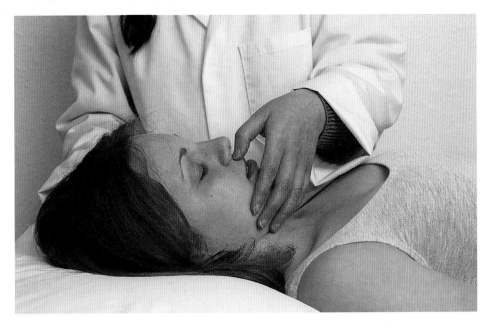

THE LUNG (LU) MERIDIAN
Treats asthma, coughs, skin rashes due to allergies and general lung problems.

THE STOMACH (ST) MERIDIAN
Treats leg problems, facial paralysis, nausea, vomiting and general stomach pains and problems.

THE HEART (H) MERIDIAN
Treats insomnia, mental problems, angina and palpitations.

THE URINARY BLADDER (UB)
Treats acute lower back pain, stiff neck and other cervical spine problems and urinary problems such as loss of bladder control.

THE PERICARDIUM (P) MERIDIAN
Treats nausea, emotional irritations such as anxiety or impatience and angina.

THE CONCEPTION MERIDIAN (REN)
Treats hernia and menstrual problems.

THE LIVER (LIV) MERIDIAN
Treats menstrual cramps, eye problems, headaches, insomnia, mental/emotional problems such as irritation and anger and high blood pressure.
The liver is the "General" in traditional Chinese medicine, ordering the smooth movement of Qi; when the liver Qi is stuck, emotional problems like anger and physical problems such as high blood pressure are the result.

THE SPLEEN (SP) MERIDIAN
Treats diarrhoea, menstrual irregularities, muscle pain and abdominal pain.

THE SMALL INTESTINE (SI)
Treats stiff neck and other cervical spine problems and chronic diarrhoea.

THE KIDNEY (K) MERIDIAN
Treats the lower back, asthma, bone pain, chronic nonspecific pain such as that caused by fibromyalgia, general weakness and ageing, stress and kidney disorders.
The kidney is the repository of constitutional energy in traditional Chinese medicine.

THE GALL BLADDER (GB) MERIDIAN
Treats migraine headaches, sciatica, pain in the ribs and gallstone pain.

THE LARGE INTESTINE (LI) MERIDIAN
Treats constipation, diarrhoea, headache and general lower intestinal problems.

THE GOVERNING MERIDIAN (DU)
Treats spinal problems such as stiffness and back pain.

THE TRIPLE WARMER (TW) MERIDIAN
Treats eye socket pain, eye problems, cheek pain, elbow pain and sweats.

EXAMPLES OF PRACTICAL POINTS

Another way to look at acupressure is to learn what each point does. In this way the therapist has flexibility over the points chosen to get results. The following examples of common practical points show the great variety of conditions that acupressure can treat. (English translations are included to show how the name of a point hints at its location, function or character.)

◆ **LI 4 HEGU ("ADJOINING VALLEYS")**
Hegu is used for elbow, groin and lower back pain, difficulty in raising the arm (shoulder complaints), sinusitis, dizziness, tinnitus, menstrual cramps, induction of labour and intestinal distress.

It also treats headaches, neck complaints, sinus problems, toothache, face and mouth problems and throat problems.
CAUTION: use of LI 4 Hegu is contra-indicated during pregnancy.

◆ **LI 5 YANGXI ("YANG CREEK")**
This point is used for an irregular heartbeat and also for palpitations.

◆ **TW 17 YIFENG ("SHIELDING WIND")**
This is good for hiccups.

◆ **P 6 NEIGUAN ("INTERNAL GATE")**
Neiguan is used for angina, irregular heartbeat, rapid heartbeat, travel sickness, insomnia, stomach spasms, knee pain, stiff neck and asthma. It is also used for most trunk problems, especially those of the Upper Jiao. It is another good point for hiccups. Neiguan is also a relaxation point.

◆ **EXTRA POINT NIUSHANGXUE ("SPRAIN POINT" – 1 CM (½ IN) LATERAL TO LI 10 SHOUSANLI**
This is an excellent first-aid point for all minor injuries and pain. It promotes circulation (moves Qi and blood), increases healing and relieves pain.
CAUTION: use of Niushangxue is contra-indicated when there is heavy bleeding.

◆ **ST 36 ZUSANLI ("THREE MILE WALKING")**
Zusanli is a very commonly used point for many problems, and helps strengthen the entire system. It can be used for a weak or distressed stomach and knee pain. It can also be helpful in long-term treatment for chest pain and heart trouble.

◆ **UB 57 CHENGSHAN ("SUPPORT THE MOUNTAIN")**
This point on the mid calf is excellent for muscle soreness and pain anywhere from overexertion, and for general overall aches as can occur from flu.

◆ **DU 14 DAZHUI ("BIG VERTEBRA")**
This point is good for relieving tailbone pain, as from a sports injury or accident. If this point is very tender, a medical check-up should be made to determine if the tailbone (or other bone) is broken.

◆ **LI 15 JIANYU ("SHOULDER BONE")**
These two points at either shoulder joint can be pressed for about five minutes before treatment in order to calm nervousness and relax the patient. It effectively drains emotional and physical trauma and stress from the body.

COMMON AILMENTS AND THEIR TREATMENT

*T*he practice of acupressure can also be approached through the ailment to be treated. For each type of condition there are some easy points upon which to apply acupressure for relief. Here are a few common ones:

LOW BACK PAIN AND SPINAL TROUBLE

BELOW

Treating low back pain and spinal trouble.

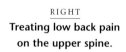

◆ **POINTS USED:** K 3 Taixi, UB 60 Kunlun. Apply pressure eight or nine times with a plucking motion to these two points, located between the Achilles tendon and the ankle. The points can also be flicked with the middle finger.

◆ **POINTS USED:** DU 14 Dazhui to DU 15 Yamen.
Find tender points between these two points on the upper spine and apply pressure. Press on your own neck and move pelvis in a circular motion at the same time.

◆ **ALSO ADD** UB 23 Shenshu.

◆ **EYE SOCKET POINTS USED:** Upper, Middle or Lower Jiao.

FINGER, TOE, HAND AND WRIST (CARPAL TUNNEL) PAIN

◆ **POINTS USED:** Extra Points:
Five Tiger Points (Wu Hu Shi)
Use thumbnail pressure on these points, which are located on each thumb, for pain relief. Grasp the thumb with the thumb and forefinger, using fingernail pressure between the first and second joints of the thumb on either side. Apply pressure with the fingernails and wiggle the affected fingers, hand, wrist or toes until pain subsides.

LIGAMENT TROUBLE

◆ **POINTS USED:** LI 13 Hand-WuLi.
Press and release this point for ligament trouble around any joints. Pinch the upper

RIGHT

Treating low back pain on the upper spine.

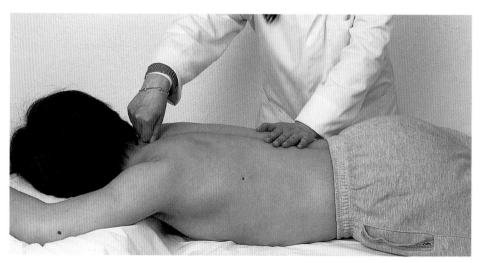

ABOVE

Point LI 4 Hegu can be used for treating colds, allergies, and headaches.

arm by holding these two points on either arm; press and release for two or three minutes or until the pain subsides. This is good for injuries such as a sprained knee. If the injury is more muscular, use UB 57 Chengshan.

PAIN ANYWHERE ALONG A MERIDIAN

◆ POINTS USED: Shu-Stream Points of the affected meridian – TW 3 Hand-Zhongzhu, SI 3 Houxi, UB 65 Shugu, ST 43 Xiangu, GB 41 Foot-Linqi, LI 3 Sanjian, LV 3 Taichong, H 7 Shenmen, SP 3 Taibai, LU 9 Taiyuan , K 3 Taixi and P 7 Daling.
Press and release the Shu-Stream Point associated with that meridian until the pain is gone.

MUSCLE PAIN

◆ POINTS USED: UB 57 Chengshan.
Use the main acupressure techniques on this point, located in the middle of the back of the calf, to relieve all types of muscle pain anywhere in the body. Press and release with the thumb until the pain is gone, usually in two or three minutes, on the same side of the body as the pain.

POOR DIGESTION

(With cold abdomen.)

◆ POINTS USED: rub the surface of the skin in a circular clockwise direction 300 times around the navel.
This technique strengthens the digestion and helps both diarrhoea and constipation. It is also good for chronic and general weakness. It warms the area around the Dantian and helps intestinal absorption, therefore promoting nutrition. It also helps the reproductive organs and the hormonal system and thus acts as an anti-ageing treatment. When the world moves too fast, we also age fast; this treatment helps to slow us down and add balance to our lives.
◆ EYE SOCKET POINTS USED: Upper Jiao, Middle Jiao, spleen and stomach.

DIARRHOEA

◆ POINTS USED: Teng's Points – the Extra Points Chang Men ("Door of the Intestines"), Gan Men ("Door of the Liver").

CHRONIC DIARRHOEA
◆ POINTS USED: add rubbing in a clockwise manner around the navel and DU 4 Mingmen on the back. Chronic diarrhoea is usually a sign of spleen and kidney deficiency and cold. Rubbing circles around the navel point and the point DU 4 Mingmen warms and tonifies the region.

ABOVE

Treating muscle pain with the point UB 57 Chengshan.

ADDITIONAL ACUPRESSURE TREATMENTS

These common but stubborn ailments can also be effectively treated with acupressure.

SHOULDER PAIN

And stiffness, restricting movement ("Forty-fifty shoulder").

◆ POINTS USED: the Jian or shoulder points are located in an arch around the shoulder: Extra Point Jianqian (also known as Jianneiling), LI 15 Jianyu, SI 9 Jianzhen, TW 14 Jianliao.

Using the press-and-release technique on tender points in a clockwise direction releases the shoulder so that the patient

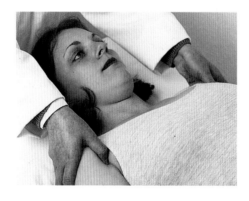

RIGHT
Treating a frozen shoulder.

can once again raise the arm.

◆ EYE SOCKET POINTS USED: Upper Jiao, large intestine, lung.

◆ Any locally tender Ahshi points may also be used.

HEMIPLEGIA

(Paralysis of one side of the body, whole or part.)

◆ POINTS USED: LI 3 Sanjian, LI 4 Hegu and LI 5 Yangxi as primary points. Also use LI 11 Quchi, GB 34 Yanglingquan, GB 39 Xuanzhong.

◆ Use points on the opposite side of the body from the hemiplegia.

◆ EYE SOCKET POINTS USED: Upper, Middle or Lower Jiao, depending on the area of the body affected.

COMMON COLD

FOR ALL COLDS

◆ POINTS USED: GB 20 Fengchi, LI 4 Hegu, ST 36 Zusanli.

FOR LUNG HEAT (FEVER AND SORE THROAT)

◆ POINTS USED: add ST 45 Lidui, P 6 Neiguan.

FOR CONSIDERABLE HEAT (FEVER)

◆ POINTS USED: add DU 14 Dazhui to clear heat from the Yang meridians and ST 36 Zusanli to bring the heat down and release it.

FOR HEAT CAUSING SORE THROAT, CONSTIPATION AND STRONGLY YELLOW URINE

◆ POINTS USED: add K 3 Taixi.

FOR A VERY BAD SORE THROAT

◆ POINTS USED: add Liv 3 Taichong.

◆ EYE SOCKET POINTS USED: Upper Jiao, lung.

INSOMNIA

There are three types of insomnia.

◆ **POINTS USED:** The "Four Gates" points Liv 3 Taichong and LI 4 Hegu are effective for each of the three types.

◆ **EYE SOCKET POINTS USED:** Upper, Middle and Lower Jiao; heart, kidney

1 INABILITY TO FALL ASLEEP

This is caused by liver Qi stagnation and is related to emotional congestion. The Four Gates points named above are the main treatment for this type of insomnia.

◆ **EYE SOCKET POINTS USED:** liver.

2 THE PATIENT FALLS ASLEEP BUT AWAKENS FREQUENTLY THROUGHOUT THE NIGHT AND EXPERIENCES MANY DREAMS

This is related to stomach trouble.

◆ **POINTS ADDED** to the Four Gates points ST 45 Lidui and SP 1 Yinbai.

◆ **EYE SOCKET POINTS USED:** stomach.

3 THE PATIENT FALLS ASLEEP AND AWAKENS ONCE IN THE NIGHT, USUALLY BETWEEN 3 AND 5 A.M., AND CAN'T GET BACK TO SLEEP

This is a common condition in the elderly and is related to kidney deficiency and high blood pressure.

◆ **POINTS ADDED:** UB 23 Shenshu, UB 52 Zhishi, K 3 Taixi and K 7 Fuliu.

◆ **EYE SOCKET POINTS USED:** kidney, urinary bladder.

CHRONIC BRONCHITIS

◆ **POINTS USED:** UB 12 Fengmen, UB 13 Fengshu, ST 36 Zusanli, LI 4 Hegu, P 6 Neiguan and the Extra Point for asthma (Dingchuan) located 1 cm (½ in) lateral to DU 14 Dazhui.

MUCUS

When the patient has a lot of mucus that can't be expelled.

◆ **POINTS USED:** carefully press REN 22 Tiantu and tap REN 17 Shanzhong in the middle of the chest.

◆ **EYE SOCKET POINTS USED:** Upper Jiao, lung.

BELOW
Treating a cold and/or headache.

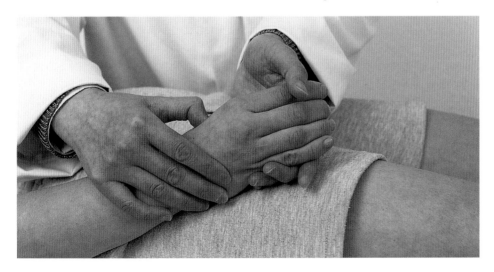

CHAPTER SIX

CHRONIC ACID INDIGESTION
With stomach or duodenal ulcer pain.

◆ POINTS USED: LI 4 Hegu, P 6 Neiguan, UB 21 Weishu, UB 20 Pishu, REN 12 Zhongwan, REN 6 Qihai, ST 25 Tianshu Extra Point Yin Tang (between the eyebrows).
◆ EYE SOCKET POINTS USED: Upper Jiao, Middle Jiao, spleen, stomach.
The patient should also use common sense and avoid fried and spicy foods.

CONSTIPATION

Constipation is often the result of a dry colon, with bowel movements occurring only every two to three days. The kidney controls the water function of the bowels and urinary tract.
◆ POINTS USED: K 6 Zhaohai and UB 57 Chengshan to adjust the Yin and Yang balance of the kidney and urinary bladder. This adjustment in turn moistens the colon.

TO ADJUST THE STOMACH AND INTESTINAL FUNCTIONS
◆ POINTS USED: add ST 36 Susanli, REN 12 Shenzhu and REN 6 Jizhong.

FOR HABITUAL, CHRONIC CONSTIPATION
◆ POINTS USED: add TW 6 Zhigou and be sure to use UB 57 Chengshan.
◆ EYE SOCKET POINTS USED: Middle Jiao.

MENSTRUAL CRAMPS

◆ POINTS USED: Most menstrual cramps can be relieved by acupressure on points ST

44 Neiting, SP 6 Sanyinjiao and LI 4 Hegu.
◆ EYE SOCKET POINTS USED: Middle Jiao, Lower Jiao, liver.

FREQUENT URINATION

Frequent urination is a sign of kidney deficiency.
◆ POINTS USED: Tap the points DU 4 Mingmen and DU 3 Yaoyangguan, then use pressure on K 7 Fuliu and SP 6 Sanyinjiao.
◆ EYE SOCKET POINTS USED: Kidney, liver.

ANGINA

This condition occurs commonly with ageing.
◆ POINTS USED: P 6 Neiguan, ST 36 Zusanli, and H7 Shenmen. On P 6 Neiguan, use the knuckle of the middle finger to apply careful and accurate pressure.
◆ EYE SOCKET POINTS USED: Upper Jiao, heart.

CANKER SORES

◆ POINTS USED: P 7 Daling and K 2 Ranggu.

MUCUS CONGESTION IN THE THROAT

For the condition in which the throat feels congested but the patient can't spit up mucus to clear the throat, the common diagnosis is liver Qi stagnation in which the emotions are stuck.
◆ POINTS USED: GB 34 Yanglingguan, LV 3 Taichong, K 3 Taixi, K 6 Zhaohai, REN 22 Tiantu and ST 40 Fenglong.

POST-TRAUMA FRIGHT

After trauma, many patients remain shaken and emotionally scattered. This is called "gall-bladder fright".
◆ POINTS USED: GB 34 Yanglingguan and LV 3 Taichong.

RECENT PHYSICAL TRAUMA

For pain at the site of new injuries, usually those less than 10 days old, a sharp jab at a tender point 1 cm (½ in) lateral to LI 10 Shousanli (Niushangxue), on the same side of the body as the pain, gives excellent relief.

HEADACHE

FOR ALL HEADACHES
◆ POINTS USED: GB 20 Fengchi, LI 4 Hegu and Extra Points Taiyang on the forehead and Yintang on the temples.

FOR HEADACHES CENTERED IN THE FOREHEAD
◆ POINTS USED: add SP 4 Gongsun, SP 9 Yinlingquan and DU 12 Zhongwan. For migraines add ST 8 Touwei, GB 41 Foot-Linqui and LU 7 Lieque.

FOR OCCIPITAL HEADACHES
◆ POINTS USED: press downwards from DU 16 Fengfu to DU 14 Dazhui and from GB 20 Fengchi to DU 14 Dazhui, and add UB 66 Foot-Tongu.

FOR SINUS HEADACHES
◆ POINTS USED: add the hand reflexology of pinching the tips of the fingers, especially the thumb and index finger.
◆ EYE SOCKET POINTS USED: Upper Jiao.

UPPER BACK TIGHTNESS

◆ POINTS USED: Use pressure on UB 10 Tianzhu, UB 40 Weizhong and TW 3 Hand-Zhongzhu.
◆ EYE SOCKET POINTS USED: Upper Jiao.

KNEE PAIN

◆ POINTS USED: ST 36 Zusanli, GB 34 Yanglingquan, GB 39 Xuanzhong, SP 9 Yinlingquan, SP 6 Sanyinjiao and LV 3 Taichong.

WRIST PAIN

◆ POINTS USED: GB 40 Quixu, ST 41 Jiexi and GB 34 Yanglingquan.

ABOVE
Treating a headache.

A PRACTICAL THERAPY

As you can see from all of the examples above, acupressure can be a very helpful therapy. Just as important, it is an eminently practical art. We can all easily learn a few points to help ourselves heal and to achieve better overall health. For the therapist, no tools are required other than some knowledge and sensitive fingers. Acupressure is so portable that it can be applied in just about any setting, whether it be on a plane to relieve anxiety and sinus problems or at work or home to loosen tired, tight muscles. Because of its powerful results and ease of use, we can expect acupressure to continue to be of great benefit to us for many centuries to come.

ACUPUNCTURE

針灸

cupuncture is a method of treatment that has been
practised for thousands of years in China and other Asian
countries, and is used as a means of treating and preventing
disease through the application of needles to the body. Although
introduced to the Western world about three centuries ago, it has gained
momentum only in the last few decades. While the debate over the
theories and usefulness of the treatment continues among medical
scientists, the popularity of acupuncture therapy has continued to grow
and it is now practised throughout the world. Benefits of acupuncture
include its effectiveness in healing a wide range of problems with few
side-effects, and its use in analgesia. Its low cost is attractive to both

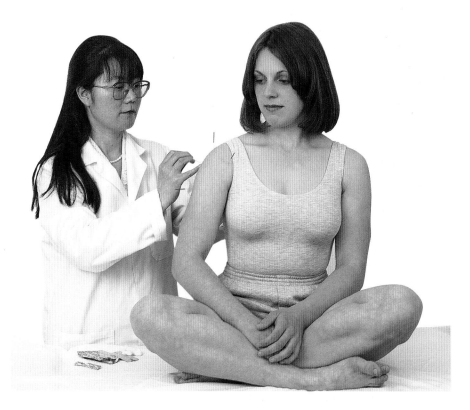

individual patients and large healthcare organizations.

Acupuncture itself is a very simple procedure administered by inserting very fine and thin needles into the acupoints along the different meridians, the pathways of energy. To achieve the best possible results, the method of treatment used and the selection of acupoints must be based on proper diagnosis and treatment principles, according to the theory of traditional Chinese medicine.

The practice of acupuncture began in ancient times in the very primitive stages of human history and, like all of the other components of traditional Chinese medicine, its techniques have undergone more than 5,000 years of refinement. The earliest known acupuncture instruments from the New Stone Age were stones with sharp edges, known as "bian". Science and technology have enabled us to continue to improve the quality of the acupuncture instruments from bone and bamboo needles to bronze and iron ones, and then to gold and silver. Now, prepackaged and

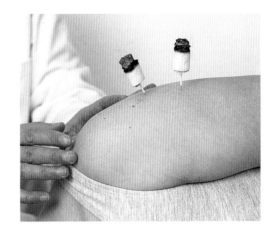

sterile stainless steel needles are commonly used. Just as the structure of the needles has been refined, so have the methods of application. One recent development has been to attach electrodes to the needles in order to conduct small amounts of electric current, increasing the stimulating effect of the treatment. The number of points on the body where acupuncture can be applied has also increased. Specific disciplines have developed within acupuncture and so, in addition to body acupuncture, a wide range of acupuncture therapies are now practised in many parts of the world, including ear needling, scalp acupuncture and hand acupuncture.

MOXIBUSTION

A long with acupuncture, the application of moxibustion is also used for treatment. *Moxa is the dried form of a herb more commonly known as mugwort, whose botanical name is* Artemisia vulgaris. *When applied to the acupoints, its warming and invigorating properties penetrate the skin and activate the channels. It was discovered after our ancestors discovered fire. At first they used heated rocks or hot sand, wrapped in animal skins or tree bark to form hot compresses. They then learned to ignite branches or hay to warm any parts of the body that were afflicted. This progressed to the various methods of moxibustion that we use today, from applying burning moxa directly to the skin to placing mediators between the moxa and the skin, to burning it on the handle of the acupuncture needle itself. A common form of moxa used today is the moxa stick, where the compressed moxa leaf is fashioned into the shape of a cigar. The end is lit and held above the skin to warm the acupuncture point or applied directly to the needle to help the body remove blockages of energy. Both acupuncture and moxibustion have a similar effect in removing blockages in the meridian pathways.*

HISTORY OF ACUPUNCTURE AND MOXIBUSTION

Recordings of acupuncture and moxibustion were seen as early as the Han Dynasty (202 BC–AD 220) in Chinese history. In an ancient tomb of that era, two silk scrolls describe the earliest outlook on the theory of meridians and collaterals (called "Jing Luo" in traditional Chinese medicine). The earliest known book on traditional Chinese medicine, *The Yellow Emperor's Canon of Internal Medicine*, is believed to have been compiled approximately 3,000 years ago. This book records the discussion of traditional Chinese medicine between the Yellow Emperor, who was one of China's most legendary rulers, reigning from 2696–2598 BC, and his minister, Qi Bo. It comprises two parts: *Simple Questions* and *Miraculous Pivot*. In *Miraculous Pivot*, acupuncture and moxibustion are systematically described in such detail that *The Classic of Acupuncture and Moxibustion.*

Throughout the centuries, studies of the theories and methods of acupuncture and moxibustion have continued to evolve. *The AB Classic of Acupuncture and Moxibustion* was written by Huang Pu Mi of the Jin Dynasty in the year AD 265. He recorded the location, indications, needling and manipulation techniques, contra-indications and cautions of 349 acupuncture points. He also recorded methods of treatment for common diseases using acupuncture and moxibustion.

Several hundred years later, these acupuncture points were further verified and illustrated. In AD 1026, during the Sung Dynasty, two life-size bronze figures were created for the education and examination of acupuncturists. Copies of the bronze figures can still be found on display at many acupuncture clinics and schools, but today live models and more detailed and accurate illustrations are also used.

During the sixth century, acupuncture was introduced to Korea and Japan, and during the seventeenth century it was introduced to Europe. However, it was not until the 1950s and 1960s that these practices were brought to Africa, and in 1975 it became legal to practise it in the United States. Just recently, due to the public's awareness of the benefits of acupuncture and the accelerating costs of healthcare in the US, more people are looking to this very different approach to medicine, which has withstood the trials of clinical practice for thousands of years. Interest in these practices and their results is attracting medical scientists and medical practitioners from all over the world. Modern science and technology are giving new life to this ancient form of treatment, and, as a result, more people will be able to benefit from its wisdom.

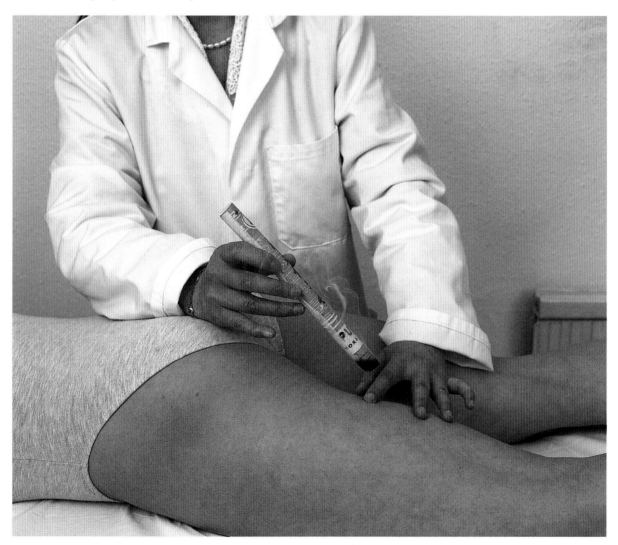

THE MERIDIAN AND COLLATERAL THEORY

The meridian and collateral theory is one of the foundations of traditional Chinese medicine, along with the theories of Yin and Yang, the Five Elements the organ systems, Qi and blood. It iplays an important role in maintaining a holistic approach to understanding human physiology and recognizing and diagnosing the causes of disease.

The meridian and collateral system consists of the meridians and collaterals whose internal pathways connect to the internal organs and whose exterior pathways connect to the surface of the body. The meridians and collaterals are the pathways through which the Qi and blood flow in our body, serving as communication lines that connect our body so that it forms an organic whole.

MERIDIANS

The main trunks in this system are the meridians, which run vertically along clearly defined pathways that begin to flow near the surface of the body, but eventually travel deep inside the body. The main meridians include the 12 regular meridians and the eight extra meridians.

THE REGULAR MERIDIANS

The 12 regular meridians are divided into six Yin channels and six Yang channels. The six Yang channels are further divided into pairings referred to as the Yang Ming, Tai Yang and Shao Yang. The six Yin channels are paired into the Tai Yin, Shao Yin and Jue Yin. These are distributed symmetrically on both sides of the body, with one of each category running along the upper limbs and one of each along the lower limbs, as well as along the back and sides of the trunk. Each of these 12 channels relates to an organ. Each of the 12 regular meridians flows to an internal organ (see table).

THE EIGHT EXTRA CHANNELS

These are in addition to the 12 regular meridians, and they are often called the extraordinary vessels. They include:

◆ The Conception vessel
◆ The Governing vessel
◆ The Penetrating vessel
◆ The Girdle vessel
◆ The Yin and Yang regulating vessels
◆ The Yin and Yang motility vessels.

These pathways act as reservoirs of Qi, blood and essence, which are drawn upon by the 12 regular channels when needed. They can also serve as receptacles for excess Qi and blood when the regular channels are full, allowing them to overflow into these vessels. These channels are closely linked with the kidneys and therefore circulate the essence which is stored in the kidneys.

COLLATERALS

The collaterals are smaller and thinner branches of the meridians, which run hor-

YIN AND YANG CHANNELS

◆ **THREE YIN CHANNELS OF THE HAND**

The hand Taiyin: lung channel

The hand Shao Yin: heart channel

The hand Jue Yin: pericardium channel

◆ **THREE YIN CHANNELS OF THE FOOT**

The foot Tai Yin: spleen channel

The foot Shao Yin: kidney channel

The foot Jue Yin: liver channel

◆ **THREE YANG CHANNELS OF THE HAND**

The hand Tai Yang: small intestine channel

The hand Yang Ming: large intestine channel

The hand Shao Yang: triple warmer channel

◆ **THREE YANG CHANNELS OF THE FOOT**

The foot Tai Yang: urinary bladder channel

The foot Yang Ming: stomach channel

The foot Shao Yang: gall-bladder channel

---

izontally and obliquely across the body and are distributed more superficially.

CONNECTING THE BODY

The meridians and collaterals connect the whole body, from the internal organs to the sensory organs, the orifices, the muscles and tendons, the skin and hair, the bones and vessels of the brain and the tissues of the body. Through these connections, the body becomes an integrated and unified organic whole. When the flow of Qi and blood is adequate, the body is capable of maintaining coordination and unification between its different parts and different functions.

Because of the interconnectedness of the body, the meridians and collaterals are able to reflect changes on the surface tissues, the organs and the sensory organs. Changes such as tenderness, numbness and pain when we are injured indicate damage to the skin, ligaments, tendons, muscles, nerves or bones. Sometimes, these symptoms occur on or along the region where the meridians and collaterals are distributed and indicate an abnormality in the internal organ system. For example, tenderness in the abdominal region can indicate abnormalities in the digestive system. However, because the meridians and collaterals of the spleen and stomach, which are the organs that are mainly related to the digestive system in traditional Chinese medicine, run along the anterior and medial aspect of the legs, we often find tenderness on the lower leg along these meridians.

Tenderness may also be found at points on the back that are related to the affected organs. In the book *Miraculous Axis,* it states that "when the pathogenic evil is in the lungs, its Qi is contained [stagnated] in the elbows; when there is pathogenic evil in the liver, its Qi is

RIGHT
This early Chinese medical figure shows some of the body's acupuncture points and the invisible meridians.

ZANG AND FU ORGANS

According to traditional Chinese medicine, the visceral organs of the body are categorized as the Zang (solid) organs or the Fu (hollow) organs. The Zang organs are the heart, the lungs, the spleen, the liver and the kidneys. The function of these organs is to transform and store Qi and the essence.

The Fu organs are the small intestines, the large intestines, the stomach, the gall-bladder and the urinary bladder. Their function is to process food and transport waste.

Each Zang organ, being more internal, has a paired relationship with one of the Fu organs, which are more external, and this connects the organs and their channels to one another

internally and superficially. For example, the hand Tai Yang meridian is related to the lungs and connected to the large intestines. The hand Yang Ming large intestine meridian is related to the large intestine and connected to the lungs.

The continuous flow of the meridians, and the criss-crossing of the meridians and collaterals, establishes relationships between other organs and so forms a very intricate and complicated connection between all the organs. For instance, the hand Yang Ming large intestine meridian flows into the foot Yang Ming stomach meridian, which is not only related to the foot Tai Yin spleen meridian, but is also directly connected with the heart.

contained in the armpit, pathogenic evil in the spleen, its Qi is contained in the thighs, and pathogenic evil in the kidneys, its Qi is contained in the knees."

The meridians and collaterals function to transport Qi and blood, which provide nutrition, warmth and a material base to nurture the interior and protect the exterior of the body. This helps the body to resist exogenous pathogens. There is a common saying in Chinese medicine that "Qi is the commander of blood, blood is the envoy of Qi." The main force here is the Qi, which helps the blood flow, and the blood also carries the Qi as it flows. The traditional theory is that this circulation and flow of Qi and blood follows a certain

direction or sequence in the body and the Yin and Yang meridians connect with each other by the starting and ending points of each meridian. According to the *Miraculous Pivot*, the three Yin meridians of the hand run from the organs to the hands, and the three Yang meridians of the hand run from the hands to the head. The three Yang meridians of the feet run from the head to the feet, and the three Yin meridians of the feet run from the feet to the abdomen.

TYPES OF QI

Traditional Chinese medicine maintains that there are different types of Qi in our bodies, which vary in their location and function. These include:

◆ The Ying Qi (or nutrient Qi)
◆ The Wei Qi (or defensive Qi)
◆ The Zong Qi (or ancestral Qi)
◆ The Yuan Qi (or primary Qi)

All these different kinds of Qi are related to the flow of Qi in the meridians. The Ying Qi and Wei Qi circulate in the body following the pathways of the meridians and collaterals.

THE YING QI

This is derived from the essences of the foods that we eat and is a vital ingredient in our blood. It circulates inside the meridians and vessels and follows a certain route between the Yin and Yang meridians. This is as shown in the table (below left).

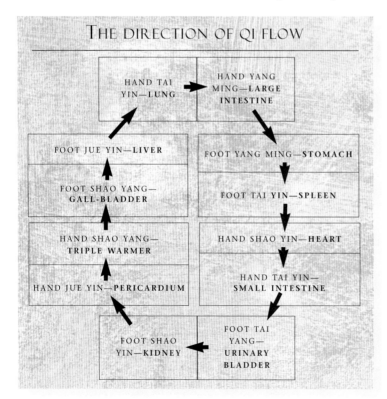

THE DIRECTION OF QI FLOW

THE WEI QI

This is also derived from the essences of foods. It is fierce by nature and has a very strong ability to spread and permeate into large areas, travelling not only inside the meridians and vessels but also spreading to the surrounding tissues. Because it is so strong and uncontrollable, the vessels cannot restrict it within its boundaries and the Wei Qi flows simultaneously into the skin and muscle of the body, moving from the head to the extremities, through the meeting and criss-crossing of the meridians and collaterals back to the head again. During the day, the Wei Qi is distributed on the surface of our body (on the face, the head, the trunk and the limbs) whereas at night it is stored and flows inside the cavities and organs of the body.

THE ZONG QI

This is the force that gives impetus to the meridians' and collaterals' ability to transport and circulate the Qi and blood. The Zong Qi is the combination of the essences from the foods we eat and the natural Qi that we inhale from the air, and it is stored inside our chest. It fills the heart vessels and energizes the blood.

THE YUAN QI

This is the Qi that is stored in our kidneys. According to traditional Chinese medicine, the kidney essence is the material source of all vital activities. The kidney Qi is the basis of our supply of the energy needed for the function of all our vital activities which, of course, includes the meridian and collateral functions.

RELATIONSHIP BETWEEN YIN AND YANG ORGANS

To comprehend the function of the meridians and collaterals further, we need to understand another theory of traditional Chinese medicine – the organ phenomenon theory. The organs and their associated meridians are categorized as Yin or Yang. The Yin organs are the heart, the lungs, the spleen, the liver and the kidneys. The Yin organs are solid and their function is to transform and store the essence and the Qi. The Yang organs are the small intestine, the large intestine, the stomach, the gall-bladder and the urinary bladder. The Yang organs are hollow and their functions are to decompose food and to pass on the wastes. The pericardium (see page 193) and the Triple Heater, also known as the Triple Burner or Triple Warmer, are not considered organs but functions, and are categorized as Yin and Yang respectively. The pericardium is the protector of the heart and the Triple Warmer relates to the upper chest, the diaphragm and the abdomen.

There are mutual relationships between the Yin and Yang organs, and each Yin organ is related to a Yang organ both superficially and internally.

The organ theory maintains that the body tissues and sensory organs are each related to an internal organ.

◆ THE HEART, which is related to the small intestines, opens into the tongue and is in charge of the vessels. The condition of the heart is reflected in the face.

◆ THE LUNGS, which are related to the large intestine, open into the nose and manifest in the skin and hair. The condition of the lungs is reflected in the skin and body hair.

◆ THE SPLEEN, which is related to the stomach, opens into the mouth and controls the muscles and limbs. The condition of the spleen is reflected in the lips.

◆ THE LIVER, which is related to the gall-bladder, opens into the eyes and is in charge of the ligaments. The condition of the liver is reflected in the nails.

◆ THE KIDNEYS, which are related to the urinary bladder, open into the ears and the two lower orifices (meaning the opening of the urethra and the anus) and are in charge of the bones. The condition of the kidneys is reflected in the hair on the head.

The dysfunction of an internal organ could also affect another internal organ through communication from the meridians and collaterals. One example is that irritability is sometimes caused by a condition of stagnated liver Qi. Some cases affect the stomach, which tends to cause hunger brought on by excessive Liver Fire. Some relieve it by over-eating. The opposite condition may occur when the Liver encroaches on the Spleen, which causes a loss of appetite.

For example, when the liver is sick, we might see symptoms related to the liver itself, but also to the organs that are related to the liver. For instance, the stomach and gall-bladder can cause nausea, stomach pains, pains on the thighs and jaundice. The tissues that are related to the liver may become affected, resulting in fragile nails, tremors or muscle spasms. The sensory organs that are related to the liver are the eyes. Therefore, redness, dryness of the eyes or vision impairment may result. Finally, the regions of the liver meridian may be affected, manifesting as inguinal hernia (of the groin area), ovary or breast problems, vertigo or headaches.

Sometimes, a problem in the internal organs will manifest itself in the sensory organs. For example, when we see a person who complains of ringing in the ears or who has a hearing impairment, we would consider the possibility of kidney deficiency because the kidneys are related to the ears.

Diseases of the internal organs often manifest on the exterior of the body as skin changes. For example, a purplish colour on the face and lips can be due to lack of oxygen from heart problems. Yellow colouring can appear in the eyes when a person has jaundice from liver disease.

Pathologically, the meridians and collaterals are pathways for the transmission of diseases. Exogenous pathogens usually invade the surface of the body and venture deeper into our body through the meridians and collaterals, causing damage to the body tissues or even the internal organs. For example, when we catch a cold, we start by feeling cold (on the skin). Then we start to sniffle as the nose drips into the ori-

fice) and a cough may develop if the problem goes a little deeper (affecting the lungs, which are internal organs). If not taken care of, we could develop bronchitis or even pneumonia if the body is weak.

In clinical practice, the application of meridian and collateral theory can be used to diagnose disease by recognizing the location and pattern of the meridians. For example, pain on the flanks of the body is usually related to liver or gall-bladder diseases because the liver and gall-bladder meridians are located along the side of the body. Headache pain can be located in different areas of the head and related to the meridian located in that region. Frontal headaches are related to the Yang Ming Meridian, while temporal headaches are related to the Shao Yang meridian. In traditional Chinese medicine, the treatment of a disease, including the use of herbs, is administered in relation to the location and pathology of the disease in the meridians. This is especially true in acupuncture and moxibustion. The needles and moxa are applied to the acupoints along the chosen meridian to regulate the Qi and blood of the affected organs or tissues through their related meridians, restoring normal flow and physiological functions to the organs and tissues, thereby reestablishing harmony within the body.

The theory of communication between the internal organs is one of the advantages of traditional Chinese medicine, providing the practitioner with the ability to recognize a patient's condition and to anticipate what it could become. Precautions are taken during the treatment process not only to treat the whole body but also to prevent further complications of the condition.

MERIDIAN AND COLLATERAL THEORY

"The meridians and collaterals can determine death and life, place a hundred diseases and regulate the deficient and the excess, so this cannot afford to be blocked." This quotation from *The Miraculous Pivot* clearly states the important role that meridian and collateral theory occupies in the practice of traditional Chinese medicine.

Acupuncture Diagnostics

To correctly diagnose conditions, a complete understanding of the patient and the patient's illness is required. There are four diagnostic methods used in traditional Chinese medicine to collect this information. They include observation (seeing), olfaction (smelling), interrogation and auscultation (hearing) and palpation (touching).

OBSERVATION

The sense of sight is used to take note of the patient's general appearance, including vigour, stance, colour of the facial complexion and the movements and responses of the patient. Also observed is the condition of the hair, eyes, nose, ears, lips, teeth, skin – and especially the tongue. In traditional Chinese medicine, the appearance, colour, condition and movements of the tongue body and the coating on the tongue all have great significance. They help in identifying the condition of the patient's Qi and blood, the changes and the location of the pathology that the patient may be experiencing and in recording the progress of a disease.

OLFACTION

This is the diagnostic tool that involves detecting odours emitted by the patient's body. The sense of smell is used to detect particular disease states by odours emanating from the patient's body.

QUESTIONING AND AUSCULTATION

Questioning the patient or their relatives employs the sense of hearing. General information is requested, such as age, address, occupation, marital status and personal and family health histories. Then more specific information is requested about the present illness, such as the date of onset, duration, location and symptoms. The practitioner is also interested in how the patient has been treated before and what the results have been. Listening is involved in order to differentiate pathological aberrations of the patient's pattern of speech, sound of voice, breathing, coughs, hiccups, belching, sighs or any other sounds.

PALPATION

The sense of touch is used by feeling various areas on the surface of the body, including the patient's pulse, in order to identify signs and symptoms. Palpation of the body can include the pulses, the skin, the extremities, the abdomen and the trigger/sensitive points. While the integration of these four diagnostic methods is important in determining a correct diagnosis, pulse diagnosis is the most essential in discovering the condition of the patient's Qi and blood, and the physiological and pathological condition of the internal organ systems.

The pulse is most commonly taken on the radial artery at the wrists. The index, middle and ring fingers apply pressure, each fingertip feeling the condition of a Yin/Zang organ and its affiliated Yang/Fu organ. Pressure is applied at three levels (deep, intermediate and superficial) and from the strength, rhythm, speed and character of the pulses, pathological conditions are recognized. There are about 28 different characteristics of pulses that are commonly felt, each indicating a different state of physiology or pathology. The pulses can be affected by factors such as seasons, time of day, temperature of the room and whether it is taken before or after meals and physical exertions. Pregnancy or menstrual cycles can also affect women's pulses.

In the diagnostic process it is most important to determine the cause of the problem and treat the cause, not the symptom. For example, a patient who has pain in the chest should be evaluated using the four diagnostic principles outlined above to determine the cause of the pain before treatment begins. According to traditional Chinese medicine, the cause could be due to blockage of energy in the stomach, gallbladder or heart meridians.

BELOW
The patient's pulse is most commonly taken on the radial artery at the wrists.

Acupuncture Treatment

*A*cupuncture requires precise placement and manipulation of the needles for the most effective treatment. Diagnosis and the treatment theory of traditional Chinese medicine determine the acupoints to be treated and the correct way of applying the needles.

Acupoints

The acupoints and meridians together form the foundation for acupuncture and moxibustion treatments. Acupoints are not only the stimulation points on the meridians but they are also points that are reactive in a disease. Acupoints are the small areas of the skin – described as vortexes of energy – that show a marked difference in electrical potential from other areas of the skin. They are identifiable with Galvinometric measurement. Acupoints can become sensitive to touch when disease is present and are therefore useful in diagnosis. They are also called reactive points, sensitive points or trigger points. The reactions can vary from localized, subjective pain to tenderness, sensitivity, colour changes of the skin or reduced electro-resistance of the tissues upon examination.

In general, acupoints are categorized into three types:
- The meridian points.
- The Extra points.
- The "Ah-shi" or "ouch" points.

The Extra points were discovered later and they supplement the meridian points. The "Ah-shi" points are supplemental to the Extra points. These are areas that are sensitive when they are palpated, but are not on the meridians and are not Extra points. The sensitivity can be anything from tenderness to sensations of pain or distension.

The meridian points

These are located along the meridians and are symmetrical on both sides of the body except for the ones that are along the midline of the body. Depending on the length of the meridians, there are different numbers of acupoints are located along the routes of the meridians. These points are mainly indicated for conditions that relate to the organ to which this meridian is linked, or for conditions relating to tissues or sensory organs where the meridian is distributed.

The lung meridian

This has 11 acupoints, which are distributed along the medial side of the arm and hand, but the meridian itself starts from the abdomen and runs upwards through the lungs to the throat and then down the medial aspect of the arm to the medial side of the thumb. So the points indicated on the meridian are used to treat problems of the chest and lungs, such as an oppressed sensation in the chest, chest pain, cough, asthma, sore throat, pain on the lateral side of the arm and shoulder pain.

THE LARGE INTESTINE MERIDIAN

This has 20 points, distributed along the anterior and anterior lateral aspect of the arm, the shoulder, the neck and the face, and are used for treating toothaches, sore throats, dry mouth, pain of the anterior aspect of the arm and pain or immobility of the shoulder.

THE STOMACH MERIDIAN

This meridian has 45 points, distributed along the anterior aspect of the legs, the abdomen, the chest and the face. The points are indicated for gastrointestinal problems, toothaches, headaches, sore throat, mental disturbances related to febrile diseases and pains and other problems along the course of the meridian.

THE SPLEEN MERIDIAN

This has 21 points, distributed along the anterior medial aspect of the leg and the abdomen and chest. They are indicated for conditions of the spleen and stomach, gynaecological disorders and other pains and conditions along the

route of the meridian.

THE HEART MERIDIAN

This has nine points, distributed along the middle of the medial aspect of the arm and chest, and they treat mental illnesses, diseases of the heart and chest and other pains and problems along its course.

THE SMALL INTESTINE MERIDIAN

This has 19 points along the posterior aspect on the medial side of the arm, the shoulder, the side of the face and around the ears and eyes. The points are used for treating ear, eye and throat problems, pain and stiffness in the neck and jaw and pain of the shoulder and arms.

THE URINARY BLADDER MERIDIAN

This has 67 points, distributed from the inner corner of the eye to the top of the head, then back down the back of the head, neck, back and the back of the legs to the lateral aspect of the foot, ending at the lateral side of the tip of the little toe. They are used to treat disorders of the head, neck, eyes, lumbar region and legs.

THE KIDNEY MERIDIAN

This has 27 points that run from the medial aspect of the foot, then up from the ankle along the posterior medial aspect of the legs to the abdomen, chest and throa, ending at the root of the tongue. The points on this meridian are indicated for treatments of the kidney, lung, throat and other conditions in the regions along the course of the meridian.

THE PERICARDIUM MERIDIAN

This meridian runs from the chest to the armpit, and then along the middle of the medial aspect of the arm to the middle finger. It has nine points, used for treating conditions of the heart, chest and stomach, as well as mental disorders and problems in the regions along the meridian.

THE TRIPLE WARMER MERIDIAN

This has 23 points, distributed along the middle of the lateral aspect of the arm, to the shoulder, neck, around the ear, and to the outer canthus (outer corner, where upper and lower lids meet) of the eye. The points are indicated for treating earache, hearing loss and pain in the jaw, around the ear, or in the shoulder, as well as in the forearm or ring and little fingers.

THE GALL-BLADDER MERIDIAN

This starts from the outer canthus of the eye, and its 44 points are distributed from the top of the head to the back of the head and neck, across to the shoulder, down the side of the trunk and leg, to the lateral side of the back of the foot. with some points around the side of the face behind the ear and on the side of the neck. The points are indicated for problems of the head, ears, and throat and for psychological disorders and other problems in the regions along the course of the meridian.

THE LIVER MERIDIAN

This has 14 points, distributed from the medial side of the tip of the big toe along the medial side of the back of the foot and up the medial side of the leg, around the genital region, up the front of the abdomen into the chest. The points on this meridian are indicated for liver problems, gynaecological disorders, diseases in the genital region and problems in the regions along the course of the meridian.

LEFT
The urinary bladder, kidney, gall-bladder and liver meridians all pass through the foot.

CHAPTER SEVEN

ACUPOINTS AND THEIR LOCATION

With the increase of acupuncture practice in recent decades more acupoints have been discovered. These are usually the result of the integration of traditional Chinese medicine and modern Western medical science, based on the meridian and collateral theories but guided by the knowledge of modern anatomy and human physiology. Some of these new acupoints include those that are located along the nerve trunks or in areas where the nerve endings are dense. The search for sensitivity is very important in the location of acupoints. Acupoints are often found in areas near joints or muscles that are sensitive when pressed with a finger.

The use of the anatomical structures of our joints and muscles as landmarks is one of the methods employed to locate acupoints. Most acupoints used in treatment are on the arms and legs.

Marks created through movements of the body, such as the creases, spaces or depressions that appear from voluntary movements of the joints, muscles or skin are also used in point location. Point LI-11, for example, is found at the lateral end of the crease in the elbow when flexing the arm. In areas where the anatomical structures of the body are not prevalent, other methods are also applied.

MEASURING METHODS
One measuring method involves using

RIGHT
The width across the span of the four fingers as they are held together is measured as three cun.

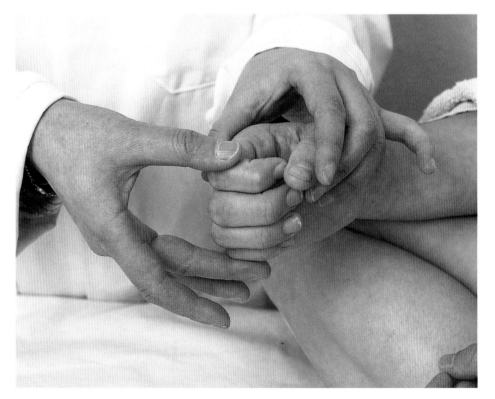

ACUPUNCTURE NEEDLES

Traditionally, there are nine types of acupuncture needle. Most commonly used is the metal filiform needle, made from silver, gold or stainless steel. The needles come in different gauges and lengths to accommodate the different areas of the body where they are to be inserted. The majority of needles used today are pre-sterilized and disposable. Apart from the filiform needles, there are other types of needle that are less commonly used in clinical practice.

THE THREE-EDGED NEEDLE
A needle with a thick and round handle, triangular body and sharp tip is used for bleeding that is achieved by pricking superficial blood vessels. The treatment is mostly used for blood letting and improving the flow of Qi and Blood in the meridians, and is indicated for severe blood stasis, pathogenic excesses, or Qi stagnation.

PLUM FLOWER NEEDLE
Another type of needle used is the plum flower needle, or seven star needle. A group of seven needles are arranged together in the shape of a flower and attached like a hammer head to a handle that is usually made of plastic or wood. The needling is done by tapping the needles on the skin lightly and swiftly and it is applied to a larger area on the skin, usually on the back and along the spine. This method can be used for any disease, but it is especially effective in treating headaches, hypertension, intercostal neuralgia and neurotic dermatitis.

SUBCUTANEOUS NEEDLES
For chronic pain and for treating addictions, subcutaneous needles are often used. These are very small, short needles that are embedded superficially under the skin, most often on the ears.

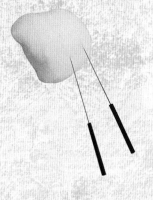

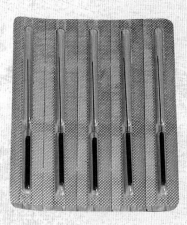

the length and width of the patient's finger as a standard of measurement for locating points. The length of the middle joint of the middle finger is measured as one "cun" (about 2 cm/1 in), as is the width of the second joint of the thumb. This measuring method is often used to locate points on the vertical length of the limbs. The width across the span of the four fingers as they are held together is measured as three cun, while the width of the index and middle fingers held in the same way is measured as one-and-a-half cun. St 36 is located four finger widths (or three cun) below the lateral side of the lower border of the patella and one thumb width on the lateral side of the margin of the tibia.

Another method of measurement used is proportional measurement. This method establishes the distance between different bone segments or certain regions of the body into a set number of cun. As the height and width of each person varies, the length of the cun may vary between individuals, yet the number of

cun is the same for a given location for every person. The distance between elbow and wrist is 12 cun, the distance between the navel and the pubic bone is 5 cun, while the distance between the navel and the apex of the sternum is 8 cun. If we measure it with a ruler, we find that the one cun in the lower abdomen is actually longer than the one cun in the upper abdomen. Proportional measurement is a basic principle in the locating of acupoints, widely used in locating points on the limbs and the trunk of the body.

Depending on the length of the meridians, there are different numbers of acupoints located along the routes of the meridians. These points are mainly indicated for conditions connected to the organ that is related to that meridian, or for conditions relating to tissues or sensory organs where the meridian in question is distributed. The chart on page 197 outlines the meridians, their distribution on the body and their indications for treatment according to meridian theory.

OTHER TYPES OF ACUPUNCTURE

Besides the body needling that is generally used and commonly practised, there are also other types of acupuncture. Needles may be applied to certain parts of the body that can be viewed as microcosms of the whole body.

◆ AURICULAR THERAPY
Needles are applied to various points on the ear to treat all kinds of diseases

◆ SCALP ACUPUNCTURE
In this type of acupuncture, the scalp is divided into different regions of the body and needles are applied in the region to treat relevant diseases

THE DISTRIBUTION OF MERIDIANS AND THEIR INDICATIONS FOR TREATMENT

CHANNEL	CHANNEL DISTRIBUTION	SYMPTOMS
Lung	Along the medial side of the arm and hand to the chest	Chest pain, cough, asthma, sore throat, pain in the lateral arm and shoulder
Large intestine	Along the anterior and anterior lateral aspect of the arm, shoulder, neck and face	Toothache, sore throat, dry mouth, pain of the anterior aspect of the arm and shoulder immobility
Stomach	Along the anterior aspect of the legs, abdomen, chest and the face	Gastrointestinal problems, facial paralysis, toothaches, headaches, sore throat, mental disturbances related to febrile disease, pain along the channel
Spleen	Along the anterior medial aspect of the leg and the abdomen and chest	Gastrointestinal disorders, gynaecological problems, pain along the meridian
Heart	Along the middle of the medial aspect of the arm	Diseases of the heart and chest, mental illness, pain along the channel
Small intestine	Along the posterior aspect on the medial side of the arm, shoulder, side of the face and around the ears and eyes	Ear, eye and throat problems, pain and stiffness of the neck and jaw, pain in the shoulders and arms
Urinary bladder	From the inner canthus of the eye to the top of the head, back down the head, neck, back and the back of the legs to the lateral aspect of the foot	Disorders of the head, neck, eyes, lumbar region and the legs
Kidney	From the medial aspect of the legs to the abdomen, the chest and the throat, ending at the root of the tongue	Conditions of the kidney, lung and throat and problems along the course of the channel
Pericardium	From the chest to the armpit, along the medial aspect of the arm to the middle finger	Conditions of the heart, chest and stomach and for mental disorders and problems along the course of the channel
Triple warmer	Along the middle of the lateral aspect of the arm, to the shoulder and neck, and around the ear to the outer canthus of the eye	Earaches, hearing loss, pain of the jaw, the ear, shoulder, forearm or ring and little fingers
Gall-bladder	From the outer canthus of the eye to the top of the head, down the back of the head and neck to the shoulder, down the side of the trunk and leg to the lateral side of foot	Problems of the head, ear, eye, the throat, psychological disorders and other problems along the channel' course
Liver	From the medial side of the big toe to the back of the foot, up the medial aspect of the leg, around the genital region, to the abdomen and the chest	Liver problems, gynaecological disorders, diseases in the genital region, and problems along the course of the meridian

Terms used: Anterior: Front Posterior: Rear Lateral: Side Aspect: Edge Canthus: Corner of the eye

TYPICAL ACUPUNCTURE TREATMENT

A typical treatment includes a detailed medical history questionnaire, followed by a patient interview and physical examination. This will ensure that the most considered and appropriate therapy is given, and that the treatment plan will be based on thorough fact-gathering. The principles of diagnosis can then be effectively applied to the individual case. Specific acupoints will be selected, based on the history and underlying cause of the disorder, in order to expel the exogenous pathogen and resolve the internal condition.

Before the insertion of the needles, the practitioner should clean the areas of the body surface where the needles are going to be inserted with alcohol to prevent infections. Acupuncture needles are then inserted, which is relatively painless and quick. After the needles pass through the skin, they are inserted into the underlying tissues to produce the "de Qi" or "receive Qi" sensation, which varies from feeling

a soreness, numbness, distention or heaviness around the point, to sometimes a cold, warm, itching feeling – or even a sensation of electric shock. There are many factors that influence the patient's needling sensations, depending on their physical constitution. A healthy patient with abundant Qi and blood will receive the needling sensation rapidly, while a patient who is seriously ill with deficient Qi and

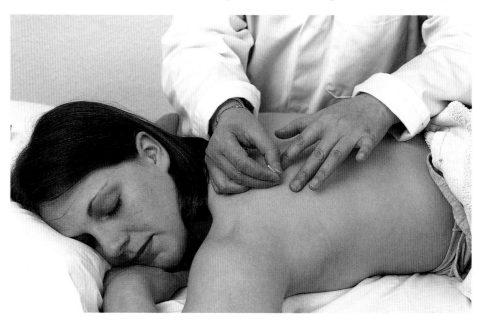

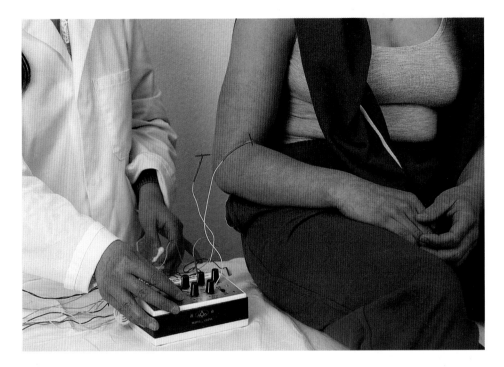

LEFT
Very light electrical stimulation may be applied to the needles to enhance the stimulation and increase the needling sensation.

Yang will tend to react very slowly to the needling sensation.

The needles may be manipulated by hand and removed rather quickly or the patient may rest quietly with the needles in place for 20 to 30 minutes – during this time they may be manipulated to achieve either a reinforcing or reducing effect, so as to correct the imbalance between the Yin and Yang and restore harmony in the body.

Very light electrical stimulation may be applied to the needles for a time to enhance the stimulation and increase the needling sensation. At the appropriate time, the needles are withdrawn from the body and pressure is applied to the punctured point with a cotton ball. Moxibustion may be applied indirectly to the point with a smouldering heat source a safe distance from the skin.

For chronic pain diseases, and for treating addictions, subcutaneous needles are often used. These are very small and short needles shaped like a thumb tack, and are embedded subcutaneously on the body, most commonly on the ears.

POSITIONS FOR ACUPUNCTURE

It is important to position the patient properly for treatment. This not only allows for better location of the points and for manipulation and retention of the needles during the treatment, but is especially effective for preventing any discomfort. In general, lying down is the best position for new patients or for patients who are nervous, elderly or seriously ill. Depending on the points being used, the patient can be in a lying or sitting position.

CHAPTER SEVEN

RESULTS OF ACUPUNCTURE

Acupuncture therapy generally produces a feeling of relaxation and well-being. Occasionally, a slight increase in symptoms can occur but this is generally moderate and very temporary. Results can be remarkably quick in some cases, but often they will take time. Several treatments are required before results can be expected, as the body gradually adjusts to the rebalancing of the body's organ systems brought about by the acupuncture. Herbal therapy may be used as adjunct therapy in

RIGHT
Moxibustion may be applied indirectly to the point with a smouldering heat source a safe distance from the skin.

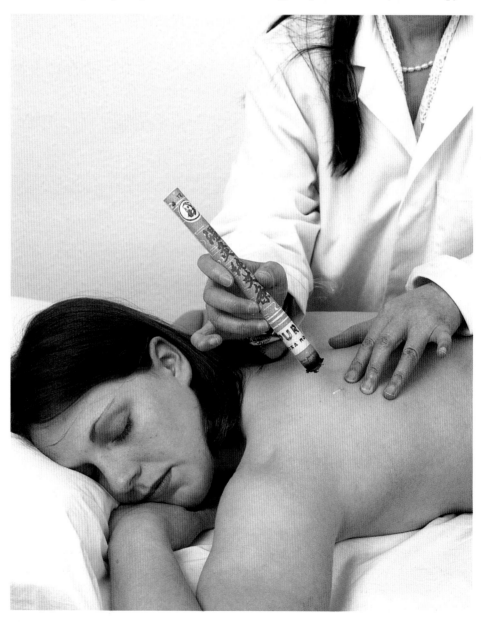

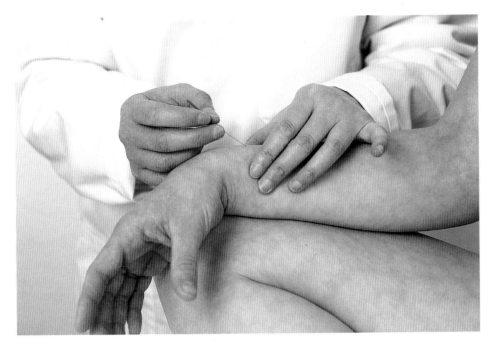

Treating asthma, coughs and respiratory problems with acupuncture.

the practice of an acupuncturist, and prescriptions are carefully selected, based on the same diagnostic treatment principles, to enhance the total therapeutic result.

FINDING A QUALIFIED PRACTITIONER

It is essential for patients to seek fully qualified and experienced practitioners for their treatment. They should be trained in the principles and theories of traditional Chinese medicine, whatever else their speciality might be. They should also be licensed according to the requirements of the country in which they are practising. A patient's best chance of success with traditional Chinese medicine is when there is close collaboration with a practitioner who is a specialist in this field. Sources of fully qualified practitioners can be found locally and through professional associations.

ACUPUNCTURE IN THE MODERN ERA

With the integration of acupuncture and moxibustion into the field of biomedicine, we are offering new explanations for the effects of acupuncture. The most common and more accepted discovery of Dr Bruce Pomeranz MD, Ph. D, Toronto, Canada, is that the stimulation of acupuncture points causes the release of opiates in the brain. These opiates have the same effect as morphine, and since it is secreted inside our own body, they are called "endorphins" (internal morphine).

These endorphins are secreted in an area called the Peri Aqueduct Grey matter (PAG) region of our brain. The endorphins block the transmission of stimulation from the thalamus, which acts as a switchboard between damaged tissues of the internal organs or body tissues and the cortex of our brain. This reduces the perception of pain by the central nervous system, thus preventing it from sending pain signals to the affected tissues, providing the affected tissues with the opportunity to heal. These opiates can also induce changes in the hypothalamic brain-stem system and influence the autonomic nervous system, which is an independent and self-controlling part of the nervous system that is connected with the internal organs and controls their functions. The opiates can influence its control over the different internal functions, obtaining optimal performance in the different organs.

Another important acupuncture effect is the stimulation of natural cortisol, with anti-inflammatory properties that are useful in treatments for pain. Acupuncture has also been shown to increase normal immune functions, for example, the stimulation of white blood cells and increased phagocytosis in laboratory animals and humans. Microcirculation has been shown to increase and thereby speed up the recovery of injured tissue. Modern research has identified many mechanisms of acupuncture, and new discoveries are being made all the time.

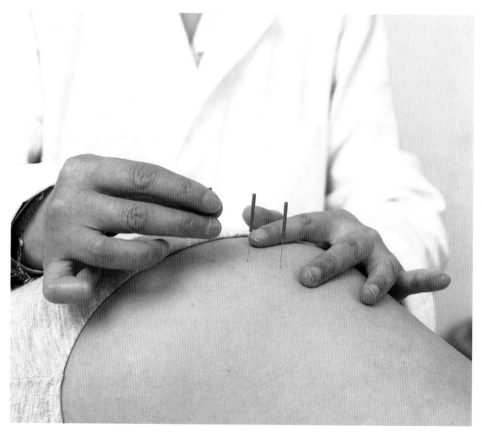

Diseases treated by acupuncture therapy

Acupuncture has been practised for thousands of years and was widely used for the treatment and prevention of many diseases, some with significant results. In 1980, the World Health Organisation of the United Nations issued a list of diseases that acupuncture is shown to treat effectively.

Respiratory tract

Acute sinusitis, rhinitis (inflammation of mucous membrane in the nose), common cold and acute tonsillitis.

Broncho-pulmonary disorders

Acute bronchitis and bronchial asthma (most effective in children and in patients without concomitant diseases).

Disorders of the eye

Acute conjunctivitis, central retinitis, myopia (children), cataract (without complications).

Disorders of the mouth cavity

Toothache, pain after tooth extraction, gingivitis, acute and chronic pharyngitis.

Gastrointestinal disorders

Spasm of the oesophagus and cardia, hiccups, indigestion, spastic colon, gastroptosis, acute and chronic gastritis, gastric hyperacidity, chronic duodenal ulcer, acute and chronic colitis, acute bacterial dysentery, constipation, diarrhoea and paralytic ileus (painful obstruction of the intestine).

Neurologic and orthopaedic disorders

Headache, migraine, trigeminal neuralgia, facial paralysis, paralysis after apoplectic fit, peripheral neuropathy, paralysis caused by poliomyelitis, Meniere's Syndrome, neurogenic bladder dysfunction, nocturnal enuresis, intercostal neuralgia, periarthritis humeroscapularis, tennis elbow, sciatica and lumbar Pain, and rheumatoid arthritis.

Other conditions

In addition to the list produced by the World Health Organization, there are many other conditions that acupuncture has been effective in treating, such as reproductive disorders, hypertension, insomnia, skin problems, sports injuries, allergies, arthritis, Bell's Palsy, addictive disorders and general acute or chronic ailments.

USEFUL ADDRESSES

UNITED KINGDOM

UMBRELLA
ORGANIZATIONS

**The Institute for
Complementary
Medicine**
Unit 15
Tavern Quay
Commercial Centre
Rope Street
London SE16 1TX
(0171) 237-5165

Details of registered
practitioners in the
principal forms of
complementary
medicine can be
obtained from:

**The British Register
of Complementary
Practitioners**
PO Box 194
London SE16 1QZ
(0171) 237-5175

**Council for
Complementary and
Alternative Medicine**
Park House
206/208 Latimer Road
London W10 6RF
(0181) 968-3862

**The British
Complementary
Medicine
Association**
39 Prestbury Road
Pittville
Cheltenham
Glos GL52 2PT
(01242) 226770

TRADITIONAL CHINESE
MEDICINE

**Register of
Traditional Chinese
Medicine**
19 Trinity Road
London N2 8JJ
(0181) 883-8431

**International
Register of Oriental
Medicine (UK)**
4 The Manor House
Colley Lane
Reigate
Surrey RH2 9JW
(01737) 242104

**Society of Chinese
Medical Practitioners
in the UK**
94 High Street
Croydon SM1 1SN
(0181) 643-4222

ACUPUNCTURE

**Academy of Western
Acupuncture**
112 Conway Road
Colwyn Bay
Clwyd LL29 7LL
(01492) 534328

**Association of
Chinese Acupuncture**
Prospect House
2 Grove Lane, Retford
Nottingham
DN22 6NA
(01777) 701509

**British Acupuncture
Association and
Register**
34 Alderney Street
London SW1V 4EY
(0171) 834-6229

**The British
Acupuncture
Council**
Park House
206 Latimer Road
London W10 6RE
(0181) 964 0222

**The British Medical
Acupuncture Society**
Newton House
Newton Lane
Lower Whitley
Warrington
Cheshire WA4 4JA
(01925) 73727

**College of
Traditional
Acupuncture**
Tao House,
Queensway
Leamington Spa
Warwickshire
England CV313LZ

**The Council for
Acupuncture**
179 Gloucester Road
London NW1 6DX
(0171) 724-5756

**European Federation
of Modern
Acupuncture**
59 Telford Crescent
Leigh
Lancashire WN 5LY
(01942) 678092

**Traditional
Acupuncture Society**
1 The Ridgeway
Stratford-Upon-Avon
Warwickshire CV37
9JL
(01789) 298798

CHINESE HERBAL
MEDICINE

**The Register of
Chinese Herbal
Medicine**
PO Box 400
Wembley
Middlesex HA9 9NZ
(0181) 904-1357

SCHOOLS OF TCM

**College of Oriental
Medicine**
Prospect House
Retford
Nottinghamshire
DN22 6NA
(01777) 701509

**The International
College of Oriental
Medicine**
Green Hedges Avenue

East Grinstead
Sussex RH19 1DZ
(01342) 313106

**School of Chinese
Herbal Medicine**
Midsummer Cottage
Clinic
Nether Westcote
Kingham
Oxfordshire
OX7 6SD
(01993) 830419

**The London Qi
Gong College**
2 St Albans Road
Reading
Berkshire RG6 2HN
(01734) 665454

**The Piu-Yong Post
Graduate School of
Traditional Chinese
Medicine**
53a Ormistone Grove
London W12 0JP
(0181) 743-0706

ASSOCIATIONS

**The Association of
Traditional Chinese
Medicine**
78 Haverstock Hill
London NW3 2BE
(0171) 284-2898

**The Association of
British Veterinary
Acupuncture**
East Park Cottage
Handcross
Hayward's Heath
Sussex RH1 6BD
(01342) 400213

**Tai Chi Union for
Great Britain**
102 Felsham Road
London SW15 1DQ

REST OF THE WORLD

AUSTRALIA

**Australian
Traditional Medicine
Society Limited**
12/27 Bank Street
Meadowbank
NSW 2114
Australia

**Qi Gong Association
of Australia**
458 White Horse
Road
Surrey Hills
Victoria 3127
Australia

CANADA

**Academy of Oriental
Heritage**
POB 35057
Station E
Vancouver
BC V6M4G1
Canada

**Canadian College
for Chinese Studies**
855-859
Cormorant Street
Victoria
BC V8W 1R2
Canada

**Chinese Medicine &
Cultural College**
3565 Rue Berri
Suite 220
Montreal
Quebec H2L 4G5,
Canada
(512) 288-2872

CHINA

**The World Academic
Society of Medical
Qi Gong**
11 Heping
Jie Nei Kou
Beijing 100029
China

JAPAN

**Meiji College of
Oriental Medicine**
Kiyoshi-Cho,
Funai-Gun
Kyoto-Pref.
629-03
Japan

UNITED STATES

**Academy of Chinese
Culture and Health**
1601 Clay Street
Oakland
CA 94612
USA
(510) 763-7787

**American College of
TCM**
455 Arkansas
San Francisco
CA 94107
USA
(415) 282-7600

**Emperor's College
of Traditional
Oriental Medicine**
1807-B Wilshire Blvd.
Santa Monica
CA 90403-5652
USA

**Five Branches
Institute**
200 Seventh Avenue
Santa Cruz
CA 95062
USA

**Meiji College of
Oriental Medicine**
1426 Fillmore Street
San Francisco
CA 94115
USA

**Pacific College of
Oriental Medicine**
7445 Mission Valley
San Diego
CA 92108
USA

**Royal University of
America**
1125 W 6th St.
Los Angeles
CA 90017
USA

**Samra University of
Oriental Medicine**
600 St. Paul Ave.
Los Angeles
CA 90017
USA

**Santa Barbara
College of Oriental
Medicine**
1919 State St., Suite 204
Santa Barbara
CA 93101
USA
(805) 682-9594

**South Baylo
University**
12012 S Magnolia Ave.
Garden Grove
CA 92641
USA
(714) 530-9650

**Yo San University
of TCM**
1314 Second St.
Suite 202
Santa Monica,
CA 90401
USA
(310) 917-2202

**Colorado School of
TCM**
1441 York St.
Suite 202
Denver, CO 80206
USA
(303) 329-6355

**Institute of Taoist
Education and
Acupuncture, Inc.**
1321 5th Street
Boulder,
CO 80302
(303) 440-3492
USA

**Tri State Institute
of TCM**
15 Bank St.
Stamford
CT 06901
(203) 469-0491
USA

**American School of
Oriental and
Homeopathic
Therapies**
933 Lincoln Road
Miami Beach
FL 33139
USA
(305) 672-4138

**Florida Institute of
Traditional Chinese
Medicine**
5335 66th Street
North Pinellas Park,
FL 34665
USA
(813) 546-6565

**Atlantic Institute
of Oriental
Medicine**
1057 SE 17 Street
Fort Lauderdale
FL 33316
USA
(305) 63-3888

**The Worsley
Institute of
Classical
Acupuncture, Inc.**
Tao House
Suite 324
6175 N.W. 153rd Street
Miami Lakes
FL 33014
USA
(305) 823-7270

**American University
of Chinese
Medicine**
2600 S. King #206
Honolulu,
Hawaii
HI 96826
USA

**Oriental Medical
Institute of
Hawaii**
1815 Kului St
Suite 206
Honolulu
Hawaii
HI 96813
USA
(808) 536-3611

**Midwest Center for
the Study of
Oriental Medicine**
4334 North Hazel,
Suite 206
Chicago
IL 60613
USA
(312) 975-8012

**Traditional
Acupuncture
Institute, Inc.**
American City
Building, Suite 108
Columbia
MD 21044
USA
(301) 917-2202

**Acupuncture Center
of Amherst**
48 North Pleasant St.
Amherst
MA 01002
USA

**The New England
School of
Acupuncture**
30 Common St.
Watertown
MA 02172
USA
(617) 926-1788

**Minnesota School of
Acupuncture and
Herbal Studies**
182 University Ave.
Suite 278
Saint Paul
MN 55104
USA

**Institute of
Chinese Medicine**
Rt. 17, Box 52-A
Santa Fe
NM 87502
USA
(505) 473-5233

Kototama Institute
935 Alto St.
PO Box 1636
Santa Fe
NM 87501
USA

**Santa Fe College of
Natural Medicine**
1590 Canyon Road
Santa Fe
NM 87501
USA
(505) 983-4569

**Southwest
Acupuncture College**
712 West San Mateo
Santa Fe
NM 87501
USA
(505) 988-3538

**College of
Acupuncture
and Electro-
Therapeutics**
800 Riverside Drive
New York
NY 10032
USA

**The New Center
School for
Acupuncture**
50 Maple Place
Manhasset
NY 11030
USA

**Pacific Institute of
Oriental Medicine**
12 W 27th St.,
9th Floor
New York
NY 10001
USA

**Tri State Institute of
TCM**
PO Box 974
Cathedral Station
New York
NY 10025
USA

**National College of
Naturopathic
Medicine**
11231 SE Market
Street
Portland
OR 97216
USA
(503) 255-4860

**North American
College of
Acupuncture**
PO Box 12128
Salem
OR 97309
USA

**Oregon College
of Oriental
Medicine**
10525 SE Cherry
Blossom Drive
Portland
OR 97216
USA
(503) 253-3443

**Academy of
Oriental Medicine**
2700 W. Anderson
Lane Suite 304
Austin
TX 78756
USA
(512) 371-3738

**Barren Land
Institute College of
Acupuncture and
Moxibustion**
4150 Pinnacle
Loc Picos, # 230
El Paso
TX 79902
USA
(915) 544-6425

**Texas College of
Oriental Medicine**
2405 S. Shepard
Houston
TX 77019
USA
(713) 529-8332

**Academy of
Oriental Heritage**
PO Box 8066
Blaine
WA 98230
USA

Bastyr University
14500 Juanita Drive
N.E.
Bothell
WA 98011
USA
(206) 823-1300

**National
Acupuncture and
Oriental Medicine
Alliance**
14637 Starr Rd
Olalla
WA 98359
USA
253-851-6883

**Northwest Institute
of Acupuncture and
Oriental Medicine**
1307 North 45th
Street
Seattle
WA 98103
(206) 633-2419
USA

WEST INDIES

**American School of
Oriental &
Homeopathic
Medicine**
C/O Castle Bay Villas
Newcastle, Nevis,
West Indies
Fax: (809) 469-9490

BIBLIOGRAPHY

General books on traditional Chinese medicine

Hoizey, Dominique, and Hoizey, Marie-Joseph, *A History of Chinese Medicine* (Bailey, Paul, trans. Edinburgh University Press, 1993)

Hsu, Hong-Yen, and Peacher, William, *Chen's History of Chinese Medical Science* (Oriental Healing Arts Press, 1971)

Porkert, Manfred, *Chinese Medicine as a Scientific System: Its History, Philosophy, and Practice, and How It Fits with the Medicine of the West* (Henry Holt and Company, New York, 1982)

Ronan, Colin A., and Needham, Joseph, *The Shorter Science and Civilization in China:1* (Cambridge University Press, Cambridge, 1988)

Schwartz, Benjamin, *The World of Thought in Ancient China* (Belnap Press of Harvard University Press, 1985)

Sivan, Nathan, *Traditional Medicine in Contemporary China, Vol. 2, in Science, Medicine, and Technology In East Asia series* (Center for Chinese Studies, The University of Michigan, 1987)

Tsuei, Wei, *Roots of Chinese Culture and Medicine* (Chinese Culture Books Company, Oakland, CA 1989)

Unschuld, Paul U., *Medicine in China, a History of Ideas* (UC Berkeley Press, Berkeley, 1985)

Qi Gong

Hallander, Jane, *Empty Force Karate Kung-Fu* (May 1986 K47355: 32–36)

Hallander, Jane, *Sum-I, the Highest Stage of Martial Training* (Inside Kung-Fu, Jan 1986, K48326: 40–43)

Hallander, Jane, *Sum-I* (Inside Kung-Fu Yearbook, Jan 1987, K48745: 78–81)

Hallander, Jane, *The Highest Level of Kung Fu Power* (Black Belt, July 1987, 47432: 56–61)

Hallender, Jane, *Xing-Yi Push Hands* (The Complete Guide to Kung Fu Fighting Styles, Aug 1987, K48745: 40–42)

Hallender, Jane, *Female of The Year – Madam Min Ou-Yang* (Inside Kung-Fu Yearbook, Jan 1988, K48745: 17)

Hallender, Jane, *Opening Qi Channels, a Direct Route to the Fountain of Youth* (Chi Power, July 1989, K48745: 36–41)

Hallander, Jane, and Doc-Fei Wong, *Xin-Yi Combat without Contact* (Official Karate, April 1990, K48289 34–37)

He Zhou, *The Magic of Qigong* (Chi Power, July 1989, K48745:54–57)

Hui Min zhang, *Qi-Gong Treatment* (Tianjin Science and Technology Publish Co. 1980)

The Chinese National Chi Kung Institute, *Chi Kung: Air Apparent to Better Health* (Chi Power, July 1989, K48745: 21–25)

Yong Nien Yu, *Standing—a Good Method for Health* (Knowledge Publish Co, 1981)

Food as Therapy

Castleman, Michael, *The Healing Herbs* (Rodale Press, Emmans, Pennsylvania, 1991)

Fuli, Wen Fang, et al., *Food Treatment for Common Diseases* (Chinese Ancient Medical Books Publishing House, Oct 1991)

Je Quan Ye, et al., *Food Treatment and Recipes* (Jiangsu People's Publishing House, 1973)

Mayer, Dr Jean, et al., *Diet and Nutrition Guide* (Pharos Books, New York, 1989)

Mei Ping Wong, et al., *Diet and Food Treatment* (People's Military Doctor Publishing House, Jan 1991)

Min Yuan Hong, et al., *Recipes of Food Treatment for Family Use* (Fujian Science Publishing House, Oct 1990)

Qing Xuan Heng, et al., 200 *Questions about Food and Nutrition* (Jindun Publishing House, Oct 1990)

Shanghai Food Treatment Research Association, *Food Treatment* (Zejiang People's Publishing Co., July 1990)

Shi Zheng Li, *Compendium of* Materia Medica (Chinese Book Publishing House, 1988)

Xue Min Zhou, *Supplement to the Compendium of* Materia Medica (Chinese Book Publishing House, 1988)

Zhang Zhong Zhao, et al., *Nutrition and Food Treatment* (Shanghai Science and Technology Publishing House, Sept 1991)

INDEX